FREEZE FRAME

FREEZE FRAME

A Samuel and Althea Stroum Book

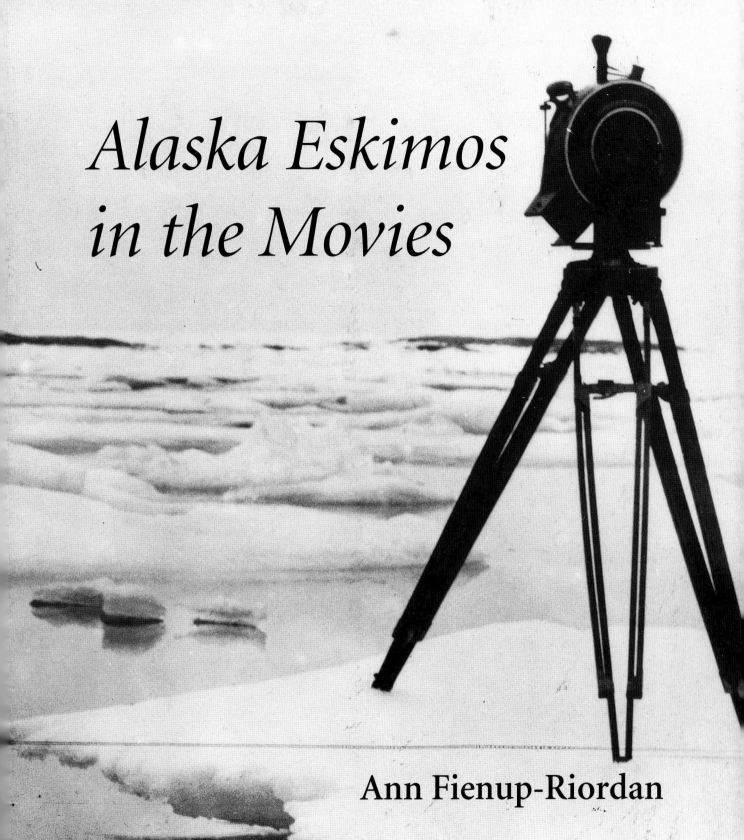

Alaska Eskimos
in the Movies

Ann Fienup-Riordan

UNIVERSITY OF WASHINGTON PRESS *Seattle & London*

Freeze Frame: Alaska Eskimos in the Movies is published
with the assistance of a grant from the Stroum Book
Fund, established through the generosity of Samuel and
Althea Stroum.

This project is supported in part by a grant from the
Alaska Humanities Forum and the National Endowment
for the Humanities, a federal agency.

Library of Congress Cataloging-in-Publication Data

Fienup-Riordan, Ann.
  Freeze frame: Alaska Eskimos in the movies /
Ann Fienup-Riordan.
    p. cm.
  Filmography: p.
  Includes bibliographical references and index.
  ISBN 0-295-97397-8 (alk. paper)
  1. Eskimos in motion pictures. I. Title.
PN1995.9.E83F54 1995   791.43'652971—dc20
94-11623 CIP

The paper used in this publication meets the minimum
requirements of American National Standard for Information Sciences—Permanence of Paper for Printed
Library Materials, ANSI Z39.48-1984. ∞

Title page photo: Filming a hunting scene for *Nanook of
the North.* Museum of Modern Art, Film Stills Archive.

For Dick and the People of Nelson Island

Given the power and depth at which the popular imagination works, it is a responsibility of the popular artist to extend and to replenish the humanity from which he has drawn his metaphors, not to permit a human type to freeze formulaic. After all, these stereotypes are only human—Maurice Yacowar, *Aspects of the Familiar*

Contents

FOREWORD

Over the course of nearly twenty-five years of reporting Native American news, I have been skeptical and critical of efforts by non-Native writers to chronicle the culture of any Native group. I have also been wary of attempts by many of those writers to gain credibility by associating with Natives or trying to establish a link by working with Native scholars and professionals.

My goal in working as a Native American journalist has been to present as accurate a picture of Native issues and peoples as possible. In pursuing my profession, I've found a few useful resources, produced by non-Native people who have honest and sincere motivations for their work and who have successfully added to the knowledge bank of information that can be trusted. Ann Fienup-Riordan's *Freeze Frame* is one of those sources.

There are many places to turn for information about the tribes in the contiguous United States, but among the indigenous peoples of this hemisphere, the true nature of Alaska's Eskimos still remains the most misunderstood. Much of what we perceive about this diverse group of people comes from the work of the outside filmmaking industry, both in documentary and in feature films.

In the most extreme cases, feature filmmakers reinforced common stereotypes by building new creations based on those old ideas—Hollywood drawing on its own false images. But both the documentaries and the big-screen movies have been at fault.

Their collective legacy has left audiences with false impressions that all Eskimos live in igloos, fight polar bears, and are peaceful, smiling nature children of the Arctic, as Ann Fienup-Riordan points out. The other side of that—with no middle ground—is the portrayal of naive, primitive savages, trying to survive in a barren environment and at the mercy of white exploiters and civilization.

In *Freeze Frame,* through lengthy and detailed research, the author has assembled very thorough and readable material on how Alaska Eskimos fared through various camera lenses. Having been in those audiences, believing those films, I find it refreshing to learn the genesis of those images and to adjust my thinking about the peoples who have thrived and developed elaborate cultures in one of the most hostile environments on the planet.

Freeze Frame details the earliest attempts by filmmakers to capture a predetermined vision of Eskimos in Alaska. It continues up through the most recent efforts by network television and feature movie-makers who are still not delivering an accurate representation of Eskimos and their cultures.

As this nation comes to grips with its true history of relations between newcomers and the indigenous populations, many tend to label such efforts as "revisionist history." Perhaps a more accurate term would be "clear-visionist history," for it is critical that the dominant society gain a new, clear understanding of the peoples who lived on this land before it. *Freeze Frame* is an important and reliable step in that direction.

GARY D. FIFE
"Heartbeat Alaska"
KSKA Public Radio, Anchorage

Eskimo Orientalism

A T THE 1992 AMERICAN ANTHROPOLOGICAL Association annual meetings in San Francisco, Donna Haraway gave a presentation describing the postmodern world and its "sites of transformation, implosion," points of extraordinary density including the Chip, the Seed, the Gene, the Bomb, and the Primate. She forgot the Eskimo, a site just as charged, just as dense, just as laden with associations. Few people on earth have been written about so prodigiously or pictured so often in an exotic light.

Representations of Eskimos occur in many places—in fiction and museum displays, in cartoons and children's books, in scholarly literature, and in popular accounts of arctic exploration. And, since the birth of the movie industry, filmmakers have fabricated countless stories using Eskimo themes. The history of these fabrications is the history of the creation and use of a cluster of representations that present themselves time and again, a series of merging strands that viewers associate with life in the High Arctic. The Eskimo theme is a "classic." Miles of film depicting Eskimo life are in cold storage in film archives all over the world. What ideas motivate and lie behind this abundant generation of images?

The issue of how Eskimos have been represented, in film and elsewhere, is more than aca-demic. Voice, the right to represent, and the cultural construction of reality are among the most important intellectual issues of our time (Clifford 1988; Hall 1992; Pearce 1953; Said 1978). If we understand the ways in which Eskimos have been imaged and the reasons for these representations, we will also understand something about how the West constructs the rest (Sahlins 1985) and appropriates exotic others for its own purposes.

The representation of Eskimos concerns the "construction of the self from the raw material of the other," the appropriation of "natural man" in the production of American culture (Haraway 1989:11). Just as representations of the Orient mirror the Occident in specific historical moments (Said 1978), so representations of Eskimos provide another window into the history of the West. Like the representation of the Orient, the representation of the Eskimo is about origins—in this case the origin of society in the "pure primitive": peaceful, happy, childlike, noble, independent, and free. The Eskimo of the movies is "essential man," stripped of social constraint and High Culture. That twentieth-century Iñupiaq and Yup'ik men and women were members of complex societies governed by elaborate cultural constraints was unimportant. Their position at the geographic and historical fringe of Western Civilization made them the perfect foils for an "Eskimo orientalism" as potent as its namesake.[1]

Chapter 1 introduces the problem posed to Euro-Americans by their encounter with America's first people. In the course of Western debate on the place of Eskimos and Indians on the "ladder of civilization," Indians came to represent the Savage Other needing to be tamed. Although the Euro-American perception of Inuit and Yup'ik peoples continued to be characterized by ambivalence, Eskimos more often represented "pure primitives" in opposition to "savage Indians." The idea of the Indian came to embody the dark side of the civilized persona, whereas nonnatives consistently employed the idea of the Eskimo to represent the childlike innocence of humanity before the Fall.

The chapter goes on to describe the Iñupiat and Yup'ik Eskimos of Alaska, both past and present, and how different their lives are in every respect from the igloo-dwelling Inuit of the Canadian Arctic on whom the original Eskimo image was modeled. The stereotypic Eskimo is seen as eking out a living in a frigid and inhospitable homeland, a tundra waste where only the fittest survive. In fact, Alaska Eskimos live in a rich environment, replete with abundant natural resources, including waterfowl and whales, seals and seabirds, many varieties of fish and land animals, not to mention berries and greens. This abundance, in turn, supported large settlements of sod and wood houses, not snow igloos. There, during the long winter months, men and women gathered for elaborate celebrations, including masked dances and distributions of great wealth. Far from an uninhabited wasteland, Alaska's Bering Sea coast was the fertile point of origin for the imaginative and complex Western Thule culture that characterized most Eskimo areas into historic times, and it continues as the home of indigenous

people bent on keeping control of their land and their lives.

With this wealth of resources and unique history, why have Euro-Americans so often confused Alaska Eskimos with the relatively impoverished Canadian Inuit? Moreover, why and how have nonnative representations of Eskimos in general been positioned in opposition to ideas about Indians? Film is a tool of narrative (Haraway 1989:41). The question is, what stories about Eskimos do films tell us? Alaska Eskimos have particular cultures that can be distinguished from those of other Inuit peoples. Film has the capability of highlighting these differences if filmmakers choose to use it in that way.

Prior to the postmodern preoccupation with issues of representation, it was common to seek out "authentic peoples," and filmmakers (among others) repeatedly engaged Eskimos to depict the "pure primitive." They looked at Eskimos both to find "the strange in the familiar and the familiar in the strange" (Hegeman 1989:145). The lives of Alaska Eskimos were dramatically altered during their two-hundred-year encounter with the outside world. Yet, until recently, many Euro-Americans remained intent on viewing them outside time, impervious to history.

Chapter 2 describes the first nonfiction films made in Alaska and what they did and did not say about Alaska Eskimos. Films involving Alaska Eskimos began as attempts by nonnatives to document indigenous peoples they encountered in the process of exploration, colonial expansion, and domination. Film made possible an "appearance of reality" that was used as vivid proof of the Eskimos' inevitable absorption into the larger world. Like turn-of-the-century exhibitions, these early explorer films made the Inuit appear simultaneously simple, childlike, entertaining, and quaint.

When the first films were made in Alaska in the early 1900s, Alaska Eskimos had already experienced more than a century of interaction with nonnatives. The first films simultaneously highlighted Alaska

---

1. I am not the first to appropriate Said's deployment of the concept "orientalism." I take my cue from Haraway, who speaks of "simian orientalism" in her book *Primate Visions* (1989:11).

Star of *Eskimo* Ray Mala, the Clark Gable of Alaska. Mala Collection, University of Alaska Anchorage Archives.

Construction of an unorthodox igloo to create the "fiction of realism" in *Nanook.* Museum of Modern Art, Film Stills Archive.

Eskimos' "primitive condition" (the difference between "us" and "them") and their adaptability to new conditions. His sense of superiority notwithstanding, William Van Valin gave audiences their first view of Alaska Eskimos actively engaged in coming to terms with goods and services newly introduced to Alaska's northern coast. Robert Flaherty's groundbreaking *Nanook of the North* would not continue this tradition, but instead showed Eskimos untouched, untroubled, and disease free. None of the original ambivalence remained.

Chapters 3 and 4 detail the history of the Hollywood representation of Eskimos. The focus is on Alaska Eskimos, although important films made in the Canadian Arctic are also discussed. What movies were made? Who made them? To say that big-budget commercial films have misrepresented Eskimos is a truism. Hollywood's "dream machine" makes no claims to an accurate portrayal of reality. Careful scrutiny of its images, however, can tell us a great deal about Euro-American preoccupations and expectations. What was it about the Arctic and its inhabitants that first attracted attention? What complex of ideas and associations gradually attached itself to the original images, and how have these images been modified over time?

Hollywood's image of the Eskimo and the effects of this representation are of more than casual interest. Recently, scholars have questioned the validity of the label "misrepresentation," as it assumes there is one and only one "right" representation (Chalfen 1992:15). We cannot dismiss "wrong" representations; they have their own social impact, and they index ideas about non-Western peoples that tell us something about our vision of ourselves.

If Eskimo films do not talk about Eskimos, what, then, do they describe? Haraway (1989:54) points out that from 1890 to 1930 the "nature movement" was at its height in the United States. Americans debated the value of "civilization," about which there was great ambivalence. Euro-Americans often blamed the "woes of civilization" on industrialization and technology. Aboriginal peoples and their

Discussing ice conditions at public hearings in Emmonak, 1982. James H. Barker

handicrafts, by contrast, became symbols of an age of innocence and purity long past. Eskimos in the movies in part represented this lost innocence. Their "primitive purity" embodied not what they were, but what Euro-Americans needed them to be. Nonnatives were engaged in a debate over the meaning of technology, and Eskimos took a starring role in morality plays constructed as part of this larger debate.

Chapter 5 moves on to Alaska Eskimo participation in the construction of documentary and ethnographic film. Again we confront the false contrast between ethnographic "fact" and film "fiction." Ethnographers are engaged in interpretations and representations as much as filmmakers, and film is just as much a medium of ideas as written ethnography. Films often succeed where written descriptions fall short, and they fail where books excel. What have filmmakers tried to tell us in the documentaries they have constructed around arctic themes? What ideas have motivated their creations?

"Tigara Eskimos have a ceremonial dance before going on a Walrus Hunt" in *Arctic Manhunt*.

Until the last decade's debate on representation, documentary films were often seen as "transparent media" (Ginsburg 1991). Many people believed they had the potential to show us what Eskimos (and others) were *really* like. The longer we have lived with film, the better we know that documentary, just like its Hollywood predecessor, is a constructed reality. The images that filmmakers recorded in Barrow and Hooper Bay, Mekoryak and Point Hope depended on a complex combination of forces—

Museum of Modern Art, Film Stills Archive

what scriptwriters and filmmakers were willing to see; what parts of themselves Yup'ik and Iñupiaq people were willing to show; and what both thought appropriate for audiences to view.

Chapter 6 discusses the media revolution in the last two decades and its impact on Alaska's first people. Previously, Alaska Eskimos were the object of Hollywood expeditions and documentary projects. They rarely watched movies. Now they view television and films (about others as well as themselves) on a daily basis. Iñupiaq and Yup'ik children learn English from *Sesame Street* and *Reading Rainbow*. *Die Hard* and the Disney channel are the background noise of daily life. As significant, Alaska natives are increasingly partners and producers in the filmmaking process.

Until recently, Alaska natives were not as involved in film and video as their Canadian neighbors. That is changing. Chapter 7 reviews the half-dozen feature films made in Alaska between 1990 and 1993. The final pages describe Yup'ik and Iñupiaq perspectives on their presentation in these films as well as their current involvement in film and video production.

Filmmakers were originally drawn to Alaska for its extreme contrasts—cold snow and warm smiles, simple people in a hard land. Ironically, Alaska Eskimos today are intent on presenting the complexity and uniqueness of the world in which they live. Whereas documentaries of the 1950s primarily described the status quo, recent films by both natives and nonnatives in Alaska not only acknowledge the imbalance of power that characterizes life in village Alaska, but seek to alter the situation with information presented on alcoholism, AIDS, pollution, even the impact of television on village life. In the hands of Iñupiaq and Yup'ik artists and technicians, film and video are becoming simultaneously a venue for participation in the larger world and a tool of empowerment.

My interest in the representation of Eskimos on film is almost as old as my involvement with Yup'ik

Eskimos in western Alaska, dating from 1978 when Barbara Lipton asked me if I would act as consultant on her documentary *Village of No River*. Ours was a stormy relationship, in part due to my lack of understanding of and impatience with the documentary film process. Since then I have advised in small ways on a number of films showcasing contemporary Yup'ik life in western Alaska, some fine and some flawed. In January 1989 I traveled to the western Alaska village of Kasigluk with Latvian filmmaker Andres Slapins to film *Selaviq,* the Russian Orthodox Christmas celebration. My job was to help introduce the filmmakers and their project to the community. Much as I admired the filmmaker, the speed and intensity with which he worked sharply contrasted with my own fieldwork style, and I went home feeling as though I had been party to a hit-and-run accident.

Though I was fascinated by the power of filmed images to reach people in our media-oriented age, their limitations also became apparent. They gave the appearance of reality but were as much a construction controlled by their creators as any book I had ever written. As an anthropologist living and working in Alaska and likely to be involved in more films in the future, I wanted to know what the film business was all about. Both what I found (the persistent use of Alaska Eskimos to represent Canadian Inuit) and what I failed to find (fiction films where Alaska Eskimos wove narratives out of their own history and traditions) surprised me.

Some films I discuss have been lost, and others are preserved in rare copies, such as MGMs classic *Eskimo* and Knud Rasmussen's *Wedding of Palo*. I have omitted a number of commercial and documentary productions involving Alaska Eskimos that people remember seeing but that I cannot locate. If there is truth in the adage we will repeat history if we forget it, then even the most inaccurate and obscure representations of Alaska Eskimos are worth viewing and reviewing. The past shapes the present, and we ignore it at our peril. Conversely, some films

dismissed as uninteresting or "merely educational" at the time they were produced now represent rare views of people and places irrevocably altered (Brownlow 1979:xiii). Although some films are hard to find, the search is worthwhile. My hope is that film preservation efforts increase so that Alaska natives can view past images for themselves, rejecting outdated metaphors and pulling the best with them into the future. In our prime-time culture, film helps create the world we reside in. To know the history of film and its present preoccupations is to gain a measure of control over the future.

One note in closing. In this book I use the term "Eskimo" and "Alaska Eskimo" for a number of reasons. First, my subject concerns image as much if not more than "reality." The Eskimo, like the Indian, is not an ethnographic fact but a complicated and contradictory idea. What authors such as Roy Harvey Pearce and Robert Berkhofer have done so well for our understanding of Euro-American ideas and images pertaining to Indians, I hope to accomplish in a more modest fashion for the Euro-American image of Eskimos, Alaska Eskimos in particular. In this sense, the book is self-examining and reflexive. Not only does it reveal something about Eskimos, but something about us and our interests in Eskimos.

In many parts of the Arctic today, including northern Alaska, Eskimo peoples prefer to be referred to as Inuit.[2] This preference derives at least in part from the pejorative and derogatory connotations of "Eskimo," whose common etymology is

2. Author Scott Young's introduction of his Inuit protagonist in *Murder in a Cold Climate* (1989) captures the dilemma: "So since then instead of police work I'd been going to conferences where I was usually identified in the program as an Inuk, or sometimes by the more specifically Western Arctic designation Inuvialuit, but often was introduced by white guys who either called me an Eskimo, or started to do that and then wound up with something like. 'um, Matthew, um, Kitologitak, an Esk . . um, In-you-it,' almost invariably using the plural Inuit rather than the singular Inuk. The farther they lived from the Arctic, the longer they took to get used to changes in terminology that had come with the Native rights programmes."

North meets an Alaska native couple (played by Graham Greene and Kathy Bates) in a scene from *North*. Bruce McBroom, Castle Rock Entertainment.

"eaters of raw flesh." Actually the name comes from a Montagnais form meaning "snowshoe-netter" (Goddard, cited in Damas 1984:6). Given our current penchant for political correctness, it might have been preferable to subtitle my text "Alaska Inuit in the Movies." But this choice would have undercut my reference to image and idea, to representation over reality. It would also involve another significant reference problem.

Yup'ik Eskimos, unlike their Canadian and Greenlandic neighbors, have not embraced the designation "Inuit," and they continue to refer to them-selves as either "Yupiit" or "Yup'ik Eskimos." As most of my work as an anthropologist has been in their part of the Arctic, I feel as uncomfortable with the designation "Inuit" as they do. My solution has been to retain the terms "Eskimo" and "Alaska Eskimo" to refer to Inuit/Iñupiaq/Yup'ik peoples in general and to ideas about them, while using specific names to talk about the particular peoples being represented.

ACKNOWLEDGMENTS

I AM NEITHER AN ETHNOGRAPHIC FILM-maker nor a film historian, but a cultural anthropologist primarily concerned with documenting the past and present patterns of life among Yup'ik Eskimos in western Alaska. Perhaps in no place in the Arctic do the images and ideas usually associated with Eskimos have so little validity. This striking mismatch between how Eskimos appear in popular representations and how I have come to understand them over the last twenty years has been an important theme in my work. In 1989 I conceived a book that would detail this mismatch, including chapters on Eskimos as depicted by explorers, Eskimos as described by missionaries, Eskimos in American popular fiction, Eskimos in children's literature, Eskimos in tourist art, and, last but not least, Eskimos in the movies. Summer came, and my children were out of school. I decided to begin with the last chapter, as I could check out Eskimo movies from the Alaska State Film Library and watch them while my kids were playing around the house. This book is that "last chapter."

The disjunction between how life is lived in Alaska and how it is represented in film was the spark that fired my original interest in this topic. Since then, many people have helped me follow through my initial burst of enthusiasm, people who

know better than I how films are made. Thanks especially to Asen Balikci, whose work on this topic supplied my original point of departure. Also special thanks to Bill Bacon, Richard Condon, Larry Kaplan, Jonathan King, Susan McKinnon, Frank Norris, Jay Ruby, David Schneider, and Elizabeth Weatherford for their comments and criticism. A number of Yup'ik and Iñupiaq men and women involved in movies about Alaska generously shared their experiences with me, including Leona and Irvin Brink, George Charles, Andrew Chikoyak, Laura George, Jeanie Greene, Charlie Kairaiuak, Steve Kaleak, Chuna McIntyre, Sadie Neakok, and Rossman Peetook. Mark Badger, Diane Benson, Sarah Elder, and Lenny Kamerling described their work for me in great detail, generously providing me the information on which I base my discussion of their contributions. Joe Aulisi made it possible for me to watch Hollywood in action on the set of the Steven Seagal film, *On Deadly Ground.* Ted Mala and Lael Morgan provided information on the late Ray Mala, and Judith Brogan and Jim VanStone, as always, gave much good advice.

The photographs also come from a number of sources. Thanks especially to the Academy of Motion Picture Arts and Sciences in Beverly Hills, Larry Edmunds Bookstore and Collectors Bookstore (both

in Hollywood), the Museum of Modern Art Film
Stills Archive in New York, the Field Museum of
Natural History in Chicago, and Centre Productions
in Boulder, Colorado. Individuals who provided
photographs include Bill Bacon, Asen Balikci, Jim
Barker, George Charles, Andrew Chikoyak, Bob
Crockett, Jeanie Greene, J. Huenergasdt, Lenny
Kamerling, Edith Kilbuck, Jonathan King, Fred and
Sara Machetanz, Jim Magdanz, Lael Morgan,
Francine Taylor, and Moses Wassilie. I also had
access to manuscripts and photographs in special
collections, including the Hubbard Collection at the
Santa Clara University Archives, the Stefansson
Collection at Dartmouth College, the University
Museum, University of Pennsylvania in Philadel-
phia, the Milotte Collection in the Alaska and Polar
Regions Department, Rasmuson Library, University
of Alaska Fairbanks, the Mala Collection at the Uni-
versity of Alaska Anchorage Archives, the National
Museum of the American Indian in New York, the
Oregon Province Archives in Spokane, the Moravian
Archives in Bethlehem, Pennsylvania, the Special
Collections Division of the University of Washing-
ton Library, the Alaska Moving Image Preservation
Association in Anchorage, the Anchorage Museum
of History and Art, and KYUK-TV in Bethel, Alaska.
I was able to view many old and out-of-print films
at the Motion Picture, Broadcasting and Recorded
Sound Division of the Library of Congress, the Film
and Television Archive of the University of Califor-
nia Los Angeles, Media Services at the Rasmuson
Library, University of Alaska Fairbanks, and the
Alaska State Film Library in Anchorage (now closed
for lack of funding).

And, as always, thanks to friends and family for
the love and support that made this book possible,
especially Nicky, Frances, Jimmy, Mom, Pop, Mary,
John, Tom, Terry, and Dick.

FREEZE FRAME

Primitive … 4a: elemental … b: of or relating to any unindustrialized people or culture not possessing a written language and commonly having a relatively simple technology and material culture … c: lacking in sophistication or subtlety of thought, feeling, or expression … d: self-taught, untutored … a simple and unsophisticated person … whose attitudes, behavior, or mentality are those of an earlier stage of society or human development. *Webster's Third New International Dictionary,* 1986

CHAPTER ONE

Primitive Pictures

A FEW YEARS AGO A SCRIPTWRITER FOR Whoopi Goldberg phoned an anthropologist at the University of Alaska to ask about Yup'ik Eskimos. Goldberg was scheduled to play a journalist in a taken-from-real-life story that begins at a press conference with George Bush. In the actual situation, a reporter had jumped up and yelled out to the president, "What about the Yup'ik Eskimos?" Now the scriptwriter was calling to find out.

I have received such calls myself, though never one quite so colorful. Filmmakers, both commercial and documentary, increasingly have come to Alaska since the state and its native peoples gained notoriety with passage of the Alaska Native Claims Settlement Act (ANCSA) of 1971 and construction of the trans-Alaska pipeline. In the mid-1980s the Alaska Department of Commerce and Economic Development went so far as to open a film/video information office to promote Alaska as a location.[1] The great whale rescue in Barrow in fall 1988 and the Prince William Sound oil spill in 1989 fueled the fire. During the fall of 1990, a German producer

filmed the award-winning movie *Salmonberries* in Kotzebue in northwest Alaska, and Warner Brothers sent a crew to Valdez in 1993 to shoot the action/adventure film *On Deadly Ground.* Alaska has also become a popular location for big-budget commercials, including ads for everything from beer and cars to toothpaste and potato chips, each with an arctic slant. The literary establishment is represented by Ken Kesey, author of *One Flew Over the Cuckoo's Nest,* who published a novel about Alaska in 1991. The book, called *Sailor Song,* is set in the next century at an economically depressed Eskimo village at which a Hollywood movie company arrives to make a motion picture of a classic children's book.

This flurry of activity raises questions about the image of Eskimos in film and video, past and present. I take my examples primarily from Alaska, although much of what I have to say may be extended to other parts of the Arctic. I will not cover all depictions of Alaska Eskimos. Although European and Japanese cinematographers have made movies about Alaska Eskimos, this review concentrates on films made by North Americans. I focus on Alaska Eskimos but have also discussed major film productions made in the Canadian Arctic, including Robert Flaherty's *Nanook of the North* and Martin Ransohoff's *White Dawn,* as these films set stan-

---

1. In 1991 the film office spent $65,000 to build a gigantic blue-tint plastic-foam iceberg (complete with fog and artificial snow) as the centerpiece for a lavish reception to attract the attention of prospective clients at the Montreal World Film Festival (Loy 1993:31).

WARM HEARTS IN A FROZEN HEAVEN!

CARL LAEMMLE Presents **IGLOO** The Strangest Adventure ever filmed!

MADE IN U.S.A

Iñupiaq Ray Mala and an all-Iñupiaq cast portrayed happy, hardy Canadian Inuit in the 1932 production *Igloo,* one of the first films to feature Alaska Eskimos. Universal Pictures.

dards against which films made in Alaska continue to be judged.

The following pages present the history of a belief and how, during the twentieth century, it has been realized in film. Primarily, Eskimos appear as "primitives," noble survivors in a hostile land. The roots of this belief are embedded in representations of Eskimos by Euro-Americans from the sixteenth century to the present, the history of which is only now beginning to be written (Balikci 1984; Fienup-Riordan 1990:10–22; Idiens 1987; King 1990;

Sturtevant and Quinn 1987; Whitehead 1987; Wright 1987). Such a history already exists for American Indians. Almost from the beginning, Americans viewed Indians as a problem, both real and intellectual, requiring debate and solution. An extensive primary and secondary literature has emerged concerning the place of Indians in American history and thought (Berkhofer 1978; Pearce 1953). Although an equally vast primary literature has developed around the details of native life in the north, Eskimos never presented a "problem" compa-

Thirty years later, Anthony Quinn and Yoko Tani continue the tradition of the noble primitive in *The Savage Innocents.* None of the film's leading roles was played by real Eskimos. Paramount Pictures.

rable to Indians for Americans. As a result, scholars have paid scant attention to how their representation differs from that of Native Americans generally. In fact, Eskimos and Indians have been treated quite differently, both in fact and in fancy.

In Roy Harvey Pearce's classic study of the Indian and the American mind, he describes the American Indian as the symbolic vehicle for the idea of the savage. Conversely, we can view the Eskimo as the symbol for the idea of the "primitive." The image of the noble survivor, battling both nature and his-

tory, is the vehicle for this symbol. The image is contradictory, evoking both positive and negative associations. When Eskimos succeed they fulfill the image of the "noble native" winning over grueling natural forces, but when they fail they are shown as poor "primitives" succumbing to civilization. Whereas Pearce presents the circumstances and character of the idea of savagery as symbolized by the Indian, I discuss the idea of primitivism as it came to be symbolized by the Eskimo.

In several important respects the representation

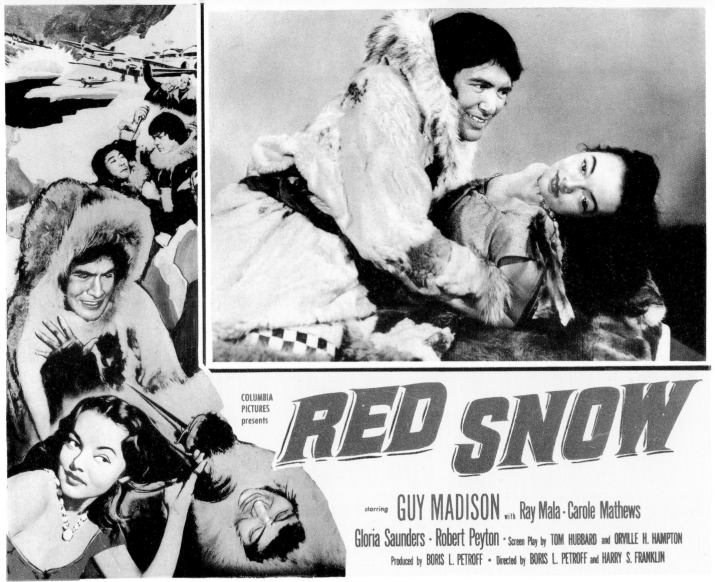

COLUMBIA PICTURES presents

RED SNOW

starring **GUY MADISON** with Ray Mala · Carole Mathews

Gloria Saunders · **Robert Peyton** · Screen Play by TOM HUBBARD and ORVILLE H. HAMPTON

Produced by BORIS L. PETROFF · Directed by BORIS L. PETROFF and HARRY S. FRANKLIN

Lobby card for *Red Snow:* Noble hunter, lovely bride. Columbia Pictures.

of Eskimos and Indians on film is essentially the same. Neither the Indians nor the Eskimos of popular culture ever really existed, yet the images are so real to most Americans that alternative ones rarely come to mind (Stedman 1982:xv). Moreover, American representations of both Eskimos and Indians are also Americans' ill-disguised representations of themselves. To rise above these representations, we must first recognize them.

Indian and Eskimo Images at Odds

The stock characters used to represent Indians in the movies are all too familiar: the sacrificial maiden, the warrior (alternately noble and ignoble), the wise chief, and the faithful Tonto (Stedman 1982). Marsden and Nachbar (1988:609) propose a similar tripartite categorization: the Pocahontas figure, the noble anachronism, and the savage reactionary. However we choose to divide them, these images did not originate in film. They formed over the last five

Lobby card for *Red Snow*. Gloria Saunders was not the first or the last to portray the sultry Eskimo maiden, naked in her igloo, opposite the noble hunter out on the ice. Columbia Pictures.

centuries from a variety of sources, from the captivity narratives of the seventeenth century to George Catlin's overseas exhibitions and Buffalo Bill's Wild West shows that toured America and Europe two hundred years later. Nor do they appear exclusively in the cinematographic arena. Rather, these stereotypes abound in many domains of popular American culture, including paperback literature, television, comic books, football and baseball teams (Redskins, Chiefs, and Braves), and children's toys.

We can see the same long history and broad spread in popular images of Eskimos, originating in the exploration literature of the sixteenth century and gradually evolving through the presentation of Eskimos at world's fairs and traveling exhibitions in the nineteenth century to the films of today. Their image was already well established by the time it was transferred to celluloid.

The film portrayal of Eskimos differed from that of American Indians from the beginning. Whereas the ignoble warrior was a standard image of Indians,

Eskimos most often were presented as the noble hunter. The environment was hostile and savage, but Eskimos were not. Rather than showing Eskimos as perpetually at war with the world, Euro-Americans most often presented them as happy and untroubled. They attributed these qualities, in turn, to their childlike nature. Like stereotypic children, Eskimos were simple and free. Finally, Eskimos embodied the essence of Darwinian logic: They survived because they were fit in a world where the weak succumbed.

Ironically, but not surprisingly, the twentieth-century Eskimo stereotype included much of what Americans had discarded from the original romantic Indian image. Christopher Columbus and his contemporaries most often depicted Indians as peaceful, innocent, and childlike, generous to a fault, sharing goods without recognition of private property, and lacking any creed or formal religion (Berkhofer 1978:5–6; Stedman 1982:20).

Rousseau and his European contemporaries focused on the naive nobility of America's first peoples of whom they had only second-hand knowledge. The primitivism espoused by Anglo-French intellectuals in the seventeenth and eighteenth centuries was a major European intellectual and imaginative tradition, and it is with us still. At base was the belief that simpler societies were happier than their Western counterpart:

> Believing thus, one would be concerned to search for and find such a society and the men who lived in it; that is to say, one would be concerned to find noble savages. . . . The question was: How noble were they? On the one side there was set in motion a current of strongly anti-primitivistic thinking. This current directly fed that American thinking about the Indian which issued into the idea of savagism. On the other side, there was set in motion a current of primitivistic thinking which swept the Indian into the work of European critics of society. Since that Indian was that noble sav-

age who theoretically embodied all that good men should be, for primitivists in the seventeenth and eighteenth centuries what he actually was came less and less to be a serious issue. What mattered was what Europeans should be. The need was to recover that portion of the primitive self which civilization had corrupted and, in the process, lay bare the faults of civilization. (Pearce 1953:136)

Although Pearce referred to the Euro-American primitivist tradition applied to Indians in the seventeenth and eighteenth centuries, no more succinct description of the filmic representation of Eskimos in the twentieth century is possible.

As Pearce points out, by the end of 1770 the American Revolution demanded a commitment on the part of colonists to a new world vision of a glorious civilization, one in which the Indian had no part. The original American notion of the noble savage gave way to the conviction that the Indian was bound to a savage past and savage society, one which was "to be destroyed by God, Nature, and Progress to make way for Civilized Man" (Pearce 1953:4). Although individual Indians might be good, as a group they were both ignoble and doomed. Indians were "forced out of American life and into American history" (Pearce 1953:58).

Commenting on the decline of the image of the American Indian, Stedman (1982:79–80) proclaims,

> It is not unusual to overlook the almost staggering turnabout in literary and dramatic portrayal of the American Indian that began in the mid-1800s. As the frontier of Indian tales changed from colonial forest, with its bowmen on foot or in canoe, to distant West, with its rifle-carrying warriors on horseback; as the theatrical milieu changed from proscenium stage to Wild West show, then flickering screen; as romantic poets abandoned the Noble Savage and the publication milieu changed from gentlemanly publishing house to mass-market industry, so did the American Indian's reputa-

UNIVERSAL-INTERNATIONAL presents

BUD ABBOTT · LOU COSTELLO LOST IN ALASKA

It's ALL NEW and a RIOT TOO!

CO-STARRING
MITZI GREEN
TOM EWELL with BRUCE CABOT

Directed by JEAN YARBROUGH
Screenplay by MARTIN A. RAGAWAY and LEONARD STERN
Produced by HOWARD CHRISTIE

Lobby card for *Lost in Alaska*, the exception to the rule. As rare as totem poles and zebraskin parkas were Eskimos shown in a humorous light. Universal Pictures.

tion decline, hastened down the path by the brutal wars in the West.

By the end of the nineteenth century, the American Indian was stereotyped most often as bloodthirsty savage. This image was fully developed in the dime novel and transferred to the Wild West Show in which Buffalo Bill and his contemporaries "used the Indians as entertainers, reenacting their vision of the 'taming of the West'" (Bataille and Silet 1985:xx).

Although the contradictory images of Native Americans as "savages noble" and "savages irredeemable" date from the founding of the nation, by the end of the nineteenth century American popular culture made much more use of the bad than of the good Indian. Just at that point in history when the Indian of American popular imagination most often was negative, his former noble qualities were not so much dispensed with as transferred to another symbol. As noble Indians limped into the wings, noble Eskimos took their place in the limelight.

The thirteenth-century Norse were the first to

EDNA FERBER'S
ICE PALACE

Presented by **WARNER BROS** · **TECHNICOLOR®** starring
RICHARD BURTON · ROBERT RYAN · CAROLYN JONES · MARTHA HYER · JIM BACKUS

6   60/178

Lobby card for *Ice Palace,* featuring Dorcas Brower of Barrow as Thor Strom's gentle, childlike wife.
Paramount Pictures.

recount the existence of Eskimos, whom they referred to as "Skrellings." Detailed descriptions of
Eskimos, however, were deferred until four centuries
later, following the exploratory voyages of Martin
Frobisher (Hakluyt 1589). Whereas the original image of the Indian gradually fell from grace, an initial
distaste for Eskimos preceded their eventual adulation. In contrast to Columbus's glowing description
of Indians, Dionyse Settle's journal account of
Frobisher's voyages depicted the Eskimos encountered on the coast of Baffinland as anything but

noble. He viewed them as men who were not men,
more animal than human.

They eate their meat all raw, both flesh, fish, and
foule, or something per boyled with blood and a
little water which they drinke. . . . If they for ne-
cessities sake stand in need of the premisses, such
grasse as the Country yeeldeth they plucke up and
eate . . . like brute beasts devouring the same. They
neither use table, stoole, or table cloth for comlines:
but when they are imbrued with blood knuckle

deepe, and their knives in like sort, they use their tongues as apt instruments to lick them cleane. (Hakluyt 1589:224)

Frobisher's accounts were, in fact, enlightened for his day, and we are lucky to have them. As Wendell Oswalt (1979:35) points out, his record most often refers to Eskimos as "countrie people" and only as villains, cannibals, and savages when they ran afoul of English interests. Frobisher may not always have approved of what he saw, but at least he considered them human.

For the next three hundred years, Euro-American explorers and adventurers continued to visit Eskimos, whom they described in numerous published accounts (Collins 1984; Oswalt 1979). European reality dominated the minds of those Old World explorers as they described the peoples they encountered. Frobisher and those who came after him were reluctant to view those they discovered as "new," preferring to interpret their finds in familiar terms. Their view of humankind remained essentially Aristotelian, with reason held out as the highest human faculty. Wherever explorers encountered humans, they judged them on a scale from beastlike to godlike, depending on the indigenous peoples' ability to control their "animal nature." Euro-Americans initially ranked Eskimos in their natural state with animals and "wild men"—devoid of civilization but capable of enlightenment through its "reasonable" charms (Colin 1987). In time—and in film—this view would be turned on its head, with Eskimos viewed as "pure primitives" whom civilization cruelly and inevitably corrupts.

Accounts of early explorers noted Inuit only in passing. Like the land and sea, the people were part of the natural environment which Europeans moved past on their way to somewhere else. They were curiosities to be remarked upon rather than the objects of study. Accurate observations were mixed with fantastic conjecture. Euro-American observers described the people's physical appearance, noting

that they were relatively short and dressed in furs. Oswalt (1979:70) remarks that the adjectives corpulent, fat, and plump are common in the descriptions. Explorers also showed some appreciation for the Eskimos' distinctive technology, including their boats, clothing, and weapons. The stereotypic Eskimo has its origins in these not-altogether-inaccurate accounts (Oswalt 1979:70).

Not until the nineteenth century and publication of the accounts of popular arctic explorers such as George Lyon (1824), William Parry (1828), and Elisha Kent Kane (1856) did the general public become better acquainted with the Inuit of Greenland and the Canadian Arctic. Alaska venues were notably absent from this repertoire. Kane's two-volume *Arctic Explorations* was especially influential, not to mention the numerous children's books and newspaper articles that further popularized his exploits in Greenland. The wide public exposure of Kane's work was at least partly responsible for the exclusion of Canadian and Alaskan counterparts. No less than Robert E. Peary (1898:xxxiv), self-proclaimed conqueror of the Pole, recalled "a chord, which, as a boy, had vibrated intensely in me at the reading of Kane's wonderful book."

Each author described the Eskimos they encountered as admirable in some respects yet decidedly inferior. Kane, for example, viewed them as good-tempered beasts of burden: "Miserable, yet happy wretches, without one thought for the future, and enjoying to the full their scanty measure of present good. As a beast, the Esquimaux is most sensible, certainly ahead of his cousin the Polar bear from whom he borrows his pantaloons" (Kane 1856, quoted in Balikci 1989:21).

Peary (1898:479, 492) would speak of Greenland's Polar Eskimos as the "fearless, hardy, cheerful little tribe of human children for whom I have the warmest regard.... Of arts, sciences, culture, manufactures and other adjuncts of civilization, they know nothing." Although they qualified their praise, explorers tended to see Eskimos as unique among the world's peoples, most often focusing on their hardiness and the rigors of their homeland. Whereas nineteenth-century Indians were perceived to have a choice between savagism and civilization, Eskimos were described in more elemental terms. Their choice was between starvation and survival. Peary's (1898:480) patronizing descriptions were typical of this attitude:

> Almost their only two objects in life [are] something to eat and something with which to clothe themselves, and their sole occupation the struggle for these objects; with habits and conditions of life hardly above the animal, these people seem at first to be very near the bottom of the scale of civilization; yet closer acquaintance shows them to be quick, intelligent, ingenious, and thoroughly human.… In disposition and temperament these people are a race of children, simple, kindly, cheerful and hospitable. (Peary 1898:492)

The turn-of-the-century arctic exhibits of the American Museum of Natural History in New York provide examples of this simultaneous adulation and ambivalence. In 1909 the museum's east corridor contained an exhibit on polar exploration put in place by the Peary Arctic Club in which Western technological superiority is a major theme: "One case contains the instruments used in exploration, such as sextant, chronometer and compass, and beside these which tell of the success of science in invention and of exploration in making use of this invention are dramatically placed various crude implements and vessels fashioned by the Eskimo from copper taken from the wreck of Sir John Franklin's ship" (American Museum 1909:209). Not only were their tools "crude," but even the copper used to make them was an inadvertent gift from a presumably greater civilization. On the floor of the exhibit, to one side, mannequins displayed Eskimos at work preparing the expedition supplies. Eskimos were important not for themselves, but for their service to the explorers' civilized endeavor.

In the same year in the same museum, Frank Stokes, an artist and member of several Peary expeditions, completed a huge mural on the ceiling of the Eskimo Hall depicting superhuman figures in dramatic natural surroundings, including panels entitled "Eskimo Goddess of the Sun," "Polar Bear at Bay," and "Walrus Hunting in the Light of the Aurora Borealis." This monumental art was intended to bring home to the observer "not only ethnological facts but the austerity of Eskimo life, its enforced simplicity" (American Museum 1909:211).

Whereas English exploration had been motivated by the search for the Northwest Passage, American explorers primarily sought a route to the Pole. The process generated a vast literature on Eskimos, both popular and scientific. No less than Rudyard Kipling was inspired to eulogize Eskimo life in the stories "Quiquern" and "The Song of the Returning Hunter" in *The Second Jungle Book* (1895). At the same time that they increased their comprehension of the "reality" of arctic life, nineteenth-century Euro-Americans began to clothe Eskimos in a new, romantic image that they wear to this day.

How was it possible for some Americans to view Eskimos so positively at the same time they held Indians in such low esteem? Frontier Americans believed that Indians had to be transformed from roaming, unreliable savages into settled, steady, and civilized beings (Pearce 1953:53). This was part of the "grand rationale of westward-moving colonialism"—the belief in the "natural and divine superiority of a farming to a hunting culture" (Pearce 1953:66). Twentieth-century missionaries, government teachers, and reformers attempted a comparable transformation of Alaska Eskimos. This encounter, however, came relatively late in American history. The nineteenth century was two-thirds past by the time the United States purchased Alaska, and the native peoples were little known. Eskimos became a problem to be confronted only after Indians had been overcome. Battles over territory, like those in the West, never occurred in the Arctic. Most of the land was unsuitable for cultivation, so the Eskimos' maintenance of rights to the land and their refusal to settle permanently was not so contemptible. Well after the press of civilization had crushed the "wild Indian," "noble Eskimos" prospered because they were perceived as no real threat.

Late nineteenth-century travelers and explorers often described encounters with Indians and Eskimos in opposite terms. Harry DeWindt, an Englishman touring Alaska in 1896, judged the Tlingit "the laziest and most impudent scoundrels" he had ever met, whereas he saw southwest Alaska Eskimos as merely "queer-looking … with a smile on his honest brown features, a contrast to the sullen, vicious faces" of Athapaskans. To the east, along the Mackenzie drainage, D. T. Hanbury described "lazy, extravagant, sullen, morose Indians who 'of late years [have] acquired a slovenly, swaggering way of going about' and who barely shielded their contempt for white men, in contrast to cheerful, jovial, more trustworthy Eskimos" (Kretch 1989:26). The dynamic between the Euro-American writer and the native peoples of the Far North involved oppositions of "nearness and distance, sameness and difference" (Hegeman 1989:144). In the construction of the distinction, Eskimos more often than not won the advantage.

The initial fascination with Eskimos by Euro-Americans was the sharp contrast between the harsh, cold, primordial conditions of arctic life and the ultimately admirable human qualities and adaptive strengths attributed to its aboriginal occupants. Such strengths presumably enabled them to cope with the severity of their environment. The Social Darwinism of the nineteenth century preached survival of the fittest, a principle that was applied to all phases of natural development. What could be more susceptible to idealization than a people who were apparently so perfectly suited for their environment, masters of their natural domain?

Eskimos were not, however, universally admired at the turn of the century, and their representation had its dark side. The flamboyant Earl of Lonsdale described the Yup'ik Eskimos of the Yukon River as having "for the most part bad and deceitful faces…. They are nasty people to be amongst and one has always to be on the look out" (Kretch 1989:72). Whereas Lonsdale entered his diatribes as private journal entries, other equally unflattering depictions greeted the public eye. In their classic family history *Cheaper by the Dozen,* Frank and Ernestine Gilbreth recalled their mother's reaction to naming pet birds Peter Soil and Maggie Mess: "Mother wouldn't let us use those full names, she said they were 'Eskimo.' (Eskimo was Mother's description of anything that was off-color, revolting, or evil minded.) We called the birds simply Peter and Maggie" (Gilbreth and Carey 1948:86). In response to her husband's suggestion that her children had "the noisiest stomachs I've ever heard," Mrs. Gilbreth "looked disapprovingly over her mending" and remarked, "I think … there are Eskimos in the house" (Gilbreth and Carey 1948:130, see also p. 91 and p. 149).[2]

Here, as elsewhere, a residual ambivalence toward Eskimos derived from contending notions of progress. Lord Lonsdale and Mrs. Gilbreth emphasized the difference between themselves and "primitive peoples" to show how far they had climbed the ladder of civilization, while doubts about progress supported the idealization of primitive life. Commitment to the notion of progress allowed people to exaggerate the difference between themselves and what they labeled "primitive." At the same time the often-violent break with the past brought on by the industrial revolution fostered doubts about progress and, coincidently, the idealization of the primitive. Many viewed "natural men" as closer than their civi-

2. Ironically, turn-of-the-century Yup'ik Eskimos used the term "white man" in an equally pointed fashion. Moravian missionary Edith Kilbuck reported in 1890, "They use the word 'white-man' to scare their children into obedience or silence as people in the states would say goblin or robbers. When the old priest wishes to intimidate the people he says 'scores of white men will come and take the women' etc. The priest himself is a native."

lized counterparts to an uncorrupted human essence. While advocates of progress had used Eskimos to show how far Western Civilization had come, romantics put them to work strengthening their critique of society.

By the end of the nineteenth century, the popular literature more and more frequently described Eskimos in the heroic mode. Their survival (like that of the explorers themselves) was proof that self-discipline, persistence, and common sense could bring success. In contrast to the disdain of the Victorians, subsequent commentators increasingly regretted the Eskimos' decline. George Byron Gordon (1906-7:70, 72) simultaneously extolled the "perfect adaptability" of the Yup'ik Eskimos of the Kuskokwim drainage and viewed them as doomed:

As a stock the Eskimos have adapted themselves perfectly to their environment.... They developed under the influence of their exceptional surroundings, a highly specialized culture type which, depending entirely on local environment for its resources, is well fitted to survive under normal conditions, but ill adapted to support radical change....

One of the most remarkable traits of the whole stock, one which has distinguished them at all times and wherever they have been encountered, may be described as a light-hearted amiability, a disposition that ... renders them cheerful in the face of hardships which would overcome any other people.... The fact that this trait becomes less pronounced ... under the influence of civilization, is one of the most dangerous symptoms in the present condition of the Western Eskimos.

Here it was not that Eskimos were flawed; rather civilization was the culprit, thwarting as it did their "perfect adaptability" and "light-hearted disposition."

Euro-Americans gradually transformed the image of the Eskimo from subhuman to superhuman.

They studied Eskimos "to understand how a primitive society dominated by an implacable environment can persevere" (Malaurie 1982:xvi). Robert Coles would write in 1977, "There is only one way Eskimos have learned to endure; they know to face up to extreme danger, to face down nature's unpredictable assaults."

The Puritan encounter with the Indian had focused on the difference between "savage" and "civilized" humanity: "Man realizes his nature as he progresses historically ... from savagism to civilization.... To civilize him was to triumph over the past. To kill him was to kill the past.... The history of American civilization would thus be conceived of as three-dimensional, progressing from past to present, from east to west, from lower to higher" (Pearce 1953:49). In contrast, the Euro-American encounter with Eskimos increasingly emphasized their similarity—people ennobled, governed by the laws of nature. Whereas the idea of progress and Manifest Destiny determined the view of the American Indian, the idea of the "primitive" determined the view of Eskimos. These inhabitants of arctic extremes were "natural men" extraordinaire, survivors and, by definition, fit.

Following Pearce, the ultimate goal of the primitivistic critique was to make people live up to "true civilization," which paradoxically meant a simpler and less sophisticated way of life. Euro-Americans viewed Eskimos as civilized ultimately because they were uncorrupted by civilization: "This was the tradition and the convention of the noble savage" (Pearce 1953:138). Serious primitivists needed a symbol for the "primitive good" (Pearce 1953:142). If the facts of life in frontier America made the application of such a tradition to Indians impossible, the facts of life in the Alaskan and Canadian Arctic provided fertile ground. The goal of the primitivist was not to know Eskimos for what they were, but rather to learn from them what had been lost yet perhaps could be regained (Pearce 1953:136).

Indians became important for the American

mind not for themselves, but rather for what they showed "civilized" people they were not and must not be (Pearce 1953:5). Eskimos showed Euro-Americans what they had been and in essentials still were. Both theories were equally fallacious, freezing the image of Indians as "savages" and that of Eskimos as "primitive first people."

The Alaska Anomaly

The popular images of Eskimos originated in Canada and Greenland (the original sites of encounter) without reference to life in Alaska. There is as much truth as fiction in these images as they apply to the lifeways of the people among whom they originated. The parka-clad, igloo-dwelling inhabitants of the High Arctic were the most widespread group of Eskimos, with a highly specialized way of life (Oswalt 1979:197). Yet they account for less than 5 percent of the approximately fifty thousand people living in the Arctic at the beginning of the nineteenth century. The extreme and exotic conditions in which they lived combined with their relatively early and well-publicized encounters with Euro-Americans, transforming them into the paradigmatic inhabitants of the Far North. Even today, if most people think about Alaska Eskimos, the images that appear in their minds derive in large part from Greenland and the Canadian Arctic and contradict the reality of life in Alaska on every count.

The stereotypic Eskimo always lives in a dome-shaped igloo or snowhouse.[3] Not so Alaska Eskimos. In the past they made their homes in semisubterranean sod houses. South of Norton Sound, men used driftwood and logs to frame these constructions, as the Yukon, Kuskokwim, and Nushagak rivers bring an ample supply from the interior

Styrofoam igloo represents life in Alaska in 1994 for the Steven Seagal film *On Deadly Ground*.

each spring. Farther north, a combination of whalebone and wood provided the necessary support.

Covered by snow in winter, these structures sometimes gave the appearance of snowhouses but were much more permanent. Villages often occupied the same sites for hundreds of years, with people patching and rebuilding their homes as needed. In the last forty years, people have replaced sod homes with frame houses, many complete with flush toilets and running water. The only igloos a visitor will see in Alaska today are those men are paid to make when a movie crew comes to town.

Not only are they placed in igloos, Eskimos are invariably imagined to eke out a living in a harsh, unforgiving land. Although residents of the arctic and subarctic environments of the north and west coasts of Alaska experienced periodic scarcity, theirs was a much richer environment than one might think, with a tremendous variety of resources. Coastal Iñupiat live in one of the best sea mammal hunting areas in the world. Under the direction of an *umialik* (boat captain), hunters continue to this day to harvest bowhead whales and walrus. Although shallow seas to the south of Norton Sound

---

3. "The igloo has a tremendous fascination for everyone who does not live in an igloo. It is the symbol of the land of the Grand North, a token of man's victory over ice" (Buliard 1951:vii).

Forty-eight belukhas taken in one day, Hooper Bay, 1934. Father John Fox, Oregon Province Archives.

limit the range of these large sea mammals, Yup'ik men hunt in pairs and threesomes for a variety of seals, walrus, and belukha whales.

Men and women supplement hunting in the open ocean by fishing for herring, tomcod, flounder, halibut, and smelt in nearshore waters. Hundreds of thousands of salmon run up the coastal rivers each spring, and the innumerable sloughs and streams that crisscross the broad, marshy, coastal plains are richly endowed with fish, including sheefish, several species of whitefish, northern pike, burbot, trout, blackfish, and stickleback.

The land and sky provide an additional array. Birds and migratory waterfowl, including geese, cranes, swans, ducks, and seabirds, nest in abundance in the delta lowlands of western Alaska. Small land mammals, such as white and red fox, rabbit and hare, land otter, muskrat, beaver, and mink, abound. Moose and bear range the river drainages, and musk oxen graze along the coast. Herds of caribou migrate across the tundra north of Norton

Sound. These diverse resources hardly match the popular representation of the Eskimos' "cruel" environment.

In northern Alaska, the coastline does resemble the environment the average schoolchild associates with Eskimos—rugged tundra, covered with snow all but two months of the year, pack ice clinging to the nearshore ice and stretching away for miles. Here driftwood is scarce, winter months devoid of light, and summers brightened by a sun that never sets. Wind can drive temperatures down to -80° F in winter, while the constant sun can boost temperatures to +80° F.

However, the majority of Alaska Eskimos live along the western, not the northern, coast. And the farther south a visitor travels along Alaska's coastline, the less the picture of a frozen wasteland applies. For thousands of years the Yukon and Kuskokwim rivers have carried silt and soil out of Alaska's interior to the delta, creating a vast alluvial fan along the coast, criss-crossed by thousands of

Ample "skirts" of herring drying at Toksook Bay. James H. Barker.

Peter Nick checks his fish trap, Russian Mission. James H. Barker.

sloughs and streams. Half the land surface is covered by water, providing the traditional highways of its native people. Yet so little precipitation falls that it qualifies as a cold desert. Except for occasional low volcanic domes breaking the surface along the coastline, the sea is shallow and the land is flat.

The Yup'ik Eskimos along this coast do not annually endure either months of frigid winter or the complete absence of sun. December day length is comparable to that in Anchorage, five hours long at the least, and men continue to hunt and fish most of the winter. Shore ice may extend thirty miles off the coast, but the sea is never frozen over. Polar bears find the maritime climate too tropical and rarely venture south of Unalakleet.

Spring does not come to the northern Arctic until mid-July. But days lengthen and snow begins to melt by mid-April in western Alaska, with breakup at the end of May. The three-month growing season is also long by arctic standards, and edible greens and berries abound. Shrubs and trees, including willows and alders, grow scattered along the coast. Spruce and birch border river drainages from above Bethel on the Kuskokwim and Pilot Station on the Yukon River.

Alaska's rich resources, including wood for building, supported the largest concentration of Eskimos in the Arctic. Eskimos comprise the world's most far-flung aboriginal population, settling along a 6,000-mile stretch from Greenland to the eastern tip of Siberia. Of the fifty thousand men and women who inhabited this vast territory when the first Europeans arrived two hundred years ago, fully half of them lived in what is now Alaska.

Alaska Eskimos are divided into two groups: the Iñupiat of northwest Alaska and the Yupiit, or Yup'ik Eskimos, of St. Lawrence Island, southern Norton Sound, and the lower drainages of the Yukon, Kuskokwim, and Nushagak rivers. The Iñupiat speak a single language, Inuit/Iñupiaq, which they share with the Inuit residents living to the east along Canada's Arctic coast and into Labrador and

Greenland. Although occupying a much smaller area, the Yupiit are internally divided into five language groups—three Siberian languages spoken on the tip of the Chukchi Peninsula and St. Lawrence Island, Central Alaskan Yup'ik spoken from Unalakleet to Bristol Bay, and Pacific Yup'ik (Alutiiq), which historically was spoken around Prince William Sound, the tip of the Kenai Peninsula, Kodiak Island, and part of the Alaska Peninsula (Jacobson 1984:28).

On the eve of the arrival of Euro-Americans, the Yup'ik and Iñupiaq men and women living in Alaska had adapted themselves to as many ecological niches as Alaska's coastal environment could support. Socially they were divided into approximately forty societies, consisting of members of closely related family groups (Burch 1980; Fienup-Riordan 1984; Pratt 1984; Shinkwin and Pete 1984). Their personal identity reflected the society into which they were born. They did not identify themselves as Alaska Eskimos and only in very specific contexts, such as contacts with speakers of another language, did they see themselves as Iñupiat or Yup'ik. Their primary allegiance was to their families and tribal groups. For example, people of Nelson Island in western Alaska thought of themselves first as Tununarmiut (people of the village of Tunuak), second as Qaluyaarmiut (people of Nelson Island), and only as Yupiit (plural, literally "real people") or Yup'ik Eskimos in comparison with people who did not speak the Yup'ik language. Genetic heritage did not carry the same weight as it does today in the recognition of an individual as an Alaska Eskimo. Language, family membership, and local residence determined personal and group identity.

Abundant resources not only meant a large and culturally diverse population by arctic standards, but a more settled life. People moved annually within a relatively fixed range in their harvesting endeavors. Each society demarcated a largely self-sufficient area within which people moved freely during the year. Dramatic fluctuations in animal populations and

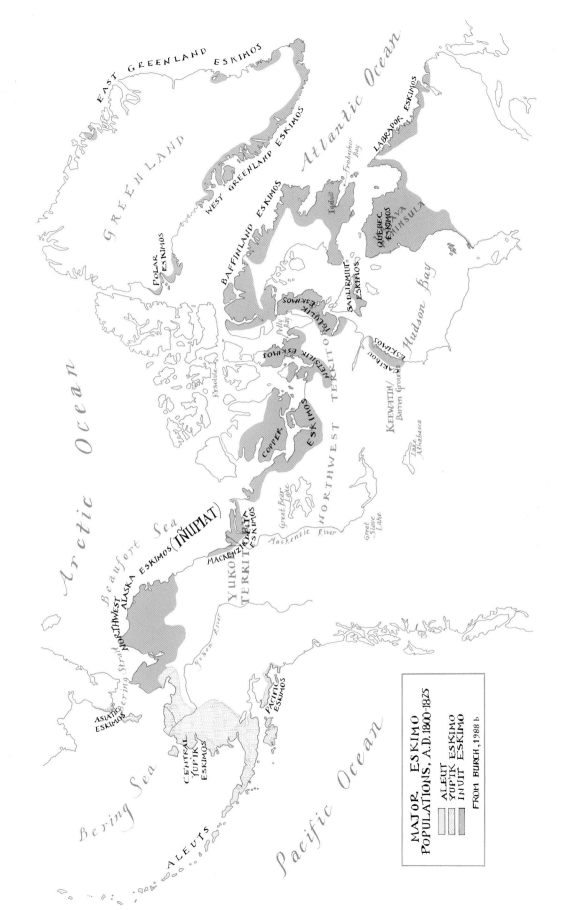

Major Eskimo populations, A.D. 1800–1825 (from Burch 1988b)

MAJOR ESKIMO
POPULATIONS, A.D. 1800-1825

ALEUT
YUP'IK ESKIMO
INUIT ESKIMO

FROM BURCH, 1988 b

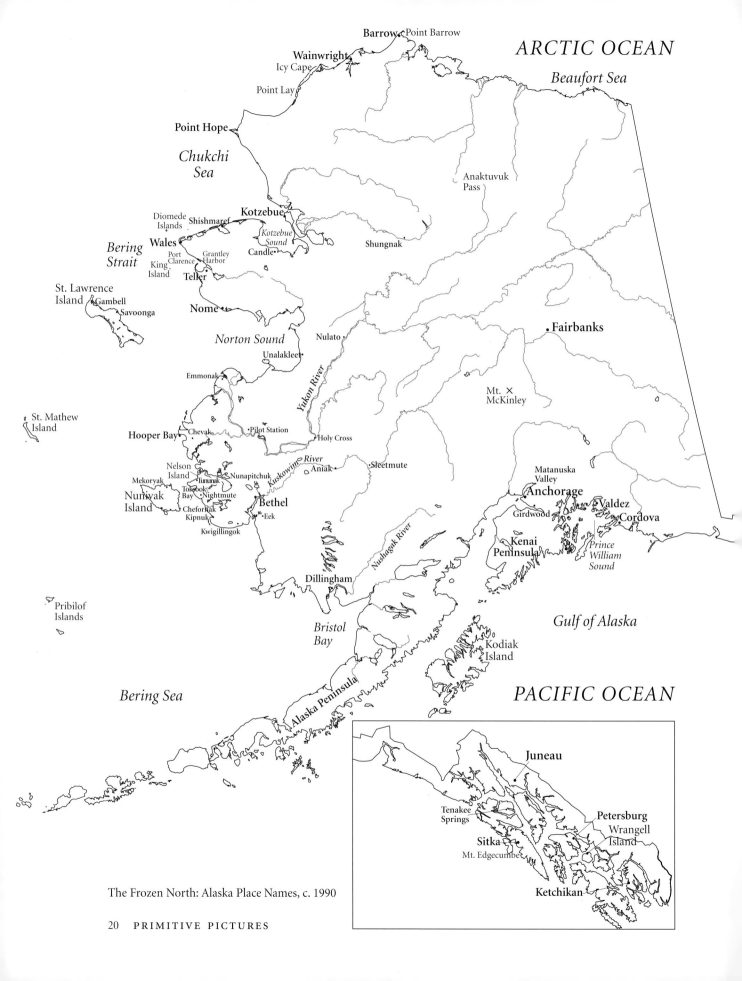

ARCTIC OCEAN

Beaufort Sea

Barrow • Point Barrow

Wainwright
Icy Cape
Point Lay

Point Hope

*Chukchi
Sea*

Anaktuvuk
Pass

Diomede
Islands
Shishmaref
Kotzebue

*Kotzebue
Sound*

Candle •
Shungnak

Wales
*Bering
Strait*
Port
Clarence
Grantley
Harbor
King
Island
Teller

St. Lawrence
Island • Gambell
Savoonga

Nome

Norton Sound

Nulato

• Fairbanks

Unalakleet

St. Mathew
Island

Emmonak

Yukon River

Mt. ×
McKinley

Hooper Bay • Chevak
• Pilot Station
Holy Cross

Nelson
Island
Mekoryak
Nunapitchuk
Kuskokwim River
Aniak
• Sleetmute

Matanuska
Valley

Tununak
Nuniwak
Island
Tokbook
Bay
Nightmute
Chefornak
Kipnuk
Bethel
• Eek

Anchorage
Girdwood
• Valdez
Cordova

Kenai
Peninsula

*Prince
William
Sound*

Kwigillingok

Dillingham

Nushagak River

Gulf of Alaska

Pribilof
Islands

*Bristol
Bay*

Kodiak
Island

PACIFIC OCEAN

Bering Sea

Alaska Peninsula

Juneau

Tenakee
Springs

Petersburg
Wrangell
Island

Sitka
Mt. Edgecumbe

The Frozen North: Alaska Place Names, c. 1990

Ketchikan

Hooper Bay in 1946. Milotte Collection, Alaska and Polar Regions Department, University of Alaska Fairbanks.

variable ice and weather conditions often made inter-regional travel and trade expedient. Social strategies that facilitated this movement included regular exchanges of food, names, feasts, and spouses.

At the turn of the century, the bilateral extended family, numbering up to thirty persons, was the basic social unit within Yup'ik and Iñupiaq societies. This is large by Greenlandic and Canadian Inuit standards. Two to four generations, including parents, offspring, and parents' parents, lived together at seasonal camps and permanent winter villages. Married siblings of either the parents or their offspring might also be included. Overlapping networks of consanguineal and affinal ties joined extended families making up a community. Members of a single residential group probably were related to one another in several different ways within four or five degrees of con-

sanguinity. In the larger villages, most marriages were within the group. Regular recruitment also occurred beyond the village, although normally within the bounds of the society.

Small family groups dispersed during the summer and fall for harvesting activities, but most Iñupiaq and Yup'ik families gathered each winter in permanent villages. Unlike their Canadian kin, Yup'ik hunter, wife, and child rarely slept under the same roof. Rather, men and boys over age five lived and worked in a central men's house, or *qasgiq*. Women and children resided in numerous smaller dwellings, where they prepared food and cared for young children. Although Iñupiaq hunters slept with their families, they, too, spent much of their time in a men's house, or *qariyi*, that they shared with fellow members of their whaling crew.

Yup'ik men working in a *qasgiq* (communal men's house) in western Alaska, early 1900s. F. Drebert, Moravian Archives, Bethlehem, Pennsylvania.

Among both Yupiit and Iñupiat, the men's house was the focus of winter community activity and the site of elaborate ceremonial exchanges such as the Messenger Feast. Although they addressed similar themes, the ceremonial round differed widely among societies. All made use of intricate ritual paraphernalia, especially to the south of Norton Sound. Some scholars have characterized the Bering Sea coast "the cradle of Eskimo civilization," as it was here that Eskimoan culture achieved the highest degree of social and technological elaboration. The complexity of their art and ceremony was anything but "primitive."

Finally, if one believes the stereotype, Eskimos are always peaceful and always friendly. In fact, prior to the arrival of the Russians in the early 1800s, bloody bow-and-arrow warfare frequently occurred both between and among Yup'ik and Iñupiaq societies. Warriors underwent rigorous training to toughen their bodies and minds for combat. Protected by slat armor made of wood or bone, they carried out surprise raids on rival groups, destroying whole villages and killing all the men among them. These armed raids did not abate in northwest Alaska until the last half of the nineteenth century. This activity stood in sharp contrast to the patterns of intergroup relations described for the sparsely populated Canadian Arctic (Burch 1974; Fienup-Riordan 1990:146–66; VanStone 1983).

Alaska Eskimos in the Public Eye

Why does the Western image of arctic life not admit the conditions found in Alaska? Why has the meager population of the High Arctic commanded world attention, while their much more numerous and culturally complex western relatives have remained, until recently, virtually unknown?

The peoples of the Far North have intrigued Euro-Americans since the two first met in the Canadian North on voyages and overland treks in search of the Northwest Passage between the Atlantic and Pacific. Subsequently Kane, followed by Peary, made front-page news with their accounts of life among Greenland Eskimos. Alaska was not a part of the "real Arctic" experienced by early explorers, and, consequently, inhabitants of Europe and the continental United States knew precious little about Alaska's indigenous people until the early years of the twentieth century. Lacking any real knowledge of Alaska Eskimos, nonnatives tended to apply to them images of Eskimos derived from experiences in better-known arctic regions. That this environment differs dramatically from its Alaska counterpart was immaterial.

As in the Canadian Arctic, the first descriptions of Alaska came as a result of voyages of exploration. Europeans did not discover the North Pacific, Bering Sea, and Arctic coast of Alaska until the eighteenth century, nearly two hundred years later than the northeastern coasts of Canada and Greenland (Collins 1984). In 1728 and 1741–42, Vitus Bering, a Dane and captain in the Imperial Russian Navy, attempted to establish Russian sovereignty in northwestern America. Although he encountered no natives, his expeditions opened the way for the Russian fur trade. The Russian-American Company subsequently sent exploratory reconnaissance into Yup'ik territory as part of the expansion of their lucrative fur trade, including expeditions led by Petr Korsakovskiy in 1818 and 1819, Mikhail Vasiliev in 1820, and Vasilii Khromchenko and Adolph Etolin in 1821 and 1822. These explorers made contacts with Yupiit and Iñupiat along the Alaska coast and

provided a foundation for future trade relations. They were followed by Ivan Vasil'ev in 1829, Fedor Kolmakov between 1829 and 1832, and, most notably, Lavrentii Zagoskin in 1842-44. Each of these men had something to say about Alaska Eskimos. Lieutenant Zagoskin was favorably impressed with the people he met and wrote: "Both his virtue and his evil are childlike. If you attach him to yourself by kind treatment … he will never forget you. To do them justice, we must admit that they are shrewd, enterprising, sound of judgment, vigilant, and gifted with a fine memory.… There are no poor among

Turn-of-the-century Nome. B. B. Dobbs, Anchorage Museum of History and Art.

them" (Michael 1967:107). Yet the results of these expeditions were closely guarded company secrets, and the explorers' comments, both positive and negative, were neither translated nor published. The details of their travels remained unknown to the English-speaking world until scholarly translations of their accounts a century and a half later (Michael 1967; VanStone 1973, 1984:150-51, 1988).

The Russians were not the only ones interested in Alaska. Captain James Cook sailed along the coast of Alaska between Bristol Bay and Icy Cape on his third and last voyage in 1778 (Beaglehole 1967:591-636). The trip produced the direct ancestor of our modern map of Alaska (VanStone 1984:152), and it opened the eyes of the world to North America's northwest coast, hitherto the playground of the Russians. Cook carried a copy of David Crantz's recently published *History of Greenland* (1767) to prepare him for any indigenous people he might meet (Beaglehole 1967:596; King 1990:3). Although he recorded only brief descriptions of the handful of Yup'ik and Iñupiaq men who paddled out to investigate his vessel, his expedition produced the earliest pictorial representation of Norton Sound Iñupiat. His remarks convey largely positive impressions of Alaska Eskimos, who he found to be both like and unlike their Greenlandic relatives. He was less enthusiastic about Alaska as a whole, in marked contrast to his more positive view of the South Pacific, primarily in reaction to the forbidding landscape and rainy weather. His most encouraging comments concerned the commercial value of the sea otter.

Such skilled and noted mariners as Otto von Kotzebue in 1815, Mikhail Vasiliev and Glieb Shishmaref in 1820, and Frederick Beechey in 1823 followed Cook's lead (Beechey 1832; Kotzebue 1821; VanStone 1984:152). Aleksandr Kashevarov's expedition traveled in Iñupiaq skinboats thirty miles east of Point Barrow in 1838, but here again his exploits and observations only became available to the non-Russian-speaking world in a 1977 scholarly translation (VanStone 1977). Although Kashevarov had

much to say on the subject of Alaska Eskimos, few heard.

These famous navigators of the eighteenth and nineteenth centuries had little impact on the Iñupiat and Yupiit with whom they came in contact. In fact, European explorers had little interest in the residents of Alaska, except insofar as the local people could give the visitors supplies and information (VanStone 1984:153). Sir John Franklin's third and fatal expedition in 1845 was one of the most dramatic incidents in arctic exploration during the nineteenth century, and its failure stunned Europe and America (Christopher 1988:262). Although the well-publicized expeditions in search of Franklin's party mentioned the natives they encountered during their search, the Euro-American fascination with the drama of lost caucasians and their fight for survival far outweighed any interest they had in Alaska's newly found indigenous population. The one notable exception was the work of John Simpson (1875), the surgeon aboard one of the Franklin search ships, who published the first detailed report about northern Alaskan Eskimos (Oswalt 1979:206).

Whaling began to have an impact on the Arctic coastline after 1850. Iñupiaq hunters sometimes worked on the whaling ships as well as at a handful of shore-based whaling stations. After their summer's work, the majority of whalers headed south for the winter, taking with them carved ivory souvenirs and stories of their Eskimo companions, both men and women. Although these encounters did not receive the publicity of Peary's exploits at the other end of the Arctic, they were among the first contexts in which some Euro-Americans began to gain more than a superficial understanding of Alaska Eskimo life. Some whalers, like Charles Brower of Barrow, established themselves as traders and stayed behind after the collapse of the market for baleen in the early 1900s, often taking Iñupiaq wives. Brower (n.d.) left voluminous accounts of his dealings with the Iñupiat over his fifty-nine-year tenure in northern Alaska. Like the writings of Russian explorers one hundred years before, his work is only now beginning to be mined by scholars.

Men such as Michael Healy (1887, 1889), Calvin Hooper (1881), and George Stoney (1900) explored the rivers flowing into Kotzebue Sound in the 1880s for the U.S. Navy on Revenue Marine steamers (VanStone 1984:152), and they were among the first to record detailed observations of life along Alaska's western coast. Even more important were the ethnographic descriptions of Edward Nelson (1882, 1899) and John Murdoch (1892), both published by the newly established Bureau of American Ethnology at the Smithsonian Institution and both masterpieces of descriptive ethnography. Murdoch was, in fact, one of the first arctic scholars to take seriously issues of representation. In 1887 he published an article debunking "popular errors in regard to Eskimos," in which he concluded, "Neither does the general belief that they drink train oil appear to be supported by reliable evidence, and some authors in various localities especially deny it. I trust that I have presented sufficient evidence to show that the popular picture of the dwarfish Eskimo, dozing in an underground den, keeping up his internal heat by enormous meals of raw blubber washed down with draughts of lamp-oil, is based on exaggeration, to say the least, rather than on actual facts" (Murdoch 1887:16).

Nelson's and Murdoch's accounts comprised major additions in what the educated person could know about Alaska Eskimo. But these publications were relatively obscure. The first printing of Nelson's monograph *The Eskimo about Bering Strait* numbered several thousand, whereas Kane's *Arctic Explorations* sold sixty-five thousand copies (Balikci 1989:23), and Peary's *Northward Over the Great Ice* enjoyed even greater distribution. John Kilbuck, a Moravian missionary who worked among Yup'ik Eskimos along the Kuskokwim between 1885 and 1921, referred to Peary's work in the opening pages of his own ethnographic manuscript "Something about the Innuit" (Fienup-Riordan 1988:3), speak-

ing of the "language of the Eskimo, whom Peary has introduced into history." Through ten thousand pages of journals and letters, Kilbuck made no mention of being aware of, let alone reading, Nelson's detailed description of the people among whom the missionary worked for more than thirty years.

By the turn of the century, commercial enterprises were drawing newcomers to Alaska in unprecedented numbers. Following the Klondike strike in 1897, thousands headed to Nome in search of gold. More modest in ambition but equally important in the development of Alaska commerce, commercial fishermen established themselves in the Nushagak drainage after 1880 (VanStone 1984:156). Alaska became a hot topic in the popular press, with authors such as John Muir, Rex Beach, and Jack London celebrating its raw, untamed beauty and the battle for survival of those who ventured there.

The plots of Beach's novels revolved around mining and commercial fishing in Alaska, with little reference to Eskimos. Later, a number of his books became movies, including *The Spoilers* (1906) and *The Silver Horde* (1909). As Eskimos played at best a supporting role in Beach's fiction, they tended to play an equally small role in the movies his books inspired.

John Muir paid more attention to Alaska's native people. Writing in the romantic tradition of William Wordsworth and Henry David Thoreau, his *Cruise of the Corwin* (1917) depicted Alaska natives as "natural men" living in harmony with their environment. The book celebrates both wild nature and its original inhabitants whose lifeways Muir, like his contemporary Gordon, contrasted to the pernicious influences of Western Civilization. People who in the past had been self-reliant and free became, under the white man's tutelage, dependent and destitute, subject to disease and drink (Jody 1969:40-44).

One of the most widely read American novelists of the world, Jack London published prodigiously on Alaska/Yukon themes, including *Call of the Wild* (1903) and *White Fang* (1905). London, who wrote more than fifty books, devoted several dozen stories to Alaska natives, the majority about Indians but a handful with Eskimo themes. His third collection of northland tales, *Children of the Frost* (1902), portrays Eskimos as simultaneously simple and free in their natural state yet doomed with the arrival of "sunlanders" set on conquest and commerce. In the tale "In the Forests of the North," Fairfax, an American who has spent years in the Arctic, describes the people among whom he lives as "honest folk" who "live according to their lights": "And then they are amazingly simple. No complexity about them, no thousand and one subtle ramifications to every single emotion they experience. They love, fear, hate, are angered, or made happy, in common, ordinary and unmistakable terms. It may be a beastly life, but at least it is easy to live…. No mistakes, no misunderstandings. It has its charm, after civilization's fitful fever" (Teacher and Nicholls 1981:266-67).

In *Children of the Frost's* "Nam-Bok the Unveracious," London describes the simple "fisherfolk" of the Yukon Delta: "They were a poor people, with

Lowland topography of western Alaska. James H. Barker.

neither gold in the ground nor valuable furs in hand, so the whites had passed them afar. Also, the Yukon, through the thousands of years, had shoaled that portion of the seas with the detritus of Alaska till vessels grounded out of sight of land. So the sodden coast, with its long inside reaches and huge mud-land archipelagoes, was avoided by the ships of men, and the fisherfolk knew not that such things were" (Teacher and Nicholls 1981:286). London's description is a succinct portrait of the isolated west coast of Alaska, home of thousands of Yup'ik Eskimos. It not only tells us why Yukon natives knew so little about the outside world at the turn of the century, but why that outside world knew so little about them.

London viewed nature and natives alike as neither benevolent nor malevolent, but a testing ground against which nonnative newcomers could measure themselves. A person needed both strength of body and spirit to survive in the Far North. Eskimos, like the forest and the sea, were part of the untamed landscape against which the white man struggled. As John Burroughs (1904:2) wrote in "In Green Alaska": "As one goes West, nature is more and more, and man less and less" (Jody 1969:55). London employed the subarctic environment and its native people, with their "elemental passions," to reveal Social Darwinism in action. The rigors of Alaska laid down the laws humans must live by, and only the fit could survive.

By 1900, the new territory of Alaska was beginning to find a place in the general American repertoire, thanks to commercial endeavors including whaling, mining, and commercial fishing. The lifeways of its native occupants, however, remained obscure. Governor Thomas Riggs, who served from 1918 to 1921, wrote that outsiders thought the Territory was "peopled by desperadoes living in huts or dugouts; a country of Eskimo and eternal snows" (Norris 1992:58). The popular image of Alaska was composed of equal parts ice, sled dogs, gold, fortune hunters, and faceless Eskimos, on whom romantics

and Social Darwinists alike might project their view of the world unencumbered by the details of everyday life.

The 1909 Alaska-Yukon-Pacific Exposition in Seattle was organized in large part to counter this ignorance and to advertise the economic potential of America's northwest corner. It was Alaska's "coming out" party and included exhibits on all the nascent commercial enterprises beginning to develop in the new territory. It also exhibited one hundred Eskimos, including men, women, and children, but no Iñupiat or Central Alaska Yupiit were among them. Rather, the promoters imported Siberian Yup'ik Eskimos to represent Alaska's first people. Moreover, the exposition displayed the troupe in a gigantic papier-mâché igloo. Brochures described them as "strange people, existing only on the products of the icy North, half civilized in their nature, knowing no god, having no laws, no government, unable to read or write, with no history of their antecedents" (quoted in *Alaska Journal* 1984:14). In the fifty years since its purchase, Alaska had begun to share its rich natural resources with the outside world. Yet its human resources were still a mystery, notable not for what they were but for what they lacked by Euro-American standards.

At the same time that Peary's exploits were making front-page news, Alaska was just beginning to be noticed, and what was reported barely gave passing reference to Eskimos. The rush for the Klondike did not do to Alaska natives what the rush for the Pole had done for the Polar Eskimos. Alaska Eskimos remained peripheral to the conquest of Alaska. Charlie Chaplin's famous film *Gold Rush* (1925) reflects the blind spot typical of this period in American history. In the film, the Little Tramp and his cohorts surmount great odds, both natural and human, to make their fortune in the untamed Northland. Natives played no part in the picture. The original occupants of Alaska were in the beginning all but nonexistent in its fictive recreation.

The "Eskimo Village" at the 1909 Alaska-Yukon-Pacific Exposition. Frank Nowell, Special Collections Division, negative no. 1766, University of Washington Libraries.

Alaska Eskimos and the Outside World

Perhaps the most damaging aspect of the generalized image of Eskimos is that, like other aboriginal peoples throughout the world, they are "people without history" (Wolf 1982). In the 1909 exposition they were viewed as "having no history of their antecedents." Even today debate too often collapses the complex history of adaptation, transformation, and invention that took place in Alaska into the catchphrase of conflict between "traditional" and "modern." In fact, the meaning of this opposition has changed dramatically since the original encounters between Alaska Eskimos and Euro-Americans two hundred years ago. To understand the situation of contemporary Iñupiaq and Yup'ik peoples in Alaska, one must understand how Alaska Eskimos

have responded to rapidly changing conditions during the last two centuries. This encounter encompasses a number of overlapping stages in the relationship between Alaska Eskimos and the people who came to live among them: resistance, coexistence, population disruption, attempted assimilation, global incorporation, dependency, and empowerment. The people on the street may have been generally unaware of the changes their northward expansion had set in motion, but this did not diminish their magnitude for those involved.

Confrontation between Alaska Eskimos and outsiders began with the arrival of Russian fur traders and European explorers in the mid-1700s. Similar to the European experience with American Indians, early contacts between Alaska Eskimos and newcomers created tensions that frequently deteriorated into violence. Most early explorers reported strained encounters with Alaska Eskimos. Yup'ik and Iñupiaq men and women demonstrated what has been characterized as "realistic opportunism" (Graburn 1969:93)—a general friendliness and willingness to trade when it suited them, mixed with a capacity to kill the intruders and take what they wanted by force if they thought they could get away with it. Early explorers and traders were painfully aware of Eskimo intergroup warfare because it disrupted their own activities.

As time went on, however, peaceful relations generally replaced hostility and suspicion between Alaska Eskimos and Euro-Americans. A period of coexistence, during which Alaska Eskimos remained largely self-sufficient, replaced the initial period of resistance. Although Russia claimed Alaska, Euro-Americans came to Alaska primarily to exploit resources rather than for territorial expansion. Except for Russian enslavement of Aleut seal hunters, Euro-Americans were not disposed to antagonize Alaska natives. They retained colonialistic attitudes, but the newcomers needed the Eskimos' help as guides and trappers and required their goodwill and instruction to see them through the perils of life in Alaska. As a result, relations between natives and nonnatives in Alaska during the nineteenth century were far less often disturbed by the murder and bloodshed that characterized Euro-American encounters with Native Americans in other parts of the New World.

Although the Russians established trading stations, they did not come in large numbers or introduce dramatic technological innovations. In western Alaska the Russians failed miserably in their attempts to get local people to increase their harvest of specific furbearers. Higher prices served only to decrease the number of pelts needed to satisfy each native's wants. Cultural need continued to be the determining factor in trade relations. The Russian attempt to foster a paternalistic pattern of dependency among Alaska Eskimos, like that of the American traders who followed them, largely failed.

Nevertheless, tremendous population disruption for Alaska Eskimos characterized the nineteenth century. Communicable disease, such as the smallpox epidemic of the 1830s, was the culprit rather than either military conquest or relocation. The vulnerable native population was devastated, and whole villages were wiped out. Populations dispersed and shifted. The population decline also undercut interregional social distinctions, undermined leadership, disrupted personal relations, and demoralized the people (Fortuine 1989; Wolfe 1982).

Harold Napoleon, a Yup'ik Eskimo from Hooper Bay, recently attributed the severe social problems found throughout western Alaska today—alcoholism, violent crime, suicide, child abuse—to the unacknowledged trauma of the "Great Death," the epidemics of the early 1900s. He likens the situation of survivors to post-traumatic stress syndrome suffered by Vietnam war veterans and others. Never resolving (let alone admitting) this trauma, several generations of natives suppressed emotions such as confusion, guilt, and feelings of inferiority (Napoleon 1990).

Some Yup'ik readers have criticized Napoleon's analysis because it lays the ultimate blame for personal problems in the 1990s on events of nearly a century before. These critics argue that to overcome such problems as alcoholism and family stress, individuals must assume responsibility for their own actions. Ironically, this characteristically Yup'ik attitude toward personal problems, including disease—the belief that they are within an individual's control—supports Napoleon's thesis. Among a people who hold themselves accountable for their own fates, the guilt and shame attending the epidemics, not to mention the pain of losing one's loved ones, must have been tremendous. Moreover, the impact of epidemic disease need not be pushed back to the turn of the century, as tuberculosis in the 1930s and 1940s took as many native lives as any single epidemic, even the "Great Death." The first comprehensive study of Alaska death rates in 1930 found that among Alaska natives who died, tuberculosis killed one in three (Oswalt 1990:145).

Although traders focused on commerce, not conversion, Alaska Eskimos were also beset by non-natives whose goal was not coexistence but rather their assimilation. Christian missionaries first attempted the cultural conversion of Alaska Eskimos. By the end of the 1800s, a dozen Protestant denominations and the Roman Catholic and Russian Orthodox churches had established mission stations throughout the state. Before 1900, Christianity spread slowly throughout the North Pacific, except in the Aleutians and a few other outposts where the Russian Orthodox Church was firmly established. But following the epidemic of 1900, whole villages converted to the foreign faith (Fienup-Riordan 1991; Kan 1988; VanStone 1964, 1984:153).

Missionaries employed an intense five-fold strategy of building, speaking, teaching, healing, and traveling to undercut traditional ways and to provide appropriate "civilized" Christian alternatives. Modern medicine showed itself superior to amulets and incantations. Likewise, the missionaries' technology worked to attract converts: the power of their goods proved the "truth" of their religion (Sahlins 1985:38). Evidence suggests, however, that Alaska Eskimos may not have viewed the missionaries as having unique or superior power, but rather power as Yup'ik and Iñupiaq people traditionally defined it.

The turn-of-the-century epidemics, as well as the widespread disruptions associated with commercial whaling, gold mining, and reindeer herding, caused some Alaska Eskimos to see the discipline and order that the missionaries preached as a novel spiritual solution to an unprecedented social and economic crisis. Combining their traditional sensitivity to the spirit world with the discipline of the Protestant work ethic, many found it possible to become fervent Christians without ceasing to be Eskimos. For example, the Moravians working among the Yupiit on the Kuskokwim committed themselves from the beginning to the transfer of responsibility and authority to a Yup'ik clergy. As a result, they provided alternatives worth considering in a situation of rapid social change, which the Yupiit were able to use according to their own practical purposes (Fienup-Riordan 1991).

Christian missionaries were not the only ones trying to transform the Alaska landscape. Following the U.S. purchase of Alaska in 1867, the first Organic Act of 1884 provided schooling for Alaska Eskimo children. As the careers of many bush educators make clear, the separation between church and state was not a deeply held belief at that time. During the late nineteenth and early twentieth centuries, Protestant missionaries conspired with the federal government to accomplish the twin goals of "civilizing" and Christianizing America's aboriginal populations. William T. Harris, head of the Bureau of Education between 1889 and 1906, wrote, "We have no higher calling in the world than to be missionaries of our idea to those people who have not yet reached the Anglo-Saxon frame of mind" (Ducker 1991:4).

Nonnatives attributed the failure of their educational efforts to assimilate Alaska Eskimos to the Eskimos' inherent inferiority. On the contrary, this presumed "failure" often was intentional, as many Yup'ik and Iñupiaq parents originally saw little value in the schooling that the bureau offered. Their reaction can be compared to that of the eighteenth-century chiefs of the Six Nations who politely declined the invitation from the government of Virginia to educate six young Indians. The chiefs stated that white men could not teach the boys what they really needed to know. However, if the white men would send them a dozen of *their* sons, they would do their best to make men of them (Benjamin Franklin, 1784, in Hughes 1972:vii).

The colonial attitude of the Bureau of Education was explicit. In 1906 the bureau chief proposed teaching natives "what a white man wants of them, so that the white man can use these men for things that are useful for his civilization" (Ducker 1991:14). One key to Eskimo usefulness in white society was

Holy Cross Mission School, early 1900s. Oregon Province Archives, Spokane, Washington.

knowledge of the English language, and the bureau zealously promoted its instruction. Its superior status as "the language of civilization" was assumed. This exclusive use of English in government and missionary schools, often harshly enforced, was a direct and intentional assault on Iñupiaq and Yup'ik identity.

The impact of teachers, like that of missionaries, was not restricted to the classroom. Under their direction the people built new houses, dug gardens, and gained access to an unprecedented array of trade goods and new technological developments. Although farming proved difficult, Reverend Sheldon Jackson, a Presbyterian educator, introduced reindeer herding in the 1890s partly in an effort to turn hunters into herders, thus moving

Alaska Eskimos one rung higher on the "ladder of civilization." Herding ultimately failed, however, mostly because it conflicted with hunting and trapping.

Though Bureau of Education personnel originally had promoted a far-reaching program of cultural assimilation, by the 1920s they sought to "preserve" Eskimos on reservations away from the "bad elements" of white society. Whereas desire for aboriginal lands elsewhere had pushed Indians onto reservations to clear the way for white settlement, government employees working in Alaska at the turn of the century sought to "buy time with space" by segregating the Eskimos from encroaching whites so that they might "learn at a measured pace" (Ducker 1989:1). Though their paternalistic percep-

Reindeer herders at Bethel, around 1910. Moravian Archives, Bethlehem, Pennsylvania.

tion of Alaska Eskimos as their "children" was based on assumptions of cultural superiority, their actions effectively provided at least some Alaska Eskimos with a new context in which to express their cultural identity. In some cases, the means of domination and assimilation turned out to be a mechanism for self-representation. Many Alaska Eskimos appropriated the new programs on their own terms as opportunities to support a way of life they valued.

Teachers and missionaries challenged Iñupiaq and Yup'ik people to selectively incorporate the trappings of Western Civilization. They not only attempted to shield Eskimos from "no-account" whites, but provided alternatives to traditional ways of doing things, some of which Alaska Eskimos accepted and some of which they did not. The missionaries and Bureau of Education employees made

only limited progress in their efforts to transform Alaska Eskimos into laborers in the larger society. Their mission of change had an undeniable impact, but in the beginning Alaska Eskimos largely dictated the terms of their success.

Although Yup'ik and Iñupiaq men and women increasingly spoke English, lived within four walls, worked for wages, and attended church, they remained independent. Their lives focused on extended family relations and the pursuit of the traditional sources of food and warmth they had relied on for centuries. In northern and western Alaska a handful of native people took up animal husbandry and gardening, trapped for furs, and seasonally worked commercial fishing. But most Alaska Eskimos ultimately ignored or modified these new activities when they conflicted with tradi-

A Yup'ik family at Tununak, Nelson Island, 1933. O.W. Geist, Alaska and Polar Regions Department, University of Alaska Fairbanks.

tional subsistence and settlement patterns. Though much had changed, much also remained of their aboriginal view of the world. Most important, for the time being they continued to be masters of their own lives.

Anglo-Protestants began to lose their dominance in American life as the twentieth century unfolded. Their effort to create a Christian nation including all inhabitants of the United States has subsided, and the colonialist aspects of their activities are now points of guilt and embarrassment (Prucha 1988).

By the 1920s, in Alaska as well as the Lower Forty-eight States, science and technology began to replace religion as the means of salvation. By 1900 the gold rush had brought miners, prospectors, and traders north. Alaska's resources were exploited as the United States industrialized. Alaska Eskimos rarely reaped the advantages from this development. Nonnative entrepreneurs employed them when it made economic sense and ignored them when it did not (Rogers 1969:22; Chance 1984:649).

During World War II, with the arrival of military personnel and attendant service industries, Alaska's nonnative population for the first time grew as large as the native population. The strategic location of Alaska in the rapidly expanding Cold War brought about a shift in the economic base from natural resource exploitation to military preparedness (Chance 1984:649). Although some Yup'ik and Iñupiaq men in the armed forces gained valuable leadership experience and exposure to the outside world, most Alaska Eskimos, even those who served, did not.

By the time Alaska became a state in 1959, the

Alaska Territorial Guardsmen. Alaska Territorial Guard Collection, Alaska and Polar Regions Department, University of Alaska Fairbanks.

relative lack of commercial resources and the geographic isolation of many Eskimo communities had reduced contacts with and innovations from the outside world. Although in some parts of the state this isolation allowed Iñupiat and Yupiit to keep their language and many aspects of their traditional way of life, in others it had disturbing economic consequences. For example, in the 1920s the standard of living of a Yup'ik fisherman along the Kuskokwim was moving ever closer to that of a typical rural resident of the continental United States (Fienup-Riordan 1991:228-309). By 1960, the economic position of Alaska Eskimos was falling further and further behind national averages (U.S. Federal Field Committee for Development Planning in Alaska 1968:528). This change did not reflect an actual economic decline, but rather the relatively

stagnant economic position of Alaska Eskimos compared to the dramatic rise in the U.S. standard of living. Outside observers found the economy of village Alaska so depressed they predicted the villages' slow but steady disappearance. This prediction has proved as fallacious as the projected total assimilation of Alaska Eskimos.

In the 1960s, the federal War on Poverty sought to diminish the widening economic gap between haves and have-nots, which included most Alaska Eskimos. State and federal agencies advocated economic development in rural Alaska to allow Eskimos "to make the transition from their present subsistence existence to a more self-supporting one with adequate income and employment" (U.S. Department of the Interior 1967:25-26). Programs emphasized equal opportunity and full participation. But as with the more blatantly assimilationist policies of the first half of the century, the implication was still that nonnative society was the goal toward which Alaska Eskimos should be striving. Critics of these policies promoted the special status of Alaska Eskimos, given their history of social and economic exploitation, supporting preferential as opposed to equal treatment (Chance 1984:651).

After statehood, Alaska Eskimos mobilized to protect their land interests, which were threatened as never before, and to address their social needs. Reacting to land selections by the new state government, native organizations made land claims throughout Alaska. Those claims remained unresolved until it became clear that oil fields discovered on Alaska's northern coast in 1968 could not be developed until native claims were settled. In 1971 Congress passed the Alaska Native Claims Settlement Act (ANCSA), which awarded Alaska natives 44 million acres and $1 billion and called for establishment of business corporations to manage those assets. Despite the rhetoric of self-determination in ANCSA, the corporate structures it established have served mainly to assimilate some Alaska natives into the larger economy and society.

Although ANCSA forces Eskimos to participate even more in society at large, it also gives them an opportunity to do so on their own terms. Since the passage of ANCSA, a diffuse yet nonetheless important cultural reformation has taken root in much of rural Alaska. The substantial changes that many Alaska Eskimos are seeking in the political system are neither total nor immediate. In an important sense the movement has restorative elements that place it in contrast with many other transformative and reformative movements (Aberle 1982:319-20). Today, the major issues that animate Yup'ik and Iñupiaq political activity are regaining control of their land, resources, and local affairs; improving economic conditions; and maintaining Yup'ik and Iñupiaq languages and values. Though these issues are not new, they focus public debate to an unprec-

edented degree. And, as we shall see, they provide the subject for numerous films and videos both by and about Alaska natives.

Many Alaska Eskimos now seek a return to the "old ways." In political and economic terms, the "old ways" refer to the 1920s, after many technological improvements had been introduced into rural Alaska but before Alaska Eskimos had experienced subordination to federal and state government control and related dependency (Fienup-Riordan 1990:221-31). We see signs of this reformation all around us—in the native sovereignty movement; debate over subsistence rights; revival of intra- and intervillage winter dance festivals; hosting of local and regional elders' conferences; increased awareness of and concern for the preservation and use of native languages and oral tradition; and, last but not least, filming of these activities for broadcast to the outside world. Such activity reveals the desire of Alaska Eskimos, often frustrated, to take control of their land and their lives, and to assert their pride in being "real people."

As yet, these trends have not developed into a single, concerted, unified movement. Nevertheless, the many small and large arenas in which issues of Iñupiaq and Yup'ik cultural identity and political control are articulated indicate an increased awareness of and value placed on being an Alaska Eskimo in the modern world.

To date, Alaska Eskimos have changed in some respects and remained the same in others as a result of exposure to and interaction with the nonnative world. Like other Native Americans, they have been much more motivated to preserve what they can of their traditional view of the world in their reactions to missionaries and agents of change in general than has been appreciated. Conversion to Christianity, for example, did not comprise a blanket denial or retreat from the old ways. Such a reading of history represents the colonial ideal, not the complex reality of culture change, simultaneously involving appropriation, resistance, and translation.

Many outsiders continue to view Alaska natives as culturally bankrupt, alternately frozen in time or as having lost their original and authentic past in their forced encounter with the nonnative world.[4] The general public and policymakers alike are fooled by appearances—Alaska Eskimos speaking English and wearing suits—into thinking that the distance between the world view of Yup'ik and Iñupiaq residents in village Alaska and nonnatives in urban centers is a short one. Nonnatives should not be so quick to assume Alaska Eskimos' loss of cultural identity. Contemporary Yupiit and Iñupiat are neither "primitive others" nor soon-to-be-white, and film and video are tools they are using to make this point to the outside world.

4. "I don't give a hoot what it means to be Aleut. I've been to the Pribilofs. They talk about the death of their culture—what culture? They just drink, smoke marijuana, hit children, shoot puffins and clobber seals on the head" (Priscilla Feral, president, Friends of Animals, quoted in the *Tundra Times,* Sept. 2, 1991, p. 2).

Kurt Bell, leader of the Hooper Bay dancers, bids an early "goodnight ladies" as he leaves the long night of dancing. Note the camera in the background. James H. Barker.

Inuit child emerging from papier-mâché igloo at the 1904 St. Louis Exposition. Carpenter Collection, Field Museum of Natural History.

CHAPTER TWO

Eskimos in the Movies: Opening Night

ALASKA NATIVES TODAY CAN USE FILM AS a tool of empowerment. This has not always been the case, however. Films involving Alaska Eskimos began at the opposite end of the spectrum—as attempts by nonnatives to document the indigenous peoples they encountered in their continued efforts to learn about, to colonize, and to dominate the world. The first films about Eskimos were made in the process of global conquest and incorporation. They were movies of exploration in the documentary tradition that highlighted the differences between "them" and "us." They were intended as a record of the first signs of the Eskimos' inexorable absorption into the larger world.

Exploration Films and the Eskimo Debut

The exploration literature of the nineteenth century had introduced the American public to Eskimos, primarily those of central Canada and Greenland. Occasionally, Eskimos also accompanied explorers south, where they were the object of intense scrutiny. Eskimos from the eastern Arctic were exhibited from the sixteenth century onward. These exhibits of living Eskimos catered to the longstanding Euro-American interest in exotic peoples and consistently depicted them as being at a purer, though lower, stage of civilization. Alaska Eskimos generally played no part in these displays, which routinely disregarded the diversity and cultural complexity that characterized arctic life. During the 1800s their venue gradually improved from sideshows, where they were exhibited like wild beasts, to major exhibitions, including the 1893 World's Columbian Exposition in Chicago, the 1904 St. Louis Exposition, and the 1909 Alaska-Yukon-Pacific Exposition in Seattle. Franz Boas had been chief assistant in anthropology at the former, at which fifty-nine Labrador Inuit and their thirty-five dogs were on display, exciting great interest. For fifty cents the public could enter the midway, and for an additional quarter they could see fur-clad Eskimos posing by papier-mâché igloos. The exhibit subsequently incorporated three children born following the group's arrival, and the remains of the Eskimos who died during their tenure in Chicago were preserved in museum collections established in the exhibition's wake (Campbell 1894:241; Harper 1986:99-100; King 1990).

Beginning in the early 1900s, Eskimos also began to be depicted in movies. Although these films appeared realistic in the sense that physical motion and form were captured through the camera's lens, they were not exactly true to life. In fact the first motion picture footage of Inuit people was shot by Thomas Edison at the 1901 Pan-American Exposition in Buffalo, New York, where they appeared alternately playing leap-frog and crack the whip, as well as racing around their "Esquimaux village" in a dog sled (Balikci 1989:33). The film, like the exhibits, both decontextualized and trivialized Inuit life (King 1990:8). No actual hunting or gathering activities were pictured. Nor were any routine domestic tasks carried out. Rather, "they present, in an ice grotto, typical Esquimaux dances, chants and athletic games, dog races, and also aquatic sports on the lake" (Ahrhart 1901:42 in King 1990:8). As in the exhibit, the film made the Inuit appear simultaneously simple, childlike, entertaining, and quaint. Also, like the exhibit, the film was organized around the theme of progress. It was visual confirmation of the metaphoric "ladder of civilization," a low rung of which was occupied by Eskimos while the top was reserved for the sons and daughters of the Industrial Revolution.

Edgar Morin (1956) has described the transformation of motion pictures—"the plaything of inspired Bricoleurs"—into the cinema—"the dream machine of the masses" (Hockings 1975:18). Two strains emerged from the beginning. On the one hand the Lumière brothers and their fleet of operators circled the globe showcasing short film reflections of the real world. On the other was the fiction film, invented by Georges Méliès in 1897 and designed to appeal to the general public (Hockings 1975:18; Sadoul 1966:32).

At the close of the nineteenth century, the race to see who would first develop experiments with film into commercial reality was as intense as the race to the Pole. Thomas Edison was a frontrunner, but in 1895 Louis Lumière won the contest with his handheld camera—the *cinématographe,* from whence the term "cinema" (Barnouw 1983:19). Lumière's "magic box" weighed only five kilograms and could, with adjustments, be transformed into a projector and also into a printing machine. The operator was

thus a working unit, who could give a show one day, shoot and develop new material the next, and show the new film that night. And the operators Lumière sent forth with his new invention did just that (Barnouw 1983:6). Within a year their stock of films grew to 750, giving audiences "an unprecedented sense of seeing the world" (Barnouw 1983:13). The Lumière operators, however, visited nations' capitals, not the unexplored hinterlands, and no arctic location either saw or became the subject of these early films.

Lumière's enterprise proved extremely popular and made clear the possibilities for profit. Throughout the world, new film enterprises began, many of which started with nonfiction items, calling them *actualités,* topicals, interest films, educationals, expedition films, travel films, and, after 1907, travelogues (Barnouw 1983:19). Entrepreneurs all over the world took up where the Lumière operators left off, and permanent cinemas were built to showcase their creations. At the same time, Lumière-style tours continued, shifting from cities to towns and far-off lands like Alaska (Barnouw 1983:21). Anchorage enjoyed its first film screening in 1915, and the Yup'ik residents of Bethel saw their first film at the local trading post in the early 1920s.

By 1907 fiction films were beginning to outnumber documentaries (Barnouw 1983:21). Except for a handful of films, early filmmakers rarely chose the Far North, let alone Eskimos, as subjects in the fiction genre. Even Méliès' own arctic adventure *La Conquête du Pôle (The Conquest of the Pole)* (1912)—reminiscent of sixteenth-century maps peopled by cannibalistic monsters and pygmies—focused on the Euro-American encounter with a fantastic land to the exclusion of the people who called that land home. Eskimos made their film debut not in Hollywood, but on the lecture circuit.

The zoologist Alfred Cort Haddon, using a Lumière camera to record his findings, produced the first ethnographic film on a Cambridge expedition to South Pacific Torres Straits in 1898 (de Brigard

Anchorage's first movie theater, Ship Creek, summer of 1915. Anchorage Museum of History and Art.

1975:16; Brownlow 1979:410). Travel films, or "scenics" as they were known in the trade, had been popular since the early 1900s; however not until 1908, when Cherry Kearton[1] accompanied Theodore Roosevelt in Africa, were films used on expeditions. The next year, Shackleton's antarctic expedition produced four thousand feet of film. Herbert G. Ponting's expertly filmed record of Scott's disastrous antarctic expedition of 1910–11 also stirred public interest. Scott wrote that no expedition ever had been illustrated so extensively and that the only difficulty would be in selecting which prints to use (Brownlow 1979:424). Ponting's footage enjoyed enormous success when shown commercially in 1912 (Barnouw 1983:30).

Although documentary in general gradually declined in favor of fiction film after the first decade of the 1900s, the explorer films continued their popularity (Barnouw 1983:30). The early Lumière

films had stimulated interest in viewing moving images of distant cities and metropolitan centers. At the same time that fiction films supplanted documentary filmmaking close to home, explorer films focused on far-away peoples (like Eskimos) and exotic locales remained popular. Among the more substantial films that followed, Alaska exploration had a prominent place.

Between 1909 and 1911, Captain Frank E. Kleinschmidt led the Carnegie Museum Expedition in Alaska and Siberia, which produced ten thousand feet of film (Vancouver Art Gallery 1979:53). Running four reels longer than Robert Flaherty's *Nanook of the North,* it is considered by some the first feature-length documentary (Brownlow 1979:473). Kleinschmidt's exploration films were also the first to capture prosaic aspects of Alaska Eskimo life on film. In the Carnegie Museum Expedition film of 1912, "… the camera tracks past Eskimo houses, built upon stilts along the shore. Eskimo children, excited by the camera and slightly alarmed by it, are dressed in department store overalls. One of them

1.   Cherry Kearton's books, photographs, and prolific wildlife films made him an unofficial guide and adventurer to a whole generation (Brownlow 1979: 434).

CARNEGIE MUSEUM
EXPEDITION. THE ORIGINAL

A
L
A
S
K
A

S
I
B
E
R
I
A
N

M
O
T
I
O
N

P
I
C
T
U
R
E
S

NEW GALLERY KINEMA,

DAILY at 2.30 and 5.30.

Advertisement for Captain Kleinschmidt's Carnegie Museum Expedition Film of 1912. Jonathan King.

sports a peaked cap. Telegraph wires stretch across the landscape ..." and huskies pull a trolley down a railroad track (Brownlow 1979:479). In the early 1920s Kleinschmidt added footage taken from aboard the submarine chaser *Silver Screen* as it traveled up the Alaska coast, and in Hollywood the combination—accompanied by a journal narration written by his wife—proved a popular draw (*Variety* 1923). His films, occasionally featuring Alaska Eskimos, were shown abroad as well as in the United States. Brownlow (1979:14-15) notes that his *Polar Hunt* was so successful that Kleinschmidt became the only American cameraman permitted to travel with the Austrian general staff.

Kleinschmidt was not the only one filming in Alaska. Fred LeRoy Granville filmed the rescue of the survivors of the Stefansson expedition in 1914. Captain Bob Bartlett, leading character in several arctic exploration films, was among those rescued. Bartlett later lost his own life making another movie (Brownlow 1979:411). The world-famous American broadcaster Lowell Thomas cut his teeth filming in Alaska, making two trips in 1914 and 1915, during which he operated his own Ernemann camera: "On these early trips to Alaska, when I carried that rather heavy movie equipment and tried to do the filming myself, I never did become too adept. The threading was complicated, and the thing frequently jammed. I came to the conclusion that the intelligent thing would be to hire the most competent cameraman available, and then direct him." The outbreak of World War I found Thomas working at Princeton University and spending weekends presenting illustrated talks about Alaska in nearby cities. These talks on Alaska won him the attention of President Wilson's Secretary of Interior Franklin K. Lane, and Thomas's career subsequently began its rapid ascent (Brownlow 1979:443).

Three years after Kleinschmidt's Carnegie triumph, Captain Jack Robertson produced *Alaskan Adventures,* a travelogue following the exploits of champion archer Arthur Young as he set out to explore the wilds of Alaska and Siberia, relying upon his skill as a bowman to supply the party with food. Although these films emphasized exploration and big game rather than Eskimos, they helped set a precedent. Explorers soon began to view cinematographers as a normal part of their equipment. Their films, however, generally never reached the commercial market (Low 1949:153–55 in Rotha 1983:39).

Since the early 1800s, arctic explorers, scholars, and even missionaries had commonly accompanied their talks with slides and photographs. The first magic lantern shows used hand-drawn slides. These early illustrated lectures on strange lands and curious peoples lead directly into the travelogues of today. The intention was the same. The use of visual imagery to underline their findings was a technique employed by popular experts on the Arctic, such as Robert Peary and Vilhjalmur Stefansson. The Peary Arctic Club Exhibit at the American Museum went so far as to include a viewing station as part of their exhibit: "The realism of the exhibit is increased by the work of a newly-invented automatic stereopticon placed in a darkened alcove at the right of the hall. Through its display of pictures (uninterrupted from nine in the morning until five in the afternoon) the visitor is carried into the heart of the Arctic. He looks on boats and men, sledges and dogs, in action; he sees in these pictures the very mountains and icebergs, the self-same pressure ridges or 'rafters' of ice and the leads of open water that the explorer whose hand held the camera saw in reality" (American Museum 1909:206).

With the advent of film, Donald MacMillan and Bob Bartlett also put this new tool to work in Greenland and the Canadian Arctic to record details of Eskimo life for educational films, newsreels, and fundraising purposes. In the process they created a photographic record of what they regarded as the Eskimos' regrettable but unavoidable contact with and corruption by the civilized world. During the Crocker Land Expedition alone, MacMillan produced more than ten thousand feet of motion picture film as well as fifty-five hundred still photographs (Allen 1962:312 in Condon 1989:61). A number of these early nitrate films are now in the process of restoration and preservation (Susan Kaplan, personal communication). This first footage is scarce, however, given the considerable expense of filming, especially during the early years.

Nations with colonial empires were also the nations that produced the majority of films during this period, and their work reflected their hierarchical, often racist, view of the world (Barnouw 1983:23). The films they created depicted Eskimos, like other native peoples, as charming and childlike. In fact, Eskimo children often provided the camera's focus.

Early filmmakers sought to capture the Eskimos' quaint customs and costumes on film, such as their tambourine-style drum dance. The Eskimos' presumed naiveté in their appropriation and use of Western technology, for example, shirts fabricated from flour sacks and gas cans used as water containers, was also routinely pictured. The Industrial Revolution had produced an expanding world search for new markets and resources. Displaying foreign peoples, and Western dominance over them, was just as important a theme in early exploration films as it had been in turn-of-the-century exhibits (Benedict 1983:43-52; King 1990).

Tip Top of the Earth

William Van Valin was among the early experimenters with film in the Arctic and the first to focus on Eskimos in Alaska. He came to Alaska in 1910 and taught school at Sinrock, northwest of Nome, in 1912 and at Wainwright in 1913. While in Alaska he became a member and eventually the leader of the John Wanamaker expedition to Point Barrow, where he remained until 1919, dividing his time between teaching, photography, and collecting—both buying artifacts and excavating them from tundra graves. What we now view as scurrilous grave-robbing was an accepted practice of the early 1900s. Many museum collections can trace their origins to men like Van Valin, who regularly were rewarded for their efforts. His agenda may have been colonialist from the perspective of the 1990s, but at the time he and his contemporaries were struggling to come to grips with a part of the Arctic still little known and poorly understood. Moreover, general audiences in the Lower Forty-eight States were as interested in his heroic stature as an adventurer in Alaska as in anything he had to say about its native people.

In his autobiography *Eskimoland Speaks* (1941:123), Van Valin described the expedition's inception:

William Van Valin dressed in spotted reindeer parka and standing next to his sled that is loaded with kayak and seal-hunting gear. Van Valin Collection, Alaska and Polar Regions Department, University of Alaska Fairbanks.

When the Hon. John Wanamaker was told by Dr. G. B. Gordon, Director of the University of Pennsylvania Museum, in Philadelphia, about the fine collection of Eskimo antiquities I had brought out of the Arctic regions and sold to the Museum, he offered to finance my return to northwest Alaska for the purpose of completing the Museum's collection of everything ancient and modern belonging to the Eskimo from Nome to Point Barrow.... It was also planned that the expedition would make a series of motion pictures covering the domestic life of the Eskimo.

To accomplish these ends, Van Valin equipped himself with an overboard Koban motor, a standard Williamson motion picture camera, a Junior Williamson, and a complete hunting and camping outfit, at a cash value of three thousand dollars (Van Valin 1941:124). Heading north, he stopped briefly in Nome, where he found he had a number of competitors in the antiquities business, including Mr. Shields, then superintendent of the Bureau of Education, Northwest Alaska Division. These men were no match for him, however, and he cleverly outflanked them in the acquisition of a Siberian graveyard collection, stolen by guests while their hosts slept. Giving us a glimpse into his attitude toward artifacts, Van Valin (1941:139) wrote: "Of course, had I known that these articles had been extracted in such a manner, I would have had serious misgivings about buying them; although I might have been influenced by the reflection that it would have been only a matter of years until the elements had ruined these priceless relics, especially the pottery."

Five years later Van Valin "returned to civilization, rich in knowledge and experience, and laden with sixty-one prehistoric Eskimos, forty-five hundred antiquities of Eskimoland, together with ten thousand feet of motion picture films of that fascinating and little-known region of the globe" (Van Valin 1941:239). Out of this raw footage he made his movie series *Tip Top of the Earth* (1912–19), which he showed on the travel lecture circuit after he returned to the States. The public was hungry to know more about both Alaska and the man who had survived its rigors, and his film-lectures were well attended and excited wide acclaim. In a period during which Native Americans were routinely denied their individuality by being homogenized into a generalized "Indian," Van Valin's films were both the exception and the rule. Although he never presented the Iñupiat as his equal, Van Valin did highlight their cultural uniqueness.

Tip Top of the Earth consists of half-a-dozen twenty-minute films. Each is a series of black-and-white moving pictures—shots of a minute or less alternating with framed written descriptive captions. The films robustly portray harvesting and subsistence activities, including whale hunting and butchering, seal hunting, and skinboat (umiak) construction. These were ordinary activities on the north coast of Alaska, but extraordinary for Eskimos as whites then commonly conceived of them. Van Valin included footage of the recently introduced reindeer industry, which was to have a substantial impact on the economy of northwest Alaska. He also filmed the "excavation" of several archaeological sites, in striking contrast to the Ukpiagvik excavation filmed near Barrow seventy years later in which paint brushes and trowels replaced the pick axes and shovels Van Valin employed. Van Valin filmed all these activities in considerable detail. For example, the sequence on whale hunting begins with the hunters cutting a trail through the pack ice. It shows their arrival at open water, setting up the whaling camp, the actual hunt, and the butchering and distribution process, followed by a blanket toss and whale festival celebrating the successful hunt. Here

Van Valin provides the first film depiction of what would become standard fare in documentary pictures of life in northwest Alaska.

Van Valin captured some unique images, including a sequence of men pulling cakes of ice to build a corral to hold eighteen hundred reindeer, villagers landing supplies from the whaler *Belvedere,* and the exhumation of a prehistoric man dressed in eider duck-skin clothing dug out of the ice and turned on edge to thaw. A photograph of the "Midnight Sun," exposed every fifteen minutes over a period of two-and-one-half hours, traces its slow march across the horizon. The film series closes with a shot of skulls and bones piled on the tundra with the caption, "Where solitude now reigns supreme, except when the wind whistles through the eye orbits and nasal cavities of these empties."

Reindeer butchering scene, probably near Wainwright. Van Valin Collection, Alaska and Polar Regions Department, University of Alaska Fairbanks.

Most of the film captions are simple and direct: "Reindeer have no barns." "They live on reindeer moss." "Herd passing by a lake." Just as often, however, Van Valin was unable to resist calling attention in words to what his audience was already conditioned to regard as exotic in relation to their own world: "50 below zero. The Eskimo eats every two hours to keep warm.… Crossing a pressure ridge 100 feet high. Hard trip home over eight miles of ice." Humorous sequences crop up here and there, including a shot of a dog eating a carcass, labeled "Dog eat dog" and a picture of the reindeer herd entitled, "Where Santa Claus might get his deer." Van Valin also employed what was already a staple in descriptions of Eskimos, filmic and otherwise—the tendency to describe Eskimos in terms of what they lacked. For example, "Primitive Eskimos had no steel picks or shovels to dig graves. They laid their dead on top of the frozen ground" and "Sanitary way of butchering taught the Eskimos." Early twentieth-century audiences still viewed Eskimos as culturally deficient. Van Valin's captions confirmed what they already knew.

In the format of the visual lecture, Van Valin's depiction takes on the character of an exotic travel film, often exploitative, with the Iñupiat as objects simultaneously marvelous in their fortitude and laughable for their quaintness. Both in his film and still photography, and finally in his book *Eskimoland Speaks,* Van Valin gives us animal-like, childlike, igloo-dwelling Iñupiat:

> Inside the humble igloo, lighted by a seal-oil lamp, Tuksarak, the mighty hunter, assembled with his wife and child around a small wooden platter of frozen raw whale meat, their last remains of food saved from the spring whaling.… They came forward and … rubbed their noses against his, sniffing simultaneously. This is the primitive Eskimo salutation, which is now almost obsolete. Perhaps the Eskimos adopted from their dogs their manner of greeting each other nose to nose.

Still, they were a jolly lot: "Taking an advantageous position, with the motion picture camera, I filmed each outfit as they pulled from the tundra to the beach and out over the Arctic Ocean.… There was always time for fun and dancing and we ate frequently. It seemed more like a picnic on the ice than like extremely strenuous work. The Eskimos are like a family of large children. They don't seem to make hard work out of anything" (Van Valin 1941:162, 171, 177).

The middle-class audiences who paid to attend Van Valin's lectures wanted information about Alaska, but they also wanted to be entertained. Van Valin attempted to give them both enjoyment and edification. The reindeer-herding scenes were mildly dramatic, and the contrast between Eskimos in cotton pants herding deer and the expected image of a parka-clad hunter provided a cameo portrait of the changes in process. Audiences wanted confirmation of what they generally believed to be true about Eskimos, but they were open to new information concerning the details of Eskimo life. Alaska was America's Arctic, and eyes turned on this last frontier in increasing numbers.

Missionaries writing home from the Bering Sea coast decried the poverty of their converts and their humble circumstances. Bureau of Education reports described the teachers' efforts to convert hunters to herders and so bring Eskimos one rung higher on the "ladder of civilization." Museum displays, like that of the American Museum in New York, contrasted primitive Eskimo tools with modern technology. Films of the period gave viewers the opportunity to visit the Arctic vicariously and make up their own minds on all these issues, or so it seemed. Sharing the same view of the world as his audience, Van Valin's constructs largely confirmed them in their biases, giving flesh to the abstract notion of the "poor primitive."

In the end Van Valin showed himself a popularizer, who used his position as school teacher to collect many candid shots of Barrow and Wainwright in

Iñupiaq girls playing hide-and-seek. According to Van Valin, the seekers assemble in a circle with their arms around each other and their heads bowed together so they can see nothing but the ground. The remaining players run and hide, and the sides change only after they are all caught. Van Valin Collection, Alaska and Polar Regions Department, University of Alaska Fairbanks.

the early 1900s. To American viewers in the early 1900s Van Valin's images of northern Alaska simultaneously highlighted what was unique about Alaska and emphasized what was generically Eskimo, the Alaska incarnation of a type of "primitive people" already well known. He gave people what they had been conditioned to expect of Eskimos, at the same time he highlighted unusual "Alaska facts." In the process, he provided succeeding generations of Iñupiat with vivid images of their past, images which they are now in the process of reclaiming (Wooley 1990).

Nanook of the North

While Van Valin shot footage in Barrow for his educational film series, Robert Flaherty engaged in a similar effort in Canada, which would have very different results. Although Flaherty never worked in Alaska, his films had a lasting impact on how Alaska Eskimos, and in fact all indigenous peoples, would henceforth be presented. His masterpiece, *Nanook of the North,* is certainly the most famous Eskimo movie ever made.

During two expeditions in 1914 and 1916, Flaherty shot what was to be a travel-adventure film about the Inuit of Hudson Bay, which he hoped to market along with a lecture about his explorations in northern Canada. Like Van Valin, Flaherty had spent long periods in the Arctic since 1910, and he knew his subject first hand. During final editing, however, Flaherty's cigarette set fire to the highly flammable nitrate-based film, and his work went up in smoke. According to Jay Ruby (1979:68), he and his wife spent the next four years screening the nonreproducible work print in an effort to raise money to finance a return trip to the Arctic to make another film. During those years they had a chance to reflect on the flaws of Flaherty's first film, flaws endemic to the travelogue including lack of continuity ("simply a scene of this and that, no relation, no thread of story") and emotional distance from their subject (Ruby 1979:68). According to their account, they determined to try a different tack in their second attempt:

Why not take, we said to each other, a typical Eskimo and his family and make a biography of their lives through the year? What biography of any man could be more interesting? Here is a man who has less resources than any other man in the world. He lives in a desolation that no other race could possibly survive. His life is a constant fight against starvation. Nothing grows; he must depend utterly on what he can kill; and all of this against the most terrifying of tyrants—the bitter climate of the North, the bitterest climate in the world. Surely this story could be interesting. (Robert Flaherty 1950, cited in Ruby 1979:68)

With this goal in mind Flaherty went back to Ungava, and during 1919 and 1920 he filmed the story of Nanook—the kindly, the brave, the simple, the stereotypic Eskimo.

In fact, Flaherty's first film probably was closer in form and content to *Nanook* than either of the Flahertys have led us to believe. Even this early footage was remarkable in its "intimacy," a quality that immediately set Flaherty's work apart from the travelogues being produced by his contemporaries (Frances Flaherty's diary, April 13, 1915, cited in Vancouver Art Gallery 1979:55). Also like its successor *Nanook,* the 1914 film focused on the life of a single family. One reviewer described how "the spectator follows the simple and sometimes adventurous life of Anunglung, his wives and his dogs with ceaseless attention" (Vancouver Art Gallery 1979:54).

When *Nanook* was released in the summer of 1922, it attained instant success. The public and critics alike judged it a realistic portrayal of Eskimos, not contrived but elicited from life. The French critics Moussinac and Delluc praised it for its "*purité*" (Rotha 1983:47). In a survey of the best films of 1922, the critic and playwright Robert Sherwood wrote, "Here was drama rendered far more vital than any trumped-up drama could ever be by the fact that it was real. Nanook was no playboy enacting a part which could be forgotten.… He was himself an Eskimo struggling to survive. The North was no mechanical affair of wind machines.… It was the North, cruel and incredibly strong" (Rotha 1983:41).

Flaherty seemed convinced that he was filming "essential truths." He wrote, "People who read books on the north are, after all, not many, but millions of people have seen this film in the last twenty-six years—it has gone round the world. And what they have seen is not a freak but a real person after all, facing the perils of a desperate life and yet always happy" (Flaherty 1950:18-19).

In fact, as Flaherty well knew, little of the film's final footage was of spontaneous behavior (Heider 1976:22).[2] This "staged" quality of *Nanook,* its character as "authentic reconstruction," drew criticism from the beginning. Arctic explorer Vilhjalmur Stefansson called *Nanook* "a most inexact picture of Eskimo life." Both in a long, unpublished manu-

2. Speaking to the issue of filmic distortion, Calder-Marshall (1963:97) quoted Flaherty as saying, "Sometimes you have to lie. One often has to distort a thing to catch its true spirit."

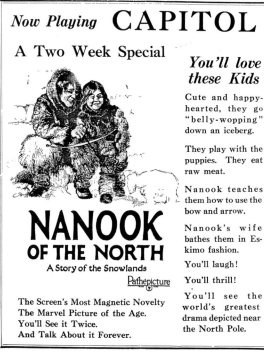

Advertisement for Flaherty's *Nanook of the North*.
Jay Ruby.

script written just after *Nanook* was released and in a shorter commentary in his book *The Standardization of Error* (1928:86–92), Stefansson detailed the myriad ways in which *Nanook* perpetrated its fraud. Stefansson (1922:3) wrote that when he first saw the film "it was not so truthful as I had hoped, nor yet (quite) as untruthful as I had feared." His interest then turned to the dramatic criticism the film received in the press the following morning, where he found his worst fears confirmed. Whether condoned or condemned, all took *Nanook* to be "real life in the North."

Stefansson commenced to detail the ways in which *Nanook* was a play, "that the action was acting, that costumes had been designed, that scenes had been rehearsed.... Taken seriously and as a truthful presentation of life on the Ungava Peninsula, the picture is harmful. It confirms most of the ordinary misconceptions; and it adds new misconceptions more numerous than those which it re-

moves" (Stefansson 1922:3–4). His scathing commentary, a combination of good analysis and pettiness, continues for twenty-two pages. He detailed the ways in which "instead of being real life this picture is a caricature." In the process, he noted so many fabrications that "you will miss something that is wrong if you ever glance away from the screen."

Stefansson points out what many would later call attention to: that these Eskimos had guns for many years as well as regular intercourse with traders and were not nearly as unsophisticated as Flaherty pretended. As to hunting techniques, the Hudson Bay Inuit did not hunt seals through the ice, and even those Eskimos who did, used methods other than those shown. Yet sealing through the ice was a dramatic activity often associated with Eskimos, and the audience expected it. So Flaherty staged it, letting Nanook pull up a seal that was already stiff and dead: "But that ... is all the realism you could expect in a play.... And what seal but a dead one could possibly be expected to allow himself to be speared in the manner shown?" (Stefansson 1928:89). Stefansson concluded his charitable interpretation: "It is possible to make the same facts look a good deal worse if you try" (1928:92).

Further, Stefansson (1922:11-16) proclaimed false caption statements that no race other than the Eskimos could survive in a dreadful country like Ungava; that the word resembling "Nyla" (Nanook's wife's name) has any meaning similar to "smiling";[3] that Eskimos wear their winter parkas in the summer; that reindeer depend on moss instead of *Cassiope tetragona,* commonly called heather; that the valiant Nanook killed seven bears with a

3. Stefansson is correct that Eastern Canada Inuktitut has no word for laughing or smiling that sounds like "Nyla." The base *qungattuq-* means "to smile," and the base *ijuq-* means to laugh. The base *nilaq-* means "to pass gas or to fart." Perhaps the Inuit offered the name "Nyla," literally, "the farting one," as a joke, or perhaps Flaherty made it up to conform to what white people expected an Eskimo name to mean (Larry Kaplan, pers. comm.).

Nyla, the smiling one. Museum of Modern Art, Film Stills Archive.

harpoon, whereas he must have used either a spear or a knife, or (most likely) a gun; that Nanook could actually be puzzled by the phonograph as they had been in use on the Ungava Peninsula since the early days of Mr. Edison's invention; that the Eskimos were continually hungry; and finally that the storm scene was actually a "threatening drifter," when in fact it was an ideal spring day, probably in April, with the temperature around zero.

Moving inside the house, Stefansson (1922:18) noted that the bedding was not laid out properly, that snow remained on people's clothing, which was bundled up hurriedly and not carefully folded, and that although the family disrobed for bed, they only went halfway, leaving on their trousers. He also pointed out the tell-tale steam puffing from the mouths of the recumbent occupants, noting that snowhouses actually are moderately warm. This, he correctly surmised, resulted from Flaherty's need for light inside the structure and his subsequent cutting away the wall of the house to film the interior. Stefansson (1928:92) commented sarcastically, "Hence the director had to explain the shivering people and their visible breathing by the harmless pretense [in the caption] that snowhouse interiors have to be colder than freezing to prevent the roof and walls from thawing."

That Stefansson was among Flaherty's first and most devoted critics was no accident. Beyond individual dramatic distortions, small and large, Stefans-

Nanook enraptured by the gramophone. Museum of Modern Art, Film Stills Archive.

son disagreed fundamentally with Flaherty's characterization of the Northland. Flaherty viewed the arctic environment as the implacable enemy:

> *Nanook* is the story of a man living in a place where no other kind of people would want to live. The tyrant is the climate, the natural protagonist in the film. It's a dramatic country and there are dramatic ingredients in it—snow, wind, ice and starvation…. These people, with less resources than any other people on the earth, are the happiest people I have ever known. (Flaherty 1949, quoted in Rotha 1983:37)

Stefansson, on the other hand, is best remembered for his portrayal of the "friendly" Arctic. In twenty-six books and more than four hundred articles, he attempted to free the Eskimos' environment from its popular image of a barren wasteland. Yet all his literary efforts paled in significance compared to Flaherty's employment of film to play out his vision of primitive life.

Stefansson's accusations of fakery, like many that would follow, can be answered in two ways. In Flaherty's defense, it can be said that Stefansson's criticism was grounded in the assumption that films about real people in real situations should never be staged, directed, or altered, but that the camera should simply record what transpires, allowing the material to speak for itself (Ruby 1979:67). In fact, selection, omission, and distortion are inevitable parts of filmmaking, as they are of any process of representation. The best that can be hoped for is that the filmmakers highlight rather than hide how and why they make their choices.

In the case of *Nanook,* critics recognized its narrative form and assumed that what they were viewing was "faked" documentary, as opposed to the film Flaherty had made in 1914, which they judged a "factual account." "The storyteller had won over the scientist," so the argument went. Rather than diminishing its value, the imposition of narrative form in *Nanook* can be viewed as the means by which the superficial travel film was transformed into true documentary (Ruby 1979:67).

Although Stefansson may have been naive in his criticism of *Nanook's* form, which was innovative and important, he was correct about the harmful power to deceive inherent in Flaherty's presentation of Nanook as the "timeless primitive," untouched and untroubled. To Flaherty, nature was the adversary, whereas the reality of Nanook's world was that it was being threatened most by the larger society. Raised on James Fenimore Cooper and Francis Parkman, Flaherty consciously chose as his stage the fringe of civilization, virgin snows, and "primitive" Eskimos. Flaherty was a romantic primitivist extraordinare, preoccupied with the "classic beauties and braveries of human existence" (Rotha 1983:156).

Flaherty was well aware that he was ignoring Eskimo reality in favor of their pure past. He justified his reconstruction as necessary to allow him to distill Eskimo life and deliver only its "incorrupt essence": "I am not going to make films about what the white man has made of primitive peoples … what I want to show is the former majesty and character of these people, while it is still possible—before the white man has destroyed not only their character, but the people as well" (Flaherty cited in Ruby 1979:72).[4] As in so many film representations of Eskimos to follow, these precivilized virtues were

paradoxically presented as the same ones Flaherty believed noblest in the human spirit—kindness, bravery, and compassion.

Flaherty plumbed the Eskimos for their resemblance to us, not their difference. Whereas travelogues such as Van Valin's had emphasized the strangeness of the Eskimos and their character as exotics, Flaherty concerned himself with the ways in which Eskimos were just like us. From the beginning his interest had been in the character of Eskimos as "essential men." In his diary of 1912 he described a farewell scene:

> To see his kind old mother packing his duffle … his father looking on silently … is all the world the same as we have it. His young wife of about 17 and their son went aboard with the first canoe, so that she didn't figure into the final farewells; I guess she felt it though. I shall never get over finding out the goodness of these people. (Quoted in Griffith 1953:35)

Van Valin had been willing to admit change and intercourse between the Iñupiat and the larger world. Flaherty, however, depicted the Inuit as untouched, almost untouchable, in their purité. Nanook was in fact already sick during the filming. While Flaherty made him appear robust and fearless on screen, the filmmaker noted in his diary that one night Nanook coughed splotches of blood (Barnouw

---

4. The same accusation was made of Edward Curtis in his still photographic work, in which he required his Indian and Eskimo subjects to dress as they had in the past and take traditional poses, blocking out all evidence of nonnative contact. Similarly, in his film *In the Land of the Headhunters* (1914), Curtis provided his Kwakiutl actors with costumes and reconstructed the living conditions of a past era, just as Flaherty would later do in *Nanook.* The film required three years of preparatory work. Curtis wrote, "Many people joined in the work to make the film as much a document of the old times as we could" (Brownlow 1979:343). Flaherty might well have said the same thing of the Inuit with whom he worked. Although Curtis's film received some excellent reviews, inadequate distribution made it a financial failure and limited its impact. Curtis never made another film.

Inuit drawing of Flaherty and camera. Museum of Modern Art, Film Stills Archive.

1983:43). Two years after *Nanook* was released, Nanook died of starvation while on a hunting trip. The reality of life in the Far North was changing, and the poverty and disease that came with these changes were lethal. The real survivor was not Nanook, but his image as happy, hardy, and intrepid.

Whereas the American encounter with the Indian often emphasized the difference between savagism and civilization, Flaherty emphasized Eskimos' similarity—humans governed by the law of nature and therefore ennobled. What Eskimos actually were grew less and less important than what Euro-Americans should be. Flaherty was not engaged in objective recording but in creatively recovering "that portion of the primitive self which civilization had corrupted." Flaherty's primitivist critique challenged people to live up to their "truly civilized nature"—simpler, less sophisticated, happier. In the process he posited an Eskimo society "to which whites should go to school," and many are still enrolled (Pearce 1953:136-42).

From the beginning Flaherty professed a desire to make a film that reflected the Inuit view of themselves: "I wanted to show the Innuit. And I wanted to show them, not from the civilized point of view, but as they saw themselves, as 'we, the people.' I realized then that I must go to work in an entirely different way" (quoted in Griffith 1953:36). Although he regularly screened his footage for the Inuit, this never prevented him from imposing his expectations on the finished film. In fact, his onsite screening of rushes was an effort to encourage their collaboration rather than to elicit their critical response: "It has always been important for me to see my rushes—it is the only way I can make a film. But another reason for developing the film in the North was to project it to the Eskimos so that they would accept and understand what I was doing and work together with me as partners" (Flaherty 1950:13–14, cited in Vancouver Art Gallery 1979:59). Partners in the process of filmmaking, perhaps, but not partners in the film's conception.

How much did Flaherty's romantic image fit with the Inuit view of themselves? Firsthand accounts indicate that the Inuit found both Flaherty and the filmmaking process laughable on many counts: "Inuit not doing things normal fashion must have appeared hilarious." Bob Stewart, the Revillon Frères factor who played himself in *Nanook,* detailed the Inuit reaction to the staged seal hunt to Dudley Copland in 1925: "In the seal hunting scene (at the breathing hole) Nanook's struggle with the supposed 'seal' was dramatized by the harpoon line being put down one hole, strung under the ice, and then up another hole where a bunch of men engaged in what amounted to a tug-of-war contest with Nanook. According to Stewart, they nearly pulled Nanook through the ice in the water, much to everyone's delight" (Vancouver Art Gallery 1979:57).

Although the Inuit may have laughed at Flaherty, they also helped him immeasurably and, for his project to succeed as it did, a number of Inuit must have been deeply involved in the filmmaking process. In an oft-quoted incident, Flaherty admonished Nanook and his companions prior to the walrus hunt that they must remember, it was the film, not the meat, that was important. According to Flaherty, they willingly, even enthusiastically concurred. Whether or not all potential conflicts of interest were resolved so amicably we will never know. But unquestionably much of what Flaherty filmed

reflected the Inuit image of their past. The filmmaker was not interested in recording their current life-style, and he asked them to draw on their memories and do things the old way. Their response was enthusiastic. *Nanook* may fail us as a record of Inuit life in Ungava in the 1920s, but it does provide a view into Inuit ideas about their traditional life, and, indeed, "a people's self-image may be a crucial ingredient in its culture, and worth recording" (Barnouw 1983:45).

Whether or not Flaherty succeeded in presenting the native point of view, he unquestionably succeeded in presenting a view of "primitive Eskimos" with which Euro-Americans could identify. John Grierson summed up Flaherty's accomplishment:

> It was a record of everyday life so selective in its detail and sequence, so intimate in its shots, and so appreciative of the nuances of common feeling, that it was a drama in many ways more telling than anything that had come out of the manufactured sets of Hollywood.... Without actors, almost without acting, he built up in his camera what he considered the essential story of their lives. (Grierson 1932:147, cited in Ruby 1979:73)

Flaherty succeeded in making the viewer feel the humanness of the Other, in this case Nanook. This empathy was Flaherty's goal, and he was untroubled by distortions in the process.

Nanook certainly presents an indelible image of an Eskimo family, living what we are told is its normal, everyday existence. While they struggle, they also accept their lot. Nanook and his family are, according to Flaherty (1949), "primitive people whose lives are simply lived and who feel strongly, but whose activities are external and dramatic rather than internal and complicated" (Ruby 1979:71). A dramatically staged fictive reconstruction, *Nanook* reflected Flaherty's paternalistic and romantic notions of the "noble savage" and the "contaminating effects" of civilization. Like primitivists before and since, Flaherty sought in the Eskimo a vision of all that good men should be: "Nanook's problem was how to live with nature. Our problem is how to live with our machines. Nanook found the solution of the problem in his own spirit" (quoted in Frances Flaherty 1960:10). Whereas the Indian stood in the path of civilization, the Eskimo stood at its foundation.

Nanook, done with great artistry, made an undeniable contribution in the development of the representation of aboriginal peoples on film. Reissued in 1947 and subsequently made available in 16mm film and video, it continues to be widely shown.[5] As the much-touted father of documentary, Flaherty was the first filmmaker to employ the method of intensive immersion, to present a specific individual rather than a faceless other, and to attempt to tell a story (Heider 1976:22). Flaherty was also the first to fix the "essential Eskimo" in film. The image he created is so powerful that all subsequent filmmakers in the Arctic work in his shadow. If anyone is ever to undo Flaherty's celluloid stereotype, they must use at least as much skill and finesse as *Nanook's* creator or they will have precious little impact.

5. Twenty-five years after its release in 1922, United Artists reissued *Nanook* as a fifty-minute film, complete with narration and orchestral accompaniment. This sound version of *Nanook* was as successful as the seventy-five-minute silent original and has been widely distributed in several languages. To accommodate the sound track, however, the film was speeded up by 50 percent, from sixteen to twenty-four frames per second. Also, continuous narration replaced the silent captions, unnecessarily anticipating the action and undercutting the drama and suspense of the original. The narration completely subverted Flaherty's original demand that the audience join him in observing the Eskimos (Heider 1976:24). In 1975, however, David Shepard restored *Nanook* for International Film Seminars. A new print was struck and the film reissued with a Tashi soundtrack, and it is now available both in film and video. See *Blackhawk Bulletin* (February 1975, p. 50) for an account of the restoration (Brownlow 1979:73).

CHAPTER THREE

Eskimos in Hollywood

T HE DEPICTION OF NATIVE AMERICANS in Hollywood films is as old as the cinema itself. With the coming of movies, Eskimos like Indians were "filmically embalmed by a coincidence of history." As Stedman (1982:155) points out, the first motion picture arrived just as theater began to seek a realism in outdoor melodrama that could only be accomplished on film. The new medium thus had both a ready-made audience and a subject.

Hollywood treated Eskimos and Indians differently from the beginning. With the frontier wars fresh in their minds, pioneer directors such as D. W. Griffith, Cecil B. DeMille, and Thomas Ince all created major Indian-fighting dramas. The infant movie industry cranked out thousands of one- and two-reel films between 1903 and 1915, several hundred of which depicted Indians (Marsden and Nachbar 1988:610). In these early films, Indians suffered such persistent indignity at the hands of moviemakers that in 1911 President William H. Taft received a delegation representing four western tribes protesting their negative screen treatment (Stedman 1982:157).

At the same time that early film energetically maligned Indians, only a handful of Hollywood movies even peripherally dealt with Eskimos. Like the frontier wars, the turn-of-the-century polar

explorations were the stuff of recent experience and contemporary newspaper reportage. Polar exploration provided a topic for a handful of expeditionary films, but Eskimo peoples did not. The few films that did deal with Eskimos gave them a positive if patronizing presentation. Unlike the overwhelmingly negative movie depiction of Indians, Eskimos were unfailingly presented as docile "primitives," not wild savages. Van Valin touted the hardy virtues of the Point Barrow Iñupiat, followed by Flaherty, whose film representation of Nanook took Eskimo nobility to a seldom paralleled extreme.

Hollywood firmly fixed the stereotypes of Native Americans and spread them more widely. Public expositions and published explorer journals had reached tens of thousands of people, but the early films reached tens of millions, including newly arrived immigrants unable to read English who derived much of their information about America from the movies. In the first decade of the twentieth century, the audiences that attended movies were largely "the young and the poor," those who lacked both the means to afford as well as the sophistication to enjoy more "refined" entertainment. Their images of Indians had developed in the stage melodramas, Wild West shows, and dime novels popular during the nineteenth century, and they took them at face value (Marsden and Nachbar 1988:609).

Beginning in 1913 the film industry replaced the one- and two-reelers with the feature-length film. As a result of rising costs, fewer films were produced, and those made were less experimental. Feature films emphasized fast action over sentimentality. The warlike Indian became a central image, and nobility (when it occurred) became synonymous with being an object of white paternalism (Marsden and Nachbar 1988:611). Good Indians ceased being heroes on screen, appearing only as the white man's trusty companion. The noble native, however, did not disappear altogether. Instead, the image of the *"belle sauvagesse"* was taken over by another more distant Native American—the Eskimo.

Films in the late 1920s and 1930s were sometimes shot in exotic locations—tropical islands, African jungles, arctic snowscapes—using local people to act out written fictional scripts with strong plot lines. This was a logical step beyond Flaherty's directed reconstructions, and these commercial ventures took advantage of the interest Flaherty had stirred. Though documentaries seldom matched popular features in box office returns, *Nanook's* financial success (it grossed $251,000 worldwide) and critical acclaim had a lasting effect on feature films. Henceforth, neither zoological garden nor studio could provide sufficient background. Audiences had experienced "the real thing" in Nanook, and they liked what they saw. Hollywood fiction films began to incorporate the values of factual films, though entertainment continued to be their primary goal (Brownlow 1978:484).

Fiction films enjoyed great popularity between the two world wars and grew increasingly imaginative in their renditions of "real life" (de Brigard 1975:21). Realism—a cultural construct with its own conventions of representation—was never an important tradition in American movies, and many conspicuous distortions characterize these films. Just as Flaherty had used Inuit to act out his vision of life

in the Far North, Hollywood producers employed Alaska Eskimos to portray the "instant Eskimo" they judged would have the strongest popular appeal.

The Girl Alaska (1919) was one of the first fiction films with Alaska footage, but it featured no Eskimos, even imaginary ones. Three years later Austin E. "Cap" Lathrop, a Fairbanks businessman, helped form the Alaska Motion Picture Corporation and set to work to make a film that would more accurately portray Alaska (Norris 1992:61). The result was the home-grown *Chechahcos* (1923), a story of Gold Rush days with scenes filmed all over Alaska, including Cordova, Girdwood, and Mount McKinley National Park. The characters include many local performers, among them an Indian housekeeper who says things like "Heap big talk, little do" and "You get 'em papoose," but no Eskimos appear. The mail carriers and miners do, however, wear handsome Iñupiaq caribou-skin parkas, and an enormous Yup'ik grass basket decorates the miners' home. The authentic props and unusual location shots add interest to the old-fashioned melodrama that Alaskans especially can still enjoy.

Another early Hollywood attempt to exploit Northland drama was the absurd parody of arctic life portrayed in Buster Keaton's *The Frozen North*, released the same year as Flaherty's triumph. This surreal burlesque opens with Keaton sauntering forth from a completely misplaced subway exit in the middle of a snowy field. The antics that follow include an attempted saloon hold-up, with the aid of a cardboard gunman, and Keaton's casual shooting of a man he thinks is invading his house and making love to his wife, only to discover it is neither his home nor his wife. Eskimos only appear as backdrops, as in a fishing tug-of-war in which Keaton tangles his line with a fur-clad angler, eventually pulling him into the hole in the ice. An igloo decorated like a frontier cabin—complete with guitar and trophy antlers hanging from the wall—provides the scene for additional gags. In the end, a theater janitor awakens Keaton, and it all turns out to be a

Buster Keaton entering the Arctic in *The Frozen North.* Academy of Motion Picture Arts and Sciences.

dream. The film was a dream in more ways than one, as Keaton employed Eskimo images derived from popular imagination rather than everyday life.

Two years later Paramount made passing use of Eskimos in its production *The Alaskan* (1924), based on the James Oliver Curwood novel by the same name and staring Thomas Meighan. Filmed in Seattle and Alberta, Canada, the film revolved around the struggle by native Alaskans—not Alaska natives—against greedy outsiders. The cameraman was the star in this overdrawn melodrama, which relied on a combination of picturesque backgrounds and fast action to move the plot along.

At the time the film was released, press kits suggested that theater owners import dog teams and reindeer from local zoos to advertise the film, as well as fix up their lobbies with "frozen north atmosphere," Eskimo igloos, fur-clad attendants, "snow,"

and pine trees.[1] They also suggested tie-ups with hotels to feature special Alaska dishes and ice cream stores that sold "Eskimo pie." Though the film portrayed Indians rather than Eskimos, the director Herbert Brenon purportedly directed an entire scene in Iñupiaq—"the first time in the history of the cinema that a scene has been directed in the language of the world's most northerly people."

It came about quite by accident and proves that the popular director is an opportunist. Enroute to location, several scenes were made on the boat as she steamed along the northern coasts. Among the passengers were several Indians and Eskimos who were pressed into service as atmosphere. From one

1. A comparable press kit accompanied *Nanook of the North,* and Jay Ruby published it in a 1980 issue of *Studies of Visual Communication.*

Buster Keaton committing a villainous deed in
The Frozen North. Academy of Motion Picture Arts
and Sciences

Buster Keaton ice fishing in *The Frozen North*.
Academy of Motion Picture Arts and Sciences.

Minutes later, after Keaton has pulled the Eskimo
through the ice. Museum of Modern Art, Film
Stills Archive.

Buster Keaton sitting in an igloo and contemplating
his fate in *The Frozen North*. Academy of Motion
Picture Arts and Sciences.

of the Eskimos, who spoke English, Brenon learned a number of words of command which he used in directing his companions.

The Eskimos who had never seen a motion picture, entered into the thing with enthusiasm, although they had only a limited comprehension of what was being done. (Press Kit 1924, Library of Congress microfilm)

Though ads predicted that the picture, with its he-man role and dime-novel melodrama, would "knock the spots off" every other Meighan record— "And that's just cold logic"—reviewers gave it mixed ratings.

Among Hollywood's first attempts to move beyond casual use of the Eskimo image was *Kivalina of the Ice Lands* (1925), featuring dramatic hunting and storm scenes filmed in north Alaska by Earl Rossman. According to reviews, shots of the ocean freezing, ice blackened by walrus, and the capture of belukha whale were dramatic highpoints. The activities of the Eskimo extras were not remarked.

The next year Columbia Pictures released *Justice of the Far North* (1926). A studio production, *Justice* received kudos for the way in which its nonnative cast took to their Eskimo roles: "A brilliant bit of screen work is done by Mr. Jasmine as the Eskimo hero, and exceptional work is also performed by Miss Manton as Wamba and Miss Winter as Nootka. These characters are made to stand out all the way" (*Variety* 1926). The plot revolved around the efforts of the noble Umluk to reclaim his sweetheart Wamba bedazzled by two rascally fur traders and carried off to their settlement. Umluk eventually finds the runaways and, after trials and tribulations, returns to his icy home with Wamba's faithful sister Nootka, leaving the degraded Wamba behind. Although the film featured no real Eskimos, it included some fine wildlife photography and scenes of the arctic seas.

Hollywood again chose a northern theme for the Fox studio production *Frozen Justice*, based on the Ejnar Mikkelsen novel and staring Lenore Ulric. Contemporary audiences would find this 1929 "talkie" racist and sexist in the extreme, although at the time it was produced its demeaning stereotypes caused no stir. Like *Justice of the Far North*, it employed no Eskimo actors, and the whites who played Eskimo parts spoke in stilted English to denote they were really using the Eskimo language. The plot is also similar to *Justice*. It focuses on the beautiful half-breed Talu caught between the world of her native husband Lanuk and the dance halls of Nome. We meet her first in Lanuk's igloo, admiring her white skin and naively dreaming of the land of her white father. A trading ship arrives, and the ruthless ship's captain tempts her to flee with him to Nome where "only the ugly [women] work and bear children. And the lovely ones … sing and laugh all day." In Nome, however, Talu finds herself more out of place than ever. She laments, "There's no place for me here, just like there's no place for me in my mother's land. There my father's blood called me away. Here my mother's blood calls me home." Trying to return to her husband, she is crushed in a pressure ridge and dies in the arms of the adoring and heartbroken Lanuk.

Frozen Justice echoed the concepts of racial superiority and "pure blood" that had determined the place of Eskimos as well as others in the turn-of-the-century exhibitions. Not only do the sailors, traders, and dancehall girls speak of "dirty Eskimos" and "ugly savages," but so does the heroine. Declining her mother's offer of oil, Talu retorts, "It makes me brown, like you.… I hate the brown skins of all of you." When the captain of the trading vessel notices Talu for the first time, he exclaims, "What's a girl like you doing in this dump? Why, you're white!" In the dramatic confrontation between Talu and her native husband, infuriated that she has disobeyed him and visited the trader, she reveals her racial superiority:

Lanuk grabs the whip. He hits her. We see blood on her white skin. Suddenly the crouched fearful

Half-breed Talu (Lenore Ulric) pleads with Lanak in *Frozen Justice*. Fox Films.

A fallen Talu in the Nome dance hall. Museum of Modern Art, Film Stills Archive.

Talu dying in Lanak's arms. Museum of Modern Art, Film Stills Archive.

Eskimo in [Talu] vanishes, leaving only the white woman. She draws herself up proudly, she faces him … an outraged white woman, her eyes blazing and her look of haughty contempt.… The age-old subservience of the dark-skinned people comes over him.… Her look holds him. Slowly his arm falls to his side and the whip drops to the floor. A smile comes to her face as she bends toward him and hisses "Eskimo!!"

Frozen Justice depicted Eskimos as racially inferior. The Eskimos were by definition childlike, foolish, and naive. The morals of the Eskimo women were loose, the dances of the men "primitive and fantastic," and the simplicity of the children ingenuous as they tried to eat the candles and bite the tin cans that the traders give them. Even Talu views her Eskimo compatriots as naive and childlike. She tells her husband, "That's child's talk, Lanuk.… Surely you do not believe all the medicine man says." At the same time, civilization appears in a less-than-favorable light. The greedy captain and his drunken crew are the villains in this morality play. Lanuk appraises their worth: "What knowledge have they ever left us but knowledge of their own evil? And they bring only discontent and unhappiness." Hollywood never again made such explicit use of the theme of racial superiority in a film involving Eskimos. However, the theme of white civilization as the inevitable corrupter of a pure primitive people would flourish. Hollywood scriptwriters discarded racism in proportion as they glorified the Eskimo image.

Frozen Justice also employed extreme sexual stereotyping. It marked the beginning of what would be a constant contrast in Hollywood representations of Eskimos: the sultry maiden lounging on fur inside her igloo and the noble hunter covered in fur out on the ice. The Eskimo woman portrayed in film is childlike, mysterious, sexy, and natural (without artifice)—simultaneously the innocent caretaker and the erotic primitive. Usually the Eskimo maiden is peripheral, with the actions of the mighty hunter,

Gloria Saunders as the glamorous Alak in *Red Snow*. Museum of Modern Art, Film Stills Archive.

like Nanook, dominating the story line. *Frozen Justice* was one of the few Eskimo films in which a woman took the starring role.

Three years after the release of *Frozen Justice*, Hollywood left the studio to film Iñupiaq men and women in a production on location. The result was *Igloo*, released by Universal Pictures in 1932. *Igloo* was more action-packed than the studio-made *Frozen Justice*, but it was far from a realistic presentation of life in the Far North. Although filmed on location in Alaska and acted by an all-native cast, *Igloo* bears little resemblance to *Nanook*. Whereas *Nanook* had been an attempt to reveal the essential humanity of a geographically distant people, *Igloo* was Hollywood melodrama at its most extreme. Like *Frozen Justice*, *Igloo*'s goal was entertainment, not revelation.

Talu lounging in her igloo in *Frozen Justice*. Fox Films.

Ray Mala: The First Alaska Eskimo Film Star

Instead of the grizzled Nanook, the young and handsome Ach-nach-chiak (Agnaqsiaq, literally, "young lady") starred as *Igloo's* leading man. Ach-nach-chiak (Ray Wise) was born in Candle, Alaska, on December 27, 1908, to an Iñupiaq mother and a Jewish American father, Bill Wise, whose family had immigrated from Russia to San Francisco at the turn of the century. The elder Wise left home at fourteen and came north with the Gold Rush to make his million. He did just that and returned to San Francisco rich enough to purchase both the Granada and Normandy hotels before he knew he had fathered a son in Alaska.

Ray's mother remained in Candle until her son was four, then moved to Kotzebue where she died in the influenza epidemic of 1918–19. The boy subsequently stayed with his Iñupiaq grandmother. He was educated at a Quaker missionary school in Kotzebue until age twelve when he ran away, taking odd jobs to support himself. Two years later, in

Nanook of the North. Museum of Modern Art, Film Stills Archive.

1922, he made his way to Nome and got a job as a cook aboard the *Silver Wave,* a vessel bound for Seattle. On board Wise met the arctic explorer and expeditionary filmmaker Captain Kleinschmidt, who hired him to carry the camera on a scientific expedition to Wrangell Island. Wise later improved this elementary knowledge when the Danish explorer Knud Rasmussen took him on an expedition to East Cape. The boy had a steady hand and the ability to manage a hand-held camera in the cold, skills that made him a valuable addition to exploring parties coming North. The men he worked with liked him and remembered him, passing his name on to those who followed them. At age sixteen, Wise also took his first bit part in a movie—dressing in a woman's parka and posing on the ice for scenes in Kleinschmidt's feature film *Primitive Love* (1926). The picture combined footage from Kleinschmidt's 1911 Alaska-Siberia expedition with fresh material. The finished product, reflecting Flaherty's influence, was not a documentary but a drama of "primitive man" struggling against the elements (Brownlow 1979:476). Unlike *Nanook,* however, this low-budget production failed at the box office.

Shortly after these experiences, Wise met a Pathé newsreel cameraman, Merle LeVoy, returning from an arctic trip in 1925. LeVoy hired him to aid in securing snow scenes for his company and took a fancy to the boy, loaning him $100 to go to Hollywood. There Captain and Mrs. Kleinschmidt put the young man up until he got a job at Fox Studio, where he worked for three years as a cameraman.

During these years Wise wrote a film script called *Modern Eskimos,* combining incidents from life in contemporary northern Alaska that he felt had film potential. The story line followed the travail of the orphan Tautuk—like the efforts of the author—to win the regard of his community, not to mention the affection of the beautiful Alak. The viewer would be treated to reindeer herding and sled races, the annual trade fair at Kotzebue, midnight games of ball involving young and old alike,

Ray Mala as Chee-ak in *Igloo.* Universal Pictures.

longshoring supplies from incoming vessels, a bloody public punishment—cutting off the lips of the town gossip—as well as a number of hunting sequences as the villagers traveled to and from seasonal camps. Iñupiaq songs would provide the musical score. The author also proposed a wedding scene: "A modern wedding would be good for a laugh, but do it in an Eskimo style such as right after the wedding, go right to work, or go hunting. With the assistance of a writer, this could be made into an original.... I feel as if it would make a sensation" (Mala 1929:3).

Although no studio ever produced the screenplay, it remains significant as the first recorded attempt by anyone, native or nonnative, to make contemporary Alaska Eskimos the subject of a commercial film. Sixty years later, this goal has yet to be realized. Ironically, had it been produced, *Modern Eskimos* would be most valuable today as an historical document.

Wise was not immediately successful as a scriptwriter. But soon after he arrived in Hollywood, the German director F. W. Murnau[2] (an admirer of Flaherty) decided to make an arctic drama of Eskimo life before the coming of the white man. Murnau was determined to tell the Ejnar Mikkelsen story, which included scenes of a whale hunt, with as much authentic detail as possible (Brownlow 1978:485). So he sent Wise north with Ewing Scott to get stock shots. Scott recalled the events that followed:

> [Murnau] fired me with the idea of making unusual pictures. He sent me to the Arctic in 1926 to prepare a Fox picture which was to be called "Frozen Justice." It didn't go through because three of our men, Capt. Jack Robinson, Charlie Clark, and Virgil Hart, got lost for three awful weeks.
>
> When we finally rescued them, they had been without food or shelter on the ice for 22 days. So the Fox people felt human lives should not be endangered in that manner and we were called home, after the company had spent $45,000. (Whitaker 1932:3)

Not only did the filmmakers have a harrowing experience getting to Barrow, but when Clarke and Robertson were well enough to leave the hospital, they found that none of the scenes they had hoped to film for *Frozen Justice* was possible. The whaling season had come and gone while they were lost on the ice. More discouraging, the "traditional" Eskimo way of life they had expected to find on Alaska's north coast was no longer there for the filming. Men used guns for the hunt, not harpoons. Their clothes were not gut and fur, but canvas and denim. And igloos were nowhere to be seen. Unlike Flaherty, who met these changes head on by having the Inuit

reconstruct their traditional lifeways, the Fox company packed up and headed home (Brownlow 1978:490). Murnau's ice film was never released, and the Lenore Ulric studio production later absconded with the title.

Wise and Scott kept in touch. According to Hollywood tradition, the idea for *Igloo* was born when the two were working together in Death Valley in scorching heat. Then and there they determined to return to the Arctic and film their own picture (Whitaker 1932:3).

Like Wise, Scott began his career as a technician in the 1920s. Inspired both by Murnau and by Flaherty's highly successful *Nanook,* Scott financed his expedition to Alaska with $5,000 of his own money after every Hollywood producer had turned him down. The three-man expedition (including Scott, Wise, and a technician) almost turned back in Fairbanks when they found it would cost $3,000 to fly them and their fifteen-hundred pounds of equipment to northern Alaska. Territorial officials wanted diphtheria antitoxin rushed to Point Barrow, so Scott decided to risk the trip, and in the end the serum helped them get a welcome (Whitaker 1932:3).

Problems did not disappear after their arrival in Point Hope, where they planned to film. The entire population of 220 Iñupiat appeared in the picture. Three times they built an igloo village to use as a set, and three times a blizzard swept it away. Scott also had difficulty finding a "suitable arctic maiden" to play opposite Wise. He judged Iñupiaq women "wooden, just lumps. They stare at one with expressionless faces." Even after finding a girl he felt he could work with, the going was rough. Influenza claimed the lives of several Iñupiat playing in important sequences, and he had to change the story to accommodate their loss. The hunting scenes also posed problems: "Another maddening thing was the elusiveness of whales, walruses, and seals—on week days.... Then on the Sabbath there would be a gorgeous run.... Those darned whales were sure in

---

2. Murnau, the director of the classic *Nosferatu,* was a German expressionist who immigrated to Hollywood. Later he worked with Flaherty in a failed partnership in a film shot in Tahiti.

league with the missionary" (Whitaker 1932:3).

Money began to run low. Scott's parents back home in Los Angeles mortgaged their house and sent him more money: "So we rushed out and got those corking crashing relentless ice-breaking sequences—even if I did go back to camp twenty pounds lighter and nearly off my head" (Whitaker 1932:3). The long-awaited whales finally made a weekday appearance, and the shoestring operation sailed home after seven months of what Scott judged "supreme endurance." On their return, however, no one rushed to grab the tribute, and studio after studio turned down the picture. Film enthusiast Edward Small then put up the money to promote the film—almost as much as the cost of the entire expedition—and at last Universal bought the picture (Whitaker 1932:3).

Like *Nanook, Igloo's* drama turned on the essential conflict between "primitive man" and a perilous environment: "A white world of perpetual snow and ice … where every living thing must battle to exist … and nature is their worst enemy." The advance advertising read:

> Away, Far Away, ADVENTURE CALLS. To the Top of the World for the Screen's Mightiest Thrills. The Strangest Adventure Ever Filmed. A Love Story of a Forgotten Land. The Romance of Chee-ak, the Great Hunter, and Kyatuk, his Eskimo Beauty. See: The raging, roaring, freezing Arctic Blizzards. A fight for life so thrilling you will gasp and wonder at its drama. See: The hunger-maddened Eskimos' walrus hunt. See: The old sealed in tombs of ice and left to die. Primitive Passions. Stark Drama. Mighty Thrills.

The narrative that opened the film read: "An authentic story based upon incidents in the life of a primitive Eskimo in the Arctic Circle. Living among these people as a member of the tribe, Ewing Scott was able to faithfully record the courageous struggle for existence of this forgotten people." The narrative continues with a grossly inaccurate characterization of the Iñupiat living in Alaska in the 1930s who, among other things, are depicted as dwelling in conical iceblock igloos on the sea ice rather than the land-based, sod-and-whalebone houses in which they actually lived. Although purportedly set in the present, nothing of that present is shown:

> This almost unknown people dwell in an ice-locked world not far from the North Pole. The Nuwuk are one of the many groups of vanishing Eskimo race, nomads of the shifting ice pack, who wrest a frigid living from the reluctant titan, their father. It is a world in itself, this northland. Ruthless. Cruel. Yet the people who are born and spend their lives upon this ice waste are a gentle and happy folk, fond of their simple sports, always ready to laugh, never known to cry.… Strange anomaly.

As in *Nanook,* the long history of contact between the Iñupiat and Euro-American civilization is dismissed in favor of the dramatic conflict between "essential men" and a harsh environment.

In the film's opening scenes we see the Iñupiat emerging from "icehouses in which they hibernate all winter." The people are hungry after the long winter and enthusiastically welcome the great hunter Chee-ak (short for Wise's real-life Iñupiaq name) who arrives to woo the beautiful Kyatuk, bringing with him gifts of meat. A feast follows in Chee-ak's honor, complete with lovemaking scenes straight out of Hollywood. The narrative accompaniment continues tongue-in-cheek: "Here is where courting is all open and aboveboard—even below zero. Imagine having to sit on a cake of ice to make love! You know the Eskimos don't kiss. They only rub noses. And what a pity they have such short noses for the longer the nose the bigger the thrill." But Kyatuk plays hard-to-get: "She tantalizes him still more and goes to tell her father that Chee-ak is a nice boy and a good hunter, but he must learn that

Chee-ak in *Igloo*. Museum of Modern Art, Film Stills Archive.

In these extreme (not to mention extremely unrealistic) circumstances, an Eskimo father is pictured deciding which of his twin toddlers he will expose to the elements, as both cannot survive. Later the narrator intones, "The law of sacrifice has been fulfilled.… The tiny one has returned to the great snow god." Infanticide was far from a routine Iñupiaq practice at any point in history. In the past it was practiced by some Eskimo groups in times of extreme food shortage, most commonly in the harsher environment of the Canadian High Arctic. Even there the Inuit, like the Greeks, only put to death nameless infants, not toddlers who had already received a name and so come to incarnate a beloved ancestor. The film script called for putting a toddler out in the snow because of its "exotic" and dramatic quality, not for its approximation to real-life Iñupiaq practice.

Following the infanticide scene, Chee-ak goes seal hunting, albeit in a most unorthodox manner. He is pictured running over the ice wearing snowshoes and looking this way and that for a breathing hole. Of course, the Iñupiat of northern Alaska hunt seals through breathing holes, but never in the manner shown. Chee-ak's quest proves unsuccessful (perhaps because of his unusual hunting methods), and he leads the tribe on a dramatic overland march south to open water: "Better to die with spear in hand than surrender like weaklings."

Before leaving, "tribal law" dictates that the old and helpless must be "buried alive. Sealed within his igloo for eternity." Like the dramatization of infanticide, senilicide is included to stimulate audience interest. Although food shortage or poor traveling conditions sometimes influenced an elderly person in the decision to be left behind without food or shelter, this was far from a routine practice or the subject of "tribal law." Stefansson (1932:12) noted that even when it did occur, it would not look like an abandonment to us: "They would travel far during a day, a weakling would drop behind, everyone would expect and hope that he would come up to

the heart of a maiden is like a walrus and cannot be slain with the first spear."

Ugly weather returns, and the men work to close the igloos from the outside against the storm: "The storm rages steadily for weeks, the temperature always at 70 below zero so that no man dare venture out into the elements." When the storm is at its height "the village looks like a deserted burial ground, and it may soon be one, for inside these ice huts there are human beings stoically facing starvation, with only a pitifully small lamp to keep them from a worse fate—being slowly frozen alive."

camp during the evening or night, but sometimes he never arrived." Moreover the Iñupiat did not view death as a final exit but as the first step in the soul's inevitable rebirth. The old and the weak might voluntarily end their lives in times of general hardship, but later, when a baby was born, the name of the deceased would pass to the child. With the passage of the name people believed some essence of that person was reborn.

The plot thickens as Chee-ak defies tribal law to rescue Kyatuk's aged father Lanak from his fate. Eskimo religion is now invoked: "Because they believe the presence of the once buried man an offense to their gods, the tribe leaves Lanak to travel behind the other sleds … for the dead may not ride with the living lest the living become as the dead." Through the remainder of the film, Chee-ak struggles against both nature and the angered gods. In the end, however, Lanak accidentally dies while crossing a pressure ridge, and Chee-ak prays for the offended deities' forgiveness. His people gather below him while the narrator's voice quivers with emotion: "O god of the wind what blows from the north, carry my prayer to Tigerak, god of the hunt. Let our arms be strong, our aim true.… Smile with favor upon these hungry children.… Let the gods forgive the presumptions of my rash spirit. Let their anger be appeased." Tigerak (*tigeraq*) literally means "index finger" and is also the name of the sand spit at Point Hope, undercutting the later claim of the press that the film was made at Nuwuk, "eighty miles beyond Point Barrow." In fact, Nuwuk is little more than eight miles from Barrow, so that the claim is either an innocent typographical error or a conscious attempt by the press to exaggerate the exotic location of the film.

In the end, Chee-ak's prayer is answered, and the men find walrus. In what one reviewer judged "a rather terrifying spectacle" (Rush 1932), the men drink the "slain monster's" blood: "Savage joy dispels all doubt of their leader [and] warm blood from ivak pledges faith renewed." The film ends in a happy feast: "And so like happy children, they laugh and play once more.… Chee-ak has proved himself. He has won the devotion of the tribe and has picked for himself its fairest flower.… And the gods themselves shall build their igloo." Stefansson (1932:15) added, "As we close on the refrain that the 'gods themselves shall build their igloo' we wonder if these are going to be conical snowhouses closed from the outside, and whether the deities are going to shape the blocks with mattocks." Stefansson attributes the film's many ethnographic blunders to the filmmaker's ignorance and carelessness, if not outright contempt, for the accurate portrayal of conditions. As in his criticism of *Nanook,* his principal objection is the contrast between the fabricated film image and the claims of the advertising that the film shows real life.

The complaints of critics such as Stefansson, however, did not affect the public response to *Igloo* any more than they had the response to *Nanook.* Originally titled *Manna,* referring to the protagonists' never-ending search for food, the film was praised by reviewers for its graphic simplicity: "Life in the raw, to say nothing of meals in the same condition, is pictured in a frozen film dainty" (Coons 1932). With its cast hired from "half-savage" natives, the film revealed a "stone age folk." According to another reviewer, the film portrayed a "stoic, strangely beautiful tribe … gaining sustenance from the frozen north, … feasting in times of plenty, starving in famine, suckling their infants in snow houses.… You see the old abandoned, according to the law of the tooth and fang.… The effect of the picture is as powerful as an iceberg" (Oliver 1932).

Not all reviewers were so complimentary. Rush's *Variety* review judged the film a novelty not meriting feature release: "It is that rare thing—a story whose realism is defeated by the absence of theatrical device" (*Variety* 1932). Both the off-screen interlocutor continually explaining the characters' motives and the melodramatic orchestral score and weird chants accompanying the unreeling undermined the film's illusion. Wise's next feature production, *Eskimo,* took both criticisms to heart and may owe its success in part to lessons learned in the production of *Igloo.*

To attract viewers, Los Angeles' Criterion Theater hired an Eskimo, Anton Entag, to stand in the lobby and talk about his life. Shown along with a Mickey Mouse cartoon, a Rudy Vallee song film, and a newsreel, *Igloo* did capacity business and made a profit. Along with *Rebecca of Sunnybrook Farm,* reviewers judged *Igloo* the best picture of the month.

When *Igloo* premiered, reviewers described the twenty-two-year-old Chee-ak as the Clark Gable of Alaska. Standing six feet tall with the face and figure of Tarzan, he became an instant celebrity—"a picturesque giant among these small Arctic dwellers" (Variety 1932). Interviews reinforced the purity of his screen image. They played down Wise's years of experience as both cameraman and scriptwriter that led up to his screen debut and billed him as Scott's "primitive discovery." The press depicted the experienced and aspiring young film star as a noble innocent:

He came from the Arctic, from frozen immensity. From his igloo he saw only sky and snow. The only colors he saw, and then but a few times a year, were in that fiery heavenspread fan, the Aurora Borealis. The only sounds he heard were lonely, weird voices of the winds.... It was Scott who had discovered Chee-ak, a Kotzebue tribesman, and had made him the star of "Manna." ...

Then he told me of his amazing discoveries in Hollywood. "People look sad and water comes from their eyes.... They do not laugh like the Eskimo, who laughs ... a good part of the time." ...

The Eskimos, I gather, are communistic anarchists.... The Eskimos have no jails, no laws, no rulers, no servants, no punishments. They have no word in their language for God, as they have no word for time—or for the hereafter, which they have never thought of! ...

"The Eskimos, before the white men came, thought there were no other people. So some of the old men and old women they think the white people are like ghosts or like dreams, not 'real.' See? In Hollywood maybe people are not real. Ha! Ha!

Chee-ak resting on the *Igloo* set. Museum of Modern Art, Film Stills Archive.

Ha! … Since I have gone to picture shows I have learned to weep." …

Long after leaving the gentle Chee-ak, … I wondered if in exchanging laughter for tears, he had not left an Arctic Garden of Eden, a simple morning-of-the-world innocence, to eat, in Hollywood, of the tragic fruit of the tree of civilization. I wondered if he had not exchanged his greatest happiness—the happiness of the mighty laughing hunter—for the dubious gift of tears. (Berthon 1932:12)

Critics complimented *Igloo* for its "descriptive incidents … the manner of life in the Far North is well put forward—even though leaning a bit to the tragic. To sum up: 'Igloo' is definitely out of the ordinary" (*New York Times Film Review* 1932:845). Out of the ordinary perhaps for movie viewers of the 1930s; however, in *Igloo* Hollywood solidified a stereotype that would become the norm in the film industry—the instant Eskimo, complete with igloo, parka, polar bear, implacable gods, and a frozen clime. Stefansson aptly aimed his criticism at this homogenized Eskimo, devoid of regional specificity. In spite of a long tradition of scholarship on Eskimos in general and increasing attention paid to Alaska Eskimos, this distorted image took hold and continues to flourish in many contexts.

MGM's Eskimo: "Life in the Raw"

Its thrills whip the blood from the heart, its drama cuts like the lash of a whip. It is life in the North. Life in the raw. Life in a land of happy huntsmen, direct in thought, direct in action, honest, fearless. (Crewe 1933)

Within months of its premiere, *Igloo's* talented leading man involved himself in a second arctic film that would solidify his position as Alaska's first real movie star. In the summer of 1932 a Metro-Goldwyn-Mayer film crew under the direction of W. S. Van Dyke set sail for Alaska in the schooner *Nanuk* to make another Eskimo movie. The screenplay was an adaptation of *Der Eskimo* (1931) and *Die Flucht ins Weisse Land* (1929) by the Danish explorer Peter Freuchen. When MGM first conceived the film, they cabled Freuchen to come to Hollywood and signed him on for a year at $300 a week. There he worked to complete the screen version of his books, originally set in Greenland. In his autobiography, *Vagrant Viking,* Freuchen (1953:245) later contended that MGM left little of his original story in the final film.

In retrospect, Ray Wise cast as the hero, Mala, seems both the obvious and perfect choice. Although he coveted the part from the first Hollywood leak that Van Dyke planned to direct an Eskimo picture, Wise's acting in the feature was far from assured. Stars were the financial backbone of the film industry, and a typical director in the 1930s would have sought a well-known white actor to play Mala. If this had been the case, Wise, a virtual unknown, would never have gotten the part. Van Dyke, however, wanted "pure Eskimos" to star in his feature and at first rejected Wise not because of his anonymity, but because of his Jewish American heritage.

Van Dyke traveled to Alaska with an experienced technical crew but without a complete cast. On his arrival he screen-tested more than one hundred and fifty Eskimos and gave the part of Mala to Robert Mayo of Wales. Filming began at once, and Van Dyke himself directed the feature's opening shots, including scenes in which Mala, the Mighty Hunter, traveled and hunted with his two sons. Van Dyke found the work tedious. He had to explain each shot to the Iñupiaq actors in great detail, but he was pleased with the results. Two months into the filming, however, with the entire summer sequence on several thousand feet of film, Robert Mayo announced that he did not want to work anymore. The result was a complete shutdown of operations.

Van Dyke, of course, tried to convince Mayo to stay. Mayo insisted that he could not work, explaining that his mother-in-law at Wales was going to have an operation, and he thought he and his wife should be there with her. No amount of cajoling could convince him to reconsider. Later it came out that some of the men in the camp had made advances to his wife, and Mayo considered it safer to take her back to Wales: "Instead of telling Van Dyke the truth and causing trouble in the unit, he told the sick mother-in-law story" (Cannom 1948:248).

It was after this that the studio contacted Ray Wise and flew him up to Teller.

He was a second cameraman at the studio in Hollywood. The studio had wanted Van Dyke to use Wise as Mala, but he had insisted on using a one hundred percent native cast. This time Woody had played a wrong hunch. Nevertheless, when he saw he was in trouble, he wasted no time in getting in touch with the studio by short wave radio to find out if Wise was still available, and before he had paid off the first Mala he had received a radio confirmation from the studio that Ray Wise was on his way. (Cannom 1948:248)

Van Dyke had decided on *Igloo's* leading man. The producer, Hunt Stromberg (1932), wired Wise saying, "Practically decided you will play Mala. Keep in training and on special diet all the way up and begin to thoroughly absorb character so you will give great performance…. Within your power and courage is now the chance to obtain sensationalism and greatness." Stromberg did not exaggerate.

In his autobiography Peter Freuchen (1953:246) gives his account of the casting of Ray Wise as Mala, indicating that he at least had seen and approved the young man for the part before leaving Hollywood: "Ray had played some bit parts for a small film company which had brought him to the United States…. He was good looking, intelligent, and he spoke the Eskimo language." Mala was engaged, although not

for the starring role. When he later took the lead, Hollywood papers reported, "Mala, the hero, is an Eskimo but not, like his companions in the cast, a wild one."

The casting of Mala was only a small part of the elaborate arrangements that went into the making of *Eskimo.* In June 1932, MGM sent the manager of the Lomen Company's Teller Reindeer Station a 100-word telegram instructing him to begin buying up reindeer skins, walrus hides, and polar bear skins: "The message also gave instructions to round up all the Eskimos they could get from Teller to Kotzebue and have them dressed in native garb and in their 'oomiaks' (large skin boats)." MGM also directed the Lomen Company to open its camp and cookhouse at the reindeer station and establish a mess for the natives:

The orders in the wire were carried out to the letter and as soon as ice conditions permitted, fifteen large oomiaks with about a hundred and fifty Eskimos arrived from Cape Prince of Wales, the Diomede Islands, Shishmaref, and other areas. Receiving no further information as to the reason for all this activity, J. I. Andersen, manager of the Teller Station for the Lomen Company requested the Nome office to wire MGM that their instructions had been carried out to the letter and they were waiting for further orders. A return wire was received stating that the schooner, "Nanuk," with a movie group in charge of a Mr. W. S. Van Dyke would arrive at Teller within twenty-four hours. Andersen was told to report to Van Dyke and he would receive all further orders from him. (Cannom 1948:241)

The *Nanuk's* arrival was dramatic, and the welcome the Iñupiat gave their first visitors from Hollywood a warm one:

Port Clarence Bay was still full of drift ice, but the second morning following receipt of the wire from

Nome, an Eskimo rushed into the store and told Andersen a vessel was approaching through the ice. Andersen took his binoculars and spotted a three-masted schooner and knew it must be the Nanuk.

As soon as the sailing schooner neared the spit between Port Clarence Bay and Grantley Harbor, a welcoming party headed by the Lomen Company's tug, "Wave," proceeded through the ice cakes to greet them. There were many oomiaks and several small boats rigged with outboard motors loaded to the gunwales with Eskimos. The sound of the motors echoed for miles around in the crystal clear atmosphere of this 65th parallel of lati-

tude. The Nanuk dropped anchor on the north side of Grantley harbor and the welcoming party made a picturesque sight as they circled the ship three times cheering and saluting their guests. The tug, "Wave," then pulled alongside and Andersen went aboard to meet Van Dyke. Mr. Anderson thought Van would be enthusiastic over this welcome, which he was, but at the moment, Woody was all business. He wanted to know how many Eskimos he had, where they were, what provisions had been made to feed and house them, how much gear he had acquired, where it was, what about locations, and when they would be able to move to their summer quarters. The Lomen Company's representa-

W. S. Van Dyke and Iñupiaq hunters aboard the *Nanuk* to film *Eskimo*. Museum of Modern Art, Film Stills Archive.

tive was beginning to think this gang the coldest-blooded outfit he had ever met. (Cannom 1948:241-42)

From the first, Van Dyke was on the trail of "primitive Eskimos" to use in his picture. Just after he arrived, Andersen told him that the natives gathered at the station needed more food, and Van Dyke ordered more fish and meat provided for them. The station manager pointed out that although the local Iñupiat were dressed in furs and were "real Eskimos," they were accustomed to white man's food, and Van Dyke would lose them unless he fed them accordingly:

Woody replied, "All right, but don't ever let it be said that we came up here and spoiled them." …

It was hard for Van to think of Eskimos as living on anything but blubber, fish and meat because that's what Peter Freuchen said they lived on in the story he was to film and that must be right. The story was right, but the period depicted was many moons back in history. (Cannom 1953:243)

Having found his "primitive Eskimos," Van Dyke had not a little trouble holding them on the set. Although they had no complaints, they continued to come and go from Teller with much more energy and ease than Van Dyke anticipated. The trouble apparently was that they were too well paid, as in addition to room and board, every man, woman and child who could be used on the film received no less than five dollars a day. This was a large sum, and when families had gathered what they thought a sufficient salary to see them through the winter they were ready to leave for the trading post, spend their earnings, and return home. Van Dyke experienced the same frustration Russian fur traders had encountered one hundred years earlier in western Alaska. The Iñupiat may have had limited means, but they also had finite needs, and when these were met they saw no reason to keep working. Higher

wages, like higher fur prices, only decreased the time a person had to work to get the money they required to secure their needs. The Iñupiat, however, caused less trouble than the Hollywood crew members, convinced as they were that they were performing heroic feats and were all martyrs for MGM. Van Dyke observed they had been just the same in Africa during the filming of Trader Horn (1930) (Cannom 1948:252).

Notwithstanding the difficulty of holding his Iñupiaq cast, Van Dyke found them easy to work with. Typical of his time and place, what impressed him most was their seeming unconcern in the face of difficulties he found intolerable: "With the variable temperatures, winds, tides and hardships, cold and hunger as a result, Van Dyke said the Eskimos were the most wonderful people he had ever seen. To his way of thinking, they had absolutely nothing to be happy about, and yet were always happy. He often said a lot of people could learn a great lesson from the Eskimos" (Cannom 1948:264). Iñupiaq happiness was both simpler and more complicated than Van Dyke imagined. Contrary to his core assumption, their rich environment and advantageous position in one of the most productive sea mammal hunting areas in the world provided them many things to be happy about. Their pleasant demeanor on a day-to-day basis, however, was no simple carefree response to their material well-being. Rather, it was grounded in elaborate social etiquette developed over thousands of years. For example, detailed rules for living required a person to withhold the expression of hostile emotions so as not to injure the mind of another. Van Dyke and his crew were both unaware of and uninterested in what lay behind the famous Eskimo smile. Their expedition was a direct descendant of the turn-of-the-century African safari, grounded in assumptions of cultural superiority and unabashedly ignorant of the complex underpinnings of so-called primitive life.

As in Africa, Van Dyke learned enough of the local language to engage in greetings and to shout

A motion picture show staged by Van Dyke for the Iñupiat at Teller. Museum of Modern Art, Film Stills Archive.

commands. Conversely, the Iñupiat developed a language to deal with the new arrivals. Ray Wise reported to the Los Angeles press that:

> Umalikpuk (big boss man) [was used] for director.… Makeup became "Minguk"—or paint … "Camera hogs" were called "Kongechak," which means in our language, "One who always pushes oneself forward but in the end is found to be a fool."
>
> "Closeups" … were called "Canitpuktoak," which means "When two people are close together." "Pitka Igh Loo Goo" (a thing that was not done well and must be done again) was their word for retakes.…
>
> There was one word the natives never found a simile for because they never could understand it. That was film. It remained film. ("Eskimo Adapts Language to Fit Hollywood Chatter")[3]

3. In current Iñupiaq orthography, Mala's observations would be rendered as follows: *umialikpak,* literally, big boat captain, often used for rich men; *minguk,* a verb stem meaning "to paint" but here used as a noun; *pitqiglugu,* literally, "do it again" (Larry Kaplan, pers. comm.).

Van Dyke's attitude remained patronizing throughout his tenure in Alaska. For instance, observing Iñupiat watching a screening of *Trader Horn:* "Some of the Eskimos had never been outside of the boundaries of their own world. When they saw all of those African lions and other beasts and carefully pondered it all, they merely shook their heads and said, 'We see 'em all right, but just the same, she is one big lie.' Van Dyke said to watch the reaction of the Eskimos while looking at the picture was the greatest show he had ever seen" (Cannom 1948:262). On another occasion, Van Dyke informed a Hollywood reporter: "We found the people to be a soft-spoken, friendly race. They had a childish curiosity concerning everything we did. And they were most obliging in attempting to help us. Had it not been for our olfactory objection to their aversion to bathing, we would have got along even better" (Tilden 1933). In fact, their "childish curiosity" was more likely intense observation of the actions and reactions of film crew members. Whereas Van Dyke worked to minimize the impact of his winter experience and to live life in Alaska as if he

Peter Freuchen at work creating *Eskimo's* igloo village. Museum of Modern Art, Film Stills Archive.

were still in Hollywood, the Iñupiat were more interested in learning from the encounter. They were probably no more interested than Van Dyke's crew in radically changing their life-style, but the eyes of the Iñupiat remained open to the possibility that their visitors had brought something useful with them.

Viewing his Eskimo employees as "primitive children," Van Dyke remained determined to show them in an "authentic, primitive light." He became a stickler for detail and wasted no time putting Iñupiaq women to work sewing caribou skin tent covers and elaborate fur clothing. Following Freuchen's directions, he insisted that everything be done exactly as it had by the Eskimos in the story. Even the tent poles had to be cut from green willows

and lashed together with rawhide (Cannom 1948:244). He also commissioned more frivolous purchases, including twelve fur coats he had promised as gifts to Hollywood actresses. Although he meant to keep his word, he had not specified size, and had each tailored a perfect twelve inches long: "The coats were packed in regular size suit boxes, insured heavily, marked 'Fur coat—handle with care' and mailed to the stars with notices written on them, 'Do not open until Christmas'" (Cannom 1948:249).

The Iñupiat were not the only ones Van Dyke employed in his efforts at reconstructing a "pure" Eskimo past. He put Freuchen to work as well. The Danish explorer recalled: "I had been thoughtless enough to let the action take place in an Eskimo

The filming of *Eskimo* on location in Teller, 1933. Mala Collection, University of Alaska Anchorage Archives.

village consisting of nineteen snow houses, thinking that the Eskimos could build the houses in no time … but none of our Eskimos had ever seen a snow house, and I had to do the whole job myself" (Freuchen 1953:255).

After the arrival of the *Nanuk* in June, Van Dyke wasted no time getting production under way. He divided the company into three units. The first left for the coast of Siberia to get shots of whaling and walrus hunting. The second stayed with the *Nanuk* in Grantley Harbor, about two miles from the MGM headquarters at the reindeer station. And the third moved with Van Dyke up the Taksak River to film the summer hunting scenes. There the Iñupiat and Hollywood people set up separate camps, the latter arranged efficiently with special tents for their can-teen, library, movie theater, and baths. Although Freuchen had naively advised the director that the crew could easily live three to a tent with each man doing his own cooking, accommodations were considerably more elaborate, including a mess hall where four cooks worked full time preparing the company's meals (Freuchen 1953:243, Cannom 1948:256).

That fall the crew moved back to the reindeer station, dubbed "camp Hollywood," located on the north shore of Grantley Harbor. From here they traveled out by dog team to shoot scenes: "It had all the earmarks of a typical bungalow court, even to the jangling noises of two or three portable victrolas, each playing a different tune at the same time. [Van Dyke] often grinned and said, 'We've got everything

Ray Mala and Lotus Long in *Eskimo*. Academy of Motion Picture Arts and Sciences.

here but the palm trees and tiled courts'" (Cannom 1948:255). The old reindeer station became the center of the settlement: "They rebuilt this building and it served as a stage for interiors, a billiard and recreation room, a gymnasium and, on occasions, a dance floor. The rest of the bungalow court consisted of small houses, carried from the United States in a knocked down condition. Then there was the kitchen, built of rough boards and stocked with everything from mushrooms to caviar. Van was determined his gang would eat well" (Cannom 1948:255-56). Emil Ottinger, once the cook for European royalty and subsequently presiding over Hollywood's Roosevelt Hotel, oversaw this culinary enterprise. When the weather kept the crew housebound, they listened to dance music over their radios from the Coconut Grove, Van Dyke's favorite Los Angeles nightspot (Cannom 1948:257).

The film crew remained in Alaska for ten months shooting *Eskimo*. Forty-two cameramen and technicians accompanied Van Dyke, including Freuchen, Emil the chef, and half-a-dozen airplane pilots. Again, the press exaggerated the size and scope of the expedition: "One hundred men and women entombed for nearly two years … in a white prison of brutal magnificence … on the ragged edge of eternity … to bring you this panorama of the uncivilized north" (*Los Angeles Times* 1934:16). This entombing was not cheap, costing MGM no less than $5,000 a day. MGM spared no expense in providing the best for all who made the trip. It cost the studio $1,600 per person just to outfit them with clothing and gear to see them through the winter (Cannom 1948:265). During that winter and spring the crew exposed more than six hundred thousand feet of film to bring ten thousand to the screen. When all was said and done, MGM spent more than $1.5 million to produce *Eskimo*.

Van Dyke also brought three Oriental actresses from Hollywood to play opposite Mala, including Ying Wong (the sister of the Chinese actress Anna May Wong), Lotus Long (part-Japanese/part-French), and a part-Chinese/part-Japanese actress. Freuchen (1953:253) ruefully lambasted these actresses as preoccupied with looking beautiful rather than looking Eskimo. It was his job to make them appear authentic, which he did by pulling down their neatly coiffured hair-dos, eliciting the response, "Help, Freuchen is attacking me!" Van Dyke's solution to their vanity was to allow them to appear wearing make-up half the time they were being filmed and relatively unadorned the other half. Little did they suspect that the cameras were actually loaded only during the second half. The ploy worked, however, and the women won kudos on their return to Hollywood for their "authentic look."

Freuchen (1953:255) never ceased finding the antics of these women ridiculous, including their insistence that they were suffering from scurvy when they found they had been served canned rather than fresh juice for breakfast: "Believe it or not, we had to cancel all work for several days while a plane was sent to Seattle for a supply of fresh fruit." He eventually got even, however, when a plane broke down near Nulato at the end of the shoot, stranding him, Emil, and two of the actresses for several days in "primitive conditions." There the women were forced to do their own cooking, and one has the sense that they were as put out as Freuchen was amused (Freuchen 1953:258).

Van Dyke was well-suited for the task of directing a major film expedition on location in Alaska. He had regularly worked on "nature stories"—pictures with leading men like Johnny Weissmuller and Max Baer. In fact, Van Dyke had directed *Tarzan the Ape Man* (1932) not many years before. His crew was equally experienced and consisted of a hand-picked group who had worked together for years. Cannom reported Van Dyke a stern but effective task-master:

> There were those who found it difficult to work for Van Dyke. There are many who find it difficult to work for one who insists upon strict obedience. To Van Dyke, these trips were not just thrilling adventures … they were serious and dangerous expeditions, not to be undertaken lightly.… A natural born leader, he was always the boss, and a hard one, but never beyond the reach of any of his troupe. Like the African trip [for the filming of *Trader Horn*] he knew just what the men would need on this expedition and hadn't passed up a thing. Fifty tons of equipment had been packed in from Hollywood. (Cannom 1948:255)

As in *Igloo,* the principal difficulties in making *Eskimo* were the three hunting scenes. The Iñupiat hunted whale, walrus, and caribou in different places, sometimes during the same season, and Van Dyke flew between hunting grounds to film what he wanted. Patience, patience, and more patience were the prerequisites for location shots. Van Dyke frequently lost his temper during the winter freeze. He wanted snow, but the weather was so cold and dry that what snow there was blew away. He wanted icicles, but it never got warm enough for them to form. When it finally did warm up, the entire igloo village melted away and had to be rebuilt. This created its own minor disaster: "Suddenly we got a frantic stop signal from Hollywood [where the finished reels were taken by plane every other day]. A cable explained that all the scenes taken in the re-built village had to be thrown away as the mountains in the background, which had been snow covered in the first scenes, were completely bare in the second setup." Cannom (1948:256-57) glorifies Van Dyke's Eskimo-like virtue in overcoming these obstacles: "Had it not been for his courage, great patience, persistence, and absolute fearlessness at times he would not have been successful on this project."

Freuchen (1953:249) gives a humorous description of Van Dyke's fit of temper during another minor shooting disaster. Just as a long-sought polar bear came within camera range, the *Nanuk's* skipper polished it off with a single shot. Never again did the crew have such an opportunity. Catching a scene of the ice floes with mountains and glaciers in the background proved just as difficult:

> The snow was so dry the wind kept the atmosphere hazy with "snowdust" and the mountains were rarely visible. Patience always had its reward and a clear day came, and a unit was on the spot instantly to make the take.… What a shot. Van Dyke was delighted. The cameras were grinding away when an unexpected, "Well, I'll be damned!" rang through the air. Van Dyke dropped his gaze from the distant mountain peak and there before the camera, bouncing down the ice having a whale of a time, was a hat—an old felt hat that only a white man would wear. He yelled "Cut!" and then before the unhappy owner could retrieve his topper, the wind began to howl and the mountains and

glaciers vanished as "snowdust" filled the air. It was as if "old Mother Nature" had imbibed the spirit of the gang and was playing a few jokes herself. She had given them a perfect day.… Then like a clown, she had flipped a … hat right down the path of the camera lens, and howled.… The crew had to wait five more days for the weather to clear up. This time the Company worked without hats. (Cannom 1948:259)

Although exciting when successful, these "shoots" were few and far between, and Van Dyke quickly became disenchanted with his arctic set. Freuchen, living in the Eskimo encampment, appears to have enjoyed himself immensely during his sojourn in Alaska, but Van Dyke found it an ordeal. From the Hollywood director's point of view "there wasn't a day but marked some sacrifice and hardly a minute but that some member of the crew's morale dropped to a new low" (Cannom 1948:265). At its best he claimed northwest Alaska as the "dirtiest, most evil smelling, dangerous, heartbreaking place on the face of the earth" (Cannom 1948:262). Papers back home quoted him as saying that nothing in the world could send him back into that "white hell": "No one knows the monotony, the unutterable tedium of ten months in the Arctic until one has done the period of time in an ice-bound purgatory. That we avoided some of the things I feared—insanity, murder—speaks volumes of the mettle of my crew" (Tilden 1933).

Van Dyke spoke in the tradition of the put-upon outsider, content to fear the worst rather than seek out the best in Alaska. His colonial expectations predisposed him to anticipate trouble and left him unprepared to appreciate the vigor and resourcefulness of the Iñupiat he had come to film. Freuchen, having spent years among the Greenland Inuit, was a much more appreciative guest. His written descriptions of his winter in Alaska focus on the film crew, not the Iñupiat, as the former was, for Freuchen, more exotic. He was familiar with Eski-

mos; working for Hollywood was a new experience.

Among Van Dyke's concerns were what he termed the "sex problem." His apprehensions, however, never materialized:

> There is something about the Arctic that makes sex relatively unimportant. The Eskimos themselves are most casual about it. Our standards, which we are pleased to call moral, are not theirs.… I threatened [my crew] to leave behind any man who acquired an Eskimo squaw. Fortunately the sex question never was troublesome. Partially this may have been due to the uninviting appearance of nearly all Eskimo women.… A white man must stay longer in the North than did our troupe to overcome revulsion of such squalor. (Tilden 1933)

Although the Iñupiat regarded sexual intercourse differently from Van Dyke and his crew, it was far from "unimportant" and unregulated. In fact sex between a man and woman was not casual and came as part of elaborate reciprocal relations, often involving the extended family. The sexual act established an ongoing relationship, and children born to either partner considered themselves related as siblings (Burch 1988:31). One wonders if the lack of sexual intercourse between the Iñupiat and their Hollywood guests reflects not only the preference of the whites but of their Iñupiaq hosts. Iñupiaq women may have looked at the soft, pampered crew members and decided they were not worth courting. The crew members' inexperience made them potentially so needy that intimate relations with them might have required more help from the Iñupiat than they were prepared to give.

Filming in Alaska did not measure up to Van Dyke's expectations:

> It wasn't like this on the other location trips I have taken with many of my crew. Africa and the South Seas presented some hardships, but none like the Arctic. The northern land was never meant to be

lived in, and don't let anyone tell you differently....

There were other thrills in the caribou, bear, and walrus hunts. But these were highlights. The rest was monotony and boredom. (Tilden 1933)

Van Dyke pledged to stay in California in future and to use corn flakes for snow without complaint.

Despite Van Dyke's laments, their time in Alaska was not all bleak boredom. Under Freuchen's direction, the film crew occupied themselves with the publication of a newspaper, the *MGM Eskimo News.* In the first issue Freuchen bantered, "A cruel fate decreed that I should become associated with the iniquitous Cinema World and travel into this Paradise of The North with the most infamous band of blackguards it has been my misfortune to meet ... a group of uncouth, un-Danish Americans." In an effort to placate the "riffraff," Freuchen benevolently agreed to act as editor on their paper's behalf. The first issue featured, among other things, a poem "The Shooting of S. Kimoo"—complete with "the gal they called Igloo"—and a weather report: "Possibly winds or calm weather, with maybe ice floes or not, depending on what day it is."

When the schooner *Nanuk* returned to Hollywood, Van Dyke and his cast received an extravagant reception as reward for their efforts.[4] Freuchen (1953:260) described their glorious return in typical tongue-in-cheek fashion:

When we arrived at Glendale we were given a hero's welcome. The film capital appeared to be vastly surprised that we had actually survived all the rigors of the Arctic—starvation and avalanches and wild animals. I heard the most fantastic stories about our great feat. According to one of them I had been carried out to sea on a tiny ice floe and

attacked by a giant polar bear which I had killed with a pocketknife....

We had brought back with us some of the Eskimos who were presented to the Mayor of Los Angeles.... But three members of our expedition were not allowed to take part in the celebration. The three Oriental actresses were smuggled away. They were deeply disappointed, but we could not afford to let it be known that the leading actresses were not genuine Eskimos.

The three Iñupiaq families that accompanied them were brought under bond to the Eskimo superintendent of the Territory of Alaska, and MGM sent them back to Alaska after they finished closeups and interiors. During their stay the Hollywood press made much of them, and MGM actively advertised their presence in an effort to reinforce the authenticity of the production.

When MGM finally finished the film, it premiered to an elaborate opening at New York's Astor Theater with a huge marquee lit up by 70,000 light bulbs. It was billed as a "drama of primitive people.... This is strong stuff. If you like sugar and water, don't see *Eskimo*" (E. Johnson 1933:17). Another reviewer wrote of sympathetic leads and villainous menaces, calling it a "swell performance" and the two female leads ("one particularly a looker") excellent (Variety 1933). Taxi tire covers and radiator cards kept the name *Eskimo* constantly before the public eye, and a Houston newspaper sent girls dressed as Eskimos to visit polar bears in the local zoo to get special press stories. Ray Wise, billboarded as "Mala the Magnificent," impressed the audience by appearing at the premier in an elaborate bird-skin parka—an "Eskimo dress suit" valued at $2,000. Peter Freuchen (1953:263) also attended the opening:

Before opening night I had to give innumerable talks in organizations of all kinds. Finally came the world premiere at the Astor Theater on Broad-

4. The *Nanuk* subsequently sailed to San Pedro where they stripped her of her gear and transformed her into the fighting ship *Bounty* for *Mutiny on the Bounty.* Over the next decade, she changed face on several occasions but never returned to the Arctic (Cannom 1948:266).

THE BIGGEST PICTURE EVER MADE

ESKIMO

ESKIMO
DARING
ESKIMO
LOVE
ESKIMO
THRILLS
ESKIMO
MORALS
ESKIMO
DRAMA
ESKIMO
ADVENTURE
ESKIMO
TERRIFIC

MAXWELL HOUSE
COFFEE
WARD
BAKING CO. MAYFLOWER DOUGHNUTS

ASTOR THEATRE
THESE WOMEN WERE
HELPLESS CREATURES OF
A STRANGE MORAL CODE

MG 34100

Marquee for *Eskimo* at New York's Astor Theater, aglow with 70,000 light bulbs. Mala Collection, University of Alaska Anchorage Archives.

way—and it was quite an ordeal. Outside the theater was an orchestra dressed in fur coats, the way our New York promoters apparently imagined an Arctic orchestra would look. I had to put up a terrible struggle to exclude a flock of penguins which were supposed to appear on stage. I insisted that there are no penguins on the northern Hemisphere, but the promoters answered that nobody knew it and that penguins were expected. A team of reindeer drove around the streets of New York advertising *Eskimo,* the Arctic-adventure film. The promoters knew their job, apparently, because the

house was packed night after night by people eager to see the movie.

As in both of its predecessors, *Nanook* and *Igloo,* the cast of *Eskimo* is almost entirely native. As in both previous films, the opening caption is a deliberate invocation of authenticity: "Entire record told by primitive Eskimos in native tongue in native costume." Also like its predecessors, the drama of *Eskimo* is built around the struggles of a mighty hunter to provide food for his people against formidable odds. The early scenes of the film are devoted to hunting episodes, which some critics explicitly compared to Flaherty's work in *Nanook*. These include a walrus hunt, a battle with a polar bear, a caribou stampede, a whale hunt, and a life-and-death struggle with a wolf, all beautifully filmed. This was not the first time a film depicted the drama of the Eskimo hunt, nor would it be the last. Opening scenes also pictured aspects of domestic Eskimo life judged particularly exotic or primitive, including tattooing, breast feeding, nose-rubbing, and wife-sharing.

As in all previous Eskimo movies, humanity's struggle against nature provides the stage. Unlike *Nanook* and *Igloo*, however, the film's melodrama revolves around the conflict between the "noble Eskimo" and corrupt civilization. Intrigued by the novelty of firearms, Mala and his family seek out the "house that floats"—a whaling vessel whose unscrupulous captain not only cheats the natives in trading but takes advantage of their women. The captain persuades Mala to loan him his wife, but when she returns drunk the next morning, Mala forces the captain to promise to leave her alone in future. ("Was he upset about his woman? You'd think he was a white man.") But while Mala is away on a hunting trip, the deceitful captain once more takes advantage of Mala's wife. Leaving the ship the next morning, she falls unconscious on the ice. The ship's mate out hunting mistakes her recumbent body for a seal and shoots her. When Mala returns, he is devastated. ("He loved his wife in his own funny way.") Mala then takes his revenge on the captain by impaling him—"One returns your harpoon."

The scene then shifts to an outpost of the Royal Canadian Mounted Police (another oddity in Alaska), who refer to the Eskimos as "Huskies": "Their code of morals is different from ours." Two sergeants receive orders to bring Mala in for trial. This they set out to do, but lose their way in a blizzard. Mala finds them near death and revives them, later naively accompanying them to Mounty headquarters.

On their return to the post, the inspector of the Mounties (played by Van Dyke) orders his men to handcuff Mala to the bench where he sleeps. ("Doesn't he realize what he's done?" asks the inspector. "No, he's just honest through and through.") Learning that the Mounties intend that he "swallow sleep" (die by hanging) for his crime, Mala makes his escape. One of the most harrowing scenes is where Mala struggles to pull his hand out of the iron manacle until he frees himself. During his long trek back to his family, the starving Mala eats his dogs one after the other. Finally, after the last dog is gone, he is attacked by a famished wolf whom he wrestles to death before collapsing in exhaustion. His family providentially discovers him, and Mala escapes the Mounties (with their mixed blessing) by jumping onto a passing ice floe and so, presumably, floating to safety. The moral of the story: "Even if your bellies are torn by the last hunger, never go to the white man!"

Eskimo, running almost two hours, was never a box-office success, even after MGM added a hot Hollywood love scene and appropriate advertising to bolster sales: "She was beautiful as a goddess! He was mighty as a god! They loved … with primitive passion … until their peace was shattered by the white man's lust." It did win critical acclaim, however, including the first Oscar awarded for best editing. At its advance showing, *Eskimo* received sensational praise, written in the largest return of preview cards in the history of the studio. *Time* magazine called it "unusual, spectacular, disturbing." The film was a dramatic story presented with the apparent realism of a documentary. Audiences were intrigued with what the industry hyped as "the strangest moral code on the face of the earth." Critics declared Ray Wise, henceforth known as Ray Mala, destined for "matinee-idol raves" and proclaimed Dortuk, the Oriental actress who played his second wife Iva, the Garbo of the North (S. Johnson 1979:18).

Unlike *Nanook* (which was silent) and *Igloo* (which was accompanied by an orchestral score), the

Mala and Aba at home in their igloo in *Eskimo.* Museum of Modern Art, Film Stills Archive.

Mala's wife Aba tempted by the ruthless captain (Peter Freuchen). Museum of Modern Art, Film Stills Archive.

Mala escapes from Mounty headquarters. Metro-Goldwyn-Mayer.

native actors in *Eskimo* spoke their own language with the words translated in subtitles on the screen, giving the film added authenticity. Critics in 1934 did not unanimously approve the film's use of the Iñupiaq language. According to one sour reviewer, "*Eskimo* could have been a really great picture if the dialogue had not been recorded and in its place a full musical score had been provided."

Such criticism serves to heighten our appreciation for just how innovative Van Dyke's use of the native language was at the time MGM produced *Eskimo*. It did not matter that they spoke Iñupiaq while (as always) playing the part of central Canadian Inuit. Reviewers judged them natural and convincing, although their praise was sometimes patronizing: "It is a remarkable film…. The acting of the Eskimos, or their ability to do what was asked of them by the director, is really extraordinary. The Eskimo in the leading male role actually gives one the impression of the moods and feeling of the character" (Hall 1933:1000).

Present-day Iñupiat of northern Alaska still look at *Eskimo* to remember how life was in the past. Mala's son, Ted, described the film as "a true picture in the details of clothing, living, and hunting, and some Eskimo parents have even named their children Mala" (S. Johnson 1979:18). Jerry Vandergriff, the owner of Pictures Inc. in Anchorage, recalled that a single frayed copy of *Eskimo* circulated in bush Alaska for more than forty years. Villagers would show it repeatedly to a full house, requesting it again and again. The costume designer for the Steven Seagal film *On Deadly Ground* (1994) sought out a video copy of the film to study its authentic costumes.

In its claim to authenticity, *Eskimo* followed in the footsteps of both *Nanook* and *Igloo*. In fact, critics explicitly and repeatedly compared *Eskimo* to *Nanook* as well as to *Grass* (1925), another groundbreaking documentary of that period. Some critics went so far as to place *Eskimo* ahead of *Nanook* because "it lets us look at the mores as well as the facts"

of Eskimo life. Reviewers predicted that "we are going to know all there is to know about the Eskimos" with its release: "Their story has been so well written and so well told and played that they are REAL to the audience" (*Hollywood Reporter* 1933). No such revelation was either the intent or the effect of *Eskimo*. In fact, with the film's release the general understanding of Alaska Eskimos may have been even more muddled than before, as the Iñupiaq dramatization of Freuchen's book required them not only to live in the past but to live the past of Inuit in another part of the Arctic.

A critical feature of *Eskimo's* "vital, primitive realism"—its presentation of "life in the raw"—was its presumably accurate treatment of Eskimo morality: "*Eskimo*, along with its revealing of the great courage and childlike simplicity and faith of these people, also attempts to bring out the unique and un-moral moral code of the Eskimos. The film accomplishes this with great charm and no little amusement" (*Hollywood Reporter* 1933).

The "un-moral moral code" referred to here is the infamous Eskimo practice of wife-sharing, which was a central theme in *Eskimo*, providing everything from humor to the motivation for dramatic acts central to the film's storyline. American society in the 1930s found this practice mildly censorious: "*Eskimo* deals with the unusual moral codes of our fur-clad neighbors without mincing words. Wives are loaned, and borrowed by the native hero, according to his customs. In fact, it is doubtful whether the PTA will place this picture on its favored list for little Junior and sister" (E. Johnson 1933).

Rather than merely reprehensible, Eskimo morality was viewed as yet another indication of the "primitive" character of Eskimos:

Probably because the tribe—in place of the family—is the unit of Eskimo civilization, physical relations are quite promiscuous where married women are concerned. These Arctic heathen seem

A caribou dance in *Eskimo*, with an unhappy Mala looking on. Academy of Motion Picture Arts and Sciences.

Teparte and his wives beckoning to lonely Mala. Museum of Modern Art, Film Stills Archive.

to consider sex a normal physical necessity instead of a religious indulgence or an economic luxury. In any event, on account of the scarcity of females, they frequently extend the hospitality of their wives to a bachelor guest; and Metro makes the most of it throughout the first half of the film. But this custom … is handled quite honestly.

Against an Arctic background of walrus, whale, and caribou slaughter, the terrible incongruity of the white man's faith is made apparent … by effective montage with a sincerity of admiration for its northern nomads shining through every frame of film. (*Hollywood Spectator* 1933)

As in the dramatization of infanticide and senilicide in *Igloo*, *Eskimo's* titillating portrayal of wife-sharing was unlike either contemporary Iñupiaq practice or the past Inuit custom on which it was supposedly

based. The soft furs and naked shoulders of the heroine placed *Eskimo's* love scenes in the hot passion/
cold climate tradition of *Frozen Justice.* The actual
practice of wife-sharing, when it occurred in northern Alaska, involved the temporary exchange of
sexual partners by two couples. Far from a random,
promiscuous expression of primitive lust or the temporary satisfaction of the sexual urges of a lonely
hunter, wife-exchange was a form of marriage and
created a permanent bond between the individuals
involved. Whether or not the sexual act which established it was ever repeated, the relationship commanded lifelong obligations of mutual support
(Burch 1988:31). Children born to either couple
were henceforth related as brothers and sisters,
and the children of these children became cousins.

The ideal view of Eskimos (wife-sharing included) presented in *Eskimo* offers a radical critique
of American society. Mala's "natural nobility" on one
level is judged inferior because he achieves his ends
by emotion, not reason, by action instead of
thought, by custom rather than law. Yet the film presents the "primitive Eskimo hero," true to the best of
primitive society, as superior to a civilized man (the
captain) corrupted by the vices of civilization. Like
Flaherty before him, Freuchen did not want to do
away with civilization but instead desired civilized
people to attain the integrity he saw in Eskimos
(Pearce 1953:149). The film version of his book
carries this message.

Mala presents the viewer with the image of
"nature's nobleman," perhaps superior to his civilized conquerors (Pearce 1953:179). Yet contemplating Eskimo nobility is like thinking about one's
childhood—a time we fondly recall yet inevitably
outgrow (Pearce 1953:195). Moreover, the details of
Mala's life explain only how Eskimos differ from the
white man—what civilized men are not, not what
Eskimos are. Mala enacted not what Iñupiat were
but what Euro-Americans should be.

Eskimo was Van Dyke's last major expedition
film,[5] and its release marked both the beginning and

the end of an era. Although not the first film to
employ Alaska Eskimos, it was the first major release
and was successful enough to break the ice for future
productions. Why, then, has Hollywood waited until
the 1990s to return to Alaska on such a grande scale?
Following *Eskimo,* elaborate expeditions would not
venture forth from Hollywood to distant lands, Arctic or otherwise, for many years: "The emergence of
back projection permitted the actors to stay in the
studio. Commercially, this was highly desirable. But
it drained a certain vitality from the cinema. Backgrounds became the most artificial parts of a film,
instead of the most authentic. Opportunities for the
documentation of exotic locales passed to the makers of travelogues" (Brownlow 1978:566). The last
twenty years has seen a return to this expeditionary
tradition, both in the production of documentaries
for television and feature films with documentary
backgrounds. But for the time, Hollywood put away
plans for yearlong sojourns in the Arctic and con-
tented themselves with prefabricated igloos and
machine-made snow.

Life in the Film Industry

After *Eskimo,* Ray Wise adopted Mala as his surname
and settled in Hollywood, where he treated swim-
ming pool owners to kayak demonstrations and
played squash with consummate skill at the Beverly
Hills Athletic Club (S. Johnson 1979:18). He also
dabbled in real estate, though with little success,
buying and subdividing acreage at Pismo Beach
between Los Angeles and San Francisco. He shared
these business dealings with his father, to whom he
introduced himself after his return from Alaska.
Though he knew his father's whereabouts long before, the young man was not entirely sure of a warm
reception and had vowed to wait until his name was

5. Brownlow (1978:566) gives this distinction to Van
Dyke's *Trader Horn.* But as this preceded *Eskimo* by three
years, the latter deserves the honor.

Mala giving a kayak demonstration in Beverly Hills. Mala Collection, University of Alaska Anchorage Archives.

on every marquee in the country before making himself known. Like his father, who had vowed to stay in Alaska until he made a million dollars, the younger Wise saw his dreams fulfilled, and Bill Wise was pleasantly surprised by his successful son.

Along with investing in real estate, Mala also tried his hand at scriptwriting. In 1934 Harrison Carroll of King Feature Syndicates reported that Mala had already completed an autobiographical volume called "Far North" and was engaged on a longer and more fictionalized story to be titled "Snow Man." Aspiring to follow in Freuchen's footsteps, Mala hoped to publish the two books, then combine them into a script which MGM would pay him to direct in Alaska. Nothing ever came of either venture. In 1941 Ewing Scott wrote the screenplay *Son of Nanook,* a story about the introduction of

Ray Mala signing autographs. Mala Collection, University of Alaska Anchorage Archives.

reindeer in Alaska, with Mala in mind, but he never produced the film.

Shortly after their return from Alaska, Van Dyke gave his opinion of Mala's potential in the film business:

One member of the party asked Van Dyke if he thought Ray Wise would get ahead in pictures because of the fine performance he had given as Mala, the lead, in *Eskimo*. Van Dyke replied, "I don't think so, and it's really too bad." Asked what he meant, he continued, "He's a type, and in the movies that's bad. Mala not only will be established in the minds of the people as an Eskimo—he actually is part Eskimo. Even if a professional actor does exceedingly well in a character study, the audience wants to see him in that kind of a role from then on." (Cannom 1948:273)

History did not entirely bear out Van Dyke's prediction on the progress of Ray Mala's career, and Mala continued to act in movies, often playing natives. After *Eskimo* was released, MGM thought they had no further need for their Iñupiaq leading man and let his contract expire. Film agent Phil Goldstone took Mala on. Then when MGM wanted Mala back, they had to sign Goldstone as a producer, and Mala was back where he started. He remained popular for a decade after *Igloo* and *Eskimo,* starring in two serials (*Robinson Crusoe of Clipper Island* and *Hawk of the Wilderness*), playing a supporting role in another (*The Great Adventures of Wild Bill Hickok*), and appearing in numerous features, including *The Tuttles of Tahiti, Coast Guard,* and *The Jungle Princess.*

Ironically, Freuchen's future in the film business, which had looked bright following *Eskimo,* suffered more than Mala's: "Louis B. Mayer called me to his

Ray Mala in a scene from the serial *Robinson Crusoe of Clipper Island. Mala Collection, University of Alaska Anchorage Archives.*

Ray Mala and Lotus Long star together again in *Last of the Pagans. Mala Collection, University of Alaska Anchorage Archives.*

office to congratulate me and promised me a fabulous career in the movie business. We were acclaimed all over Hollywood." After sending him on a trip to Hudson Bay to complete an outline for a new film, however, MGM allowed Freuchen's contract to expire:

> I was quite relieved to be able to leave Holly-wood.... My film had been good enough, MGM told me, but there was no market now for films of that kind....
>
> When I arrived in New York I found a cable from MGM. I was asked to stand by in readiness for a trip to Alaska. MGM wanted me to look into the possibility of making a film about the colonization of the Matanuska Valley. I waited for a week and finally sent a wire to Hollywood asking for further information. The answer came in due time—I was to proceed to Denmark! They did not want to keep me waiting in New York. They would get in touch with me again about the film. I am still waiting. (Freuchen 1953:266)

Significantly, the theme of Freuchen's proposed film may have had as much to do with MGM's reluctance as the market for things Eskimo. Freuchen (1953:264) had agreed to make the Hudson's Bay Company film on one condition—that he could show the company as a blessing to the Eskimos rather than a curse: "Well, I said, all films about primitive people make a point of proving that the white man always ruined the natives who had lived in paradise until contaminated by civilization.... I could not understand why the white man should always picture himself in this role, I explained, particularly as it was far from the truth—at least as far as Eskimos were concerned." The time to set the record straight had, apparently, not come.

Though Freuchen bid the film industry adieu following *Eskimo,* Ray Mala continued to live and work in Hollywood, taking the part of the quintessential native. Although his later films were most often set in the South Seas, Mala also played in a handful of grade-B movies dealing with the North in which Eskimos played peripheral roles. These later films, including *Call of the Yukon* (1938) and *Girl From God's Country* (1940), featured Eskimos and arctic snowscapes but never starred them.

Call of the Yukon, from the James Curwood novel *Swift Lightning* (1919), is set on the Arctic coast of Alaska, title notwithstanding. The film draws a clever parallel between human and animal characters—the love of the rough trapper for a young woman writer who has come to stay in the little Eskimo village of Topek and the devotion of the Eskimo dog, Swift Lightning, for Firefly, a sophisticated collie. In the end both females—human and canine—choose the half-wild, uncivilized males over their civilized counterparts. Eskimos, when they appear, serve only to emphasize the untamed character of the land in which this double love story is played out. Eskimos are the backdrop that signifies the primitive and elemental.

The 1940 Republic production *Girl From God's Country* also made use of Eskimo actors—chiefly Ray Mala speaking a Hollywood patois resembling the pig-Latin equivalent of Esperanto—to move a love triangle to resolution. Starring Chester Morris, Charles Bickford, and Jane Wyatt as the love interest, the story focused on the mysterious withdrawal of a young doctor from civilization. Hounded by a suspicious stranger from the States, the doctor eventually wins both a clear name and the love of his recalcitrant nurse. The film had the dubious distinction of being the first to make use of euthanasia as part of a screen plot—the doctor was suspected of killing his own terminally ill father. Moreover, witnessing a Caesarian delivery performed on an Eskimo woman is the act that transforms the reluctant nurse into a lover. One critic wrote that "hokum is most attractive when it is unabashed and it is for that reason that one is inclined to be gentle" with the film (*New York Times Film Review* 1940:1731).

The 1940 film censor board worked to preserve

Ray Mala in *Call of the Yukon.* Museum of Modern Art, Film Stills Archive.

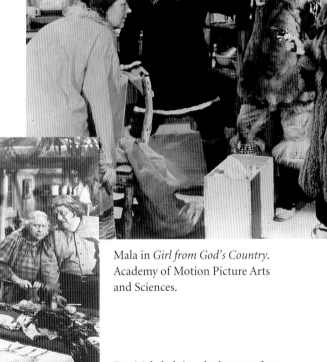

Mala in *Girl from God's Country.* Academy of Motion Picture Arts and Sciences.

Ray Mala helping the hero perform an operation in *Girl from God's Country.* Museum of Modern Art, Film Stills Archive.

the screen purity of the film's Eskimo actors. They ruled that the underlined portion of the dialogue by the Eskimo woman, Koda, be eliminated from all release prints: "Long time ago—Klondike strike days—I know all cards—all men too. I bad girl." They allowed Eskimo Ninimook's skull to be fractured, but not on screen. Similarly a scene in which an old grandmother "instinctively smeared a baby" with oil is hidden from view. Like *Call of the Yukon, Girl From God's Country* is not about Eskimos, but only uses them as background for the major players, who are white.

Mala's last feature film *Red Snow* (1952) was an exception. The independent producer Boris Petroff created this unusual documentary/spy thriller from a combination of studio shots and stock Alaska footage he had left from his 1949 release *Arctic Fury*. Mala's old associate Ewing Scott, who had filmed so much frozen footage in the past, handled the Alaska direction, bringing with him footage from *Igloo* that Petroff adroitly incorporated into his celluloid collage. The movie's budget was modest—less than $100,000—and the producers had the satisfaction of selling their finished film to Columbia Pictures for immediate release.

Red Snow is typical of the patriotic spy movies popular in the postwar period. Starring Guy Madison as Lieutenant Johnson and Ray Mala as Sergeant Koovuk, the film opens with heroic music and a dedication to "loyal American Eskimos." The story tells how the U.S. Air Force, alarmed over strange lights and sounds from the Russian side of the Bering Strait, sends Eskimo soldiers back to their tribes to investigate. Working with Eskimo troops, the Air Force saves an important base from enemy destruction. In the process, Sergeant Koovuk (dressed all in white while his contemporaries wear darker colors) also saves his people on Little Diomede Island from starvation, winning the hand of the lovely Alak in the process. *Red Snow* was the only American-made motion picture dealing with the Soviet Union's invasion of Alaska, not to men-

Mala helps Lieutenant Johnson in *Red Snow*. Museum of Modern Art, Film Stills Archive.

tion the only Hollywood movie before or since to deal with the Eskimo Territorial Guard. Although the words "Russia" and "communism" did not appear in the script, the dialogue included "Siberia," "Uncle Joe's borscht," "political commissar," and "die for the party."

The film proceeded at a slow pace, occasionally quickened with scenes of Eskimos hunting and killing walrus, whales, and polar bears, escaping ice breakups, and trekking across the frozen wastes to the mainland—scenes not just reminiscent of scenes in *Igloo,* but taken directly from it. Although generally complementary of Petroff's use of Alaska scenery, critics judged his attempt to blend documentary footage on Eskimos with a routine spy story confusing. The tale would have been much stronger, they said, if it had concentrated on the Eskimo angle.

Although twenty years had passed since the filming of *Eskimo,* and although the subject was supposedly contemporary Alaska Eskimos rather than nineteenth-century Canadian Inuit, *Red Snow's* Eskimos were still the "pure primitives" of Hollywood's earlier productions. Men battle the elements, women chew hides, and children are always happy even in the face of hunger. Koovuk describes the preparations for his wedding:

> With the help of some of my friends it will not take long to build a new igloo for my bride for our honeymoon.... The bride is captured in the old custom by the young men of the tribe, like they say in the Army, whoo! Now I must find my bride and rescue her. They toss her to the heavens. The higher she goes will be her happiness. It is time for the ritual of our ancestors. We must first pass thru the valley of the love spirit.... Now we go to the Chief and the mother. In our ancient law, the wedding pants are given to the bride, she offers me this promise of my authority."

Although routine in its idealization of primitive Eskimos, *Red Snow* is unusual in its use of an

Eskimo villain to counter Koovuk's nobility. Koovuk's adversary, in both love and war, is the "alien [Siberian] Eskimo" Putu, who is eventually revealed as a spy and killed by our hero. *Red Snow* is painfully patronizing in its rendition of Eskimo dialogue as pidgin English reminiscent of Tonto talking to the Lone Ranger. The film is still featured occasionally on late-night television.

Between the releases of *Eskimo* and *Red Snow,* the homogenized image of Eskimos had changed but little. Even members of the Eskimo Territorial Guard were pictured living in igloos, rubbing noses with their sweethearts, and praying to ancient gods. In fact, by the end of World War II, the lives of Iñupiat and Yupiit living in Alaska had undergone dramatic changes. Both mining and whaling had all but evaporated from northwest Alaska, and men and women were leaving the villages in increasing

Ray Mala and his film sweethearts, demonstrating the famous Eskimo kiss. In Yup'ik, *cingar-* (translated today as "kiss") originally meant a gesture of affection, consisting of a slight pressure of the nose against another's face, accompanied by a quick upward motion. Grandparents typically expressed their fondness for young children in this way. Into the 1950s, elderly Yup'ik men and women watching romantic scenes in Hollywood movies could still be heard remarking, "What are those *Kass'ats* (White people) doing with their mouths?" *Red Snow* (left) Museum of Modern Art, Film Stills Archives; and *Eskimo* (right), Mala Collection, University of Alaska Archives.

The treacherous Putu, a Russian spy, visiting Sergeant Koovuk's girlfriend in *Red Snow*. Academy of Motion Picture Arts and Sciences.

Putu does his worst. Museum of Modern Art, Film Stills Archive.

Mala's sweetheart emerging from her igloo. Museum of Modern Art, Film Stills Archive.

Mala (far right) at work as a cameraman. Mala Collection, University of Alaska Anchorage Archives.

numbers. They were in the midst of a tuberculosis epidemic that would prove more devastating than any previous epidemic. Housing was ramshackle and unsanitary by national standards. Social scientists in the late 1950s predicted the slow but steady decline in the population of rural Alaska and the eventual disappearance of village life as it was then known. While Mala pursued his career in Hollywood, played squash, and looked after real estate investments, his relatives in Teller and Kotzebue were experiencing economic stagnation.

Hollywood was cool to Eskimo themes during the 1940s. Then the war curtailed location films outside the continental United States, putting an end to Polynesian pictures. Mala's original place in the film industry was as a competent cameraman, and he graciously returned to it when his acting career dipped. Although some would have found this change of fortune untenable, he took it in stride. Fellow union men respected his work in the trade, and he lived well.

A satisfying personal life probably did much to see Mala through hard times. He had returned from Alaska with his Iñupiaq wife, Gertrude Becker from Nome, but the couple divorced after several years and she returned home (Blackman 1989:90-91). Like Mala, however, she was a modern, relatively emancipated Alaskan, and she kept her hand in the film industry, eventually returning to the West Coast to live out her life. Mala later fell in love with and married a beautiful expatriated Russian, Galina Liss, with whom he had one son, Ted. Their marriage was a happy one, and they counted such luminaries as Stan Laurel and Bob Hope as personal friends.

In the early 1950s Mala's phone had just begun to ring again. Television was getting started, and demand resurfaced for the now-mature actor. After ten years off screen, he came back in 1952 to co-star in *Red Snow*. Other films were in the works. Although suffering from a weak heart, he went ahead with a location shoot in the California mountains. He died soon after his return, the same year *Red Snow* was released, at the age of forty-four. To this day, his handsome face decorates the walls of homes all across northern Alaska, and he remains the most prolific film star the state has yet produced.

Leni Riefenstahl is carried to safety in the grande finale of *S.O.S. Iceberg*. Universal.

CHAPTER FOUR

Hollywood After Eskimo: Innocence Lost

Although Ray Mala was the single most important Iñupiaq actor to appear on film and epitomized the Hollywood Eskimo for a generation of moviegoers, he was not the only Eskimo in the movies. Following *Igloo* and *Eskimo,* Hollywood continued to look north, occasionally at Eskimos. In collaboration with the German filmmaker Arnold Frank, pioneer of the distinctive genre of "mountain" films known for their last-minute rescue scenes and celebration of heroic images, Universal Pictures produced one fantastic melodrama, *S.O.S. Iceberg,* in northwestern Greenland in 1933. Leni Riefenstahl stars, and in the concluding scene we see her dramatically draped over kayaks as Eskimos dutifully bear her to safety.[1] Riefenstahl was Hitler's favorite at the time, and the film is generally considered a proto-Nazi production. Interiors were made in Berlin, and only the finished negative went to Hollywood.

1. Peter Freuchen (1953:271) had this to say about Leni Riefenstahl's activities while filming in Greenland: "During the film expedition she had lived in Umanak in a tent right in the middle of the colony. With their insatiable curiosity the Eskimos had kept a close guard by the tent at night. They had even cut a couple of peepholes in her abode and had eagerly observed the activities of the German beauty and her visitors. There had been plenty to see, according to my Eskimo friends." Riefenstahl not only acted in films but directed them as well. For details of her filmmaking career, see Barnouw (1983:100-111).

Reversing the normal pattern of Alaska Eskimos pretending to be Canadian Inuit, in *Iceberg* Greenlanders play the parts of Iñupiat. The film concerns a party of lost explorers and attempts to rescue them. A biplane crash lands in what is supposed to be the Beaufort Sea, and the fully-clothed hero swims from iceberg to iceberg to reach an isolated Eskimo village for help. Eskimos figure only in the last five minutes of the film as they run to the edge of the ice to greet the understandably exhausted swimmer. The film ends with the magnificent spectacle of a flotilla of kayaks speeding to the rescue, a duplication of the ride in *Birth of a Nation,* the chariots in *Ten Commandments,* and similar massed effects—theatrically striking but bearing little relationship to the prior action (Hall 1933). Reviewers acclaimed the ice masses the most spectacular part of the film—a picture in which nature outshone both the story and the players, Eskimo and European alike. This would be a recurrent problem in films featuring the Arctic.

One reviewer noted a "screening blunder" at the film's premier in permitting the use of a Universal newsreel with a clip of the Lindbergh party in Greenland. The short included a scene of Eskimo girls dancing modern steps on the deck of a steamer which, the reviewer thought, detracted from the

A flotilla of kayaks to the rescue in *S.O.S. Iceberg.* Universal Pictures.

native scenes at the end of the picture: "This was corrected with the replacement by the next news release" (anonymous reviewer, September 26, 1933).

Polar explorer Knud Rasmussen assisted in the production of *Iceberg,* as well as another unusual movie, *The Wedding of Palo,* which premiered in 1938, the year after his death. Although not a Hollywood film, *Palo* is in many respects the Greenlandic counterpart of *Eskimo.* Based on a traditional Inuit tale, it is a reenactment of an Eskimo love story. Rasmussen wrote the screenplay, and Inuit acted the parts on location in eastern Greenland. Thanks to both, the film is ethnographically quite accurate, as in the depiction of the Greenlandic song duel, an indigenous method for dealing with interpersonal conflict in which two antagonists face each other

Filming the kayak scene in *S.O.S. Iceberg.* Museum of Modern Art, Film Stills Archive.

and publically declare their grievances in emotionally powerful songs. The song duel was a public performance relying in part on audience appreciation for its effectiveness, and this filmed version, although decontextualized, is quite powerful. *Palo* also features an "evil" Eskimo—the villainous Samo—who, dressed in dark colors, unsuccessfully battles the white-clad Palo for the hand of the beautiful and virtuous Navarana.

As in both *Nanook* and *Eskimo,* critics judged the "primitive simplicity" of the film an authentic reflection of Eskimo life: "If Rasmussen used his camera with less sophistication [than Flaherty], he had at least as much appreciation for the heart of his subject. He gives us here a simple story of Eskimo life that is most noteworthy because of its simplicity" (*Stage Magazine* 1940). Another anonymous but equally enthusiastic reviewer reported, "Behind the simplicity of the story you get all the shapes of that lonely and sterile, yet somehow lovely, country, lived in by people full of life's joy, struggle and primitive meaning." When it was released in New York, *The New York Times* applauded: "It must be regarded as

Knud Rasmussen directing *S.O.S. Iceberg.*
Universal Pictures.

one of the most accurate, absorbing, and truly dramatic native pictures that we have seen, … a splendid monument to Greenland's greatest historian."

Following the work of Ray Mala in Alaska and Rasmussen in Greenland, Hollywood virtually ignored Eskimos—Inuit, Iñupiat, and Yup'ik—for nearly thirty years. After Mala's appearances in *Igloo* and *Eskimo,* Eskimos rarely starred in Hollywood movies, nor did their way of life provide the dramatic focus. Hollywood still regularly featured the Northland, however, and sometimes made use of Eskimo extras to carry these plots along. MGM's *Petticoat Fever* (1936), starring Robert Montgomery, Myrna Loy, and Reginald Owen, is a classic example. This featherweight farce concerns a befuddled Englishman and his beautiful fiancee whose plane is forced down near a remote Labrador outpost, where Montgomery, the young wireless operator, and his Eskimo servant take them in. Our hero falls instantly in love with his fair guest, to whom he lays siege, shamelessly neglecting the Englishman and making only perfunctory efforts to return them to civilization.

On location in Greenland filming *S.O.S. Iceberg.* Museum of Modern Art, Film Archive.

Palo and Samo during the song duel in *The Wedding of Palo.* Museum of Modern Art, Film Stills Archive.

he is mistaken for a missionary and falls in love with an Eskimo girl. In the spring, however, the investigators fly in, and Conrad is drowned while trying to escape.

Critics panned the film for its leisurely pace: "The story takes much too long to get started, and consequently rambles along like some of the Eskimo dogs in the film" (*Variety* 1949). Once again a non-native actress (Carol Thurston) is complemented for her "skillful handling of a difficult part—that of an Eskimo gal—makes role believable at all times" (*Variety* 1949). The film was a conventional adventure drama of the Far North, with Eskimos and dog teams and a white man enduring incredible hardships that never quite managed to be convincing: "The portions of the yarn where the hero is alone and lost amid the snowy wastes north of Nome,

Some critics judged the film diverting, charming, and cute, while others appraised it overdrawn and idiotic. The Japanese actor who played the Eskimo man-of-all-work, Kimo, got universally good reviews. The two walk-on characters (played by Bo Ching and Iris Yamaoka) giggled and blushed enough to be judged convincing Eskimos. Critics noted that the studio sets representing the Arctic were particularly bad and complained that the picture failed to make use of the comic material its setting provided (Cameron 1936; Delehanty 1936; Mishkin 1936; Pelswick 1936).

The late 1940s saw the production in quick succession of three films with "Arctic" in the title. In *Arctic Manhunt* (1949) Mala's longtime associate Ewing Scott adroitly combined footage he shot at Point Hope and Point Barrow during the winter of 1947 with studio shots he directed at home in Hollywood. The cops-and-robbers plot revolves around Mikel Conrad, an ex-con being tracked over arctic wastes by insurance investigators trying to locate a missing quarter-of-a-million dollars. After many mishaps, Conrad arrives in an Eskimo village where

Myrna Loy pursued by a polar bear in *Petticoat Fever.* Academy of Motion Picture Arts and Sciences.

Myrna Loy and Robert Montgomery shooting *Petticoat Fever*. Academy of Motion Picture Arts and Sciences.

Reginald Owen getting ready for a sled ride in *Petticoat Fever*. Academy of Motion Picture Arts and Sciences.

Robert Montgomery and his man-Friday, Kimo, in *Petticoat Fever*. Museum of Modern Art, Film Stills Archive.

The "Labrador hula" danced by Iris Yamaoka and Bo Ching. According to Robert Montgomery, this was "probably the only floor show ever seen in Labrador." Museum of Modern Art, Film Stills Archive.

Alaska, tend to grow very monotonous, even with Chet Huntley's narration to explain his sufferings, but things brighten up considerably when he reaches the Eskimo village where the natives add color and variety."

The Iñupiaq woman listed as Quianna in the credits was judged particularly attractive. Flown to Los Angeles to shoot interiors, newspaper articles hailed her as a "cool customer ... too hot after Alaska": "In an interview, Quianna, which means 'thank you' to an Eskimo, revealed her real name as Wilma Bernhardt, that she is one of 13 children; that her mother is Eskimo and her father of German descent; that Hollywood is an exciting place, and that she is busy, when not before the camera, collecting autographs of stars for friends and relatives in

Nome" (*Los Angeles Times* 1949). Born in Teller, Wilma took first place in a Miss Alaska contest staged in Nome. She surprised Californians on two counts: She spoke good English and needed dark makeup to make her "look more like an Eskimo" for the picture.

After the completion of *Arctic Manhunt*, Ewing Scott helped to write and produce *Arctic Flight* (1952). As in *Red Snow*, the plot revolved around the Cold War tension at the Soviet/American border. Mike Jarvis, Alaska bush pilot operating out of Kotzebue, picks up an apparently wealthy businessman, Harold Wetherby, who subsequently gets acquainted with Dave Karluk, Eskimo reindeer herder, his modern native girlfriend Saranna Koonuk (again played by Carol Thurston), and others at Kotzebue.

Eskimo students attend to Saranna (Carol Thurston) and Mike Jarvis (Mikel Conrad) in *Arctic Manhunt*. Museum of Modern Art, Film Stills Archive.

Mikel Conrad points the way in *Arctic Manhunt*. Museum of Modern Art, Film Stills Archive.

Friendly enough at first, Wetherby turns out to be a Russian spy bound for the border carrying concealed microfilm disclosing U.S. miliary secrets. Although he makes a break over the ice toward Big Diomede, Russian sentries shoot him on approach. The bush pilot and Kotzebue Eskimos live happily ever after.

A third arctic billboard, *Arctic Fury* (1949), was a fiction film that used documentary footage to tell the story of Alaska's flying doctor Thomas Barlow. In the opening scene the doctor learns that a mysterious "plague" is ravaging a band of Eskimos "on the eastern slope of the Brooks Range" and sets out in his plane on a five-hundred-mile journey to help them. The plane crashes, and the bulk of the film follows the doctor in his journey through the Alaska wilderness, eluding bears, musk oxen, wolves, and cougars. After wandering in his shirt-sleeves for two months through forested country looking nothing like the Brooks Range, he makes it to the supposed Eskimo village, consisting of log houses and totem poles, only to find it deserted. Rescue is at hand, however, and the film ends happily: "[The Eskimos] look up to the sky and wonder. For Dr. Barlow has met the fury of the Arctic and mastered it."

Eskimos do no more than "add interest and color" (*Hollywood Reporter* 1949). Their most significant scene depicts them leaping dramatically from ice floe to ice floe, as the plague is "driving these men toward the doubtful aid of civilization." Boris Petroff, who directed Mala in *Red Snow,* lifted this scene directly from the closing reel of *Igloo,* and audiences purportedly found it both believable and entertaining.

Of all three arctic films, *Arctic Fury* had perhaps the most unusual history. Norman Dawn originally directed its production in 1935 for some $30,000. A crew of five men made three different attempts within eighteen months to tell Dr. Barlow's story and finally emerged with what was released as *Tundra,* an elongated featurette, distinguished by "delightful scenes in which Arctic animals played the

leading parts" (Joseph 1949). Petroff subsequently reedited the *Tundra* footage and tried to roadshow it without success. After a few test runs, he realized he had footage but no story. He subsequently redid the film for $10,000, doubling its length by adding fresh material—mostly interiors filmed in Hollywood. As in *Tundra,* survival is the theme: "The frozen Arctic demands a man be a hero." The moral is "that hope and courage will sometimes overcome the greatest of odds. All this is good stuff, especially for children" (*Herald* 1949).

In 1953 Universal Pictures returned briefly to northland drama in their production of James Oliver Curwood's durable classic *Back to God's Country,* complete with sterling hero and heroine and sneering villain. Starring Rock Hudson and Steve Cochran, the feature also made use of peripheral Eskimos to tell its tale—principally the treacherous native guide Uppy, played by Pat Hogan. The Great Dane Walpi, "an Eskimo name meaning walrus," shares the spotlight, adding both the doggy touch, without which no Curwood story would be complete, and as much human interest as all the peripheral Eskimo players combined.

Ice Palace (1959) was another much more influential example of Eskimo-abusing Alaskana from this period. Based on Edna Ferber's best-selling novel, the film championed the cause of statehood for Alaska. Although the Eskimo interest is again peripheral to the plot, the scenes in which Eskimos appear are memorable as among the worst in film history (S. Johnson 1979:21). At one point the hero, Thor Strom, flees civilization to find brief happiness with an igloo-dwelling Eskimo wife, Una, living within sledding distance of Juneau! Nineteen-year-old Dorcas Brower of Barrow appeared in this role as a simple, fur-clad primitive, as did her screen parents Helen and Chester Seveck, manager of the U.S. government's reindeer herd near Kotzebue. After Una's death, Strom returns to civilization with their son, who later elopes with his rival's daughter. One of the phoniest scenes in the movie depicts the

Captain Peter Keith (Rock Hudson) distrusts the native Uppy (Pat Hogan) in *Back to God's Country*. Universal Pictures.

Eskimos stand by while Captain Keith inspects a fake map given him and his wife Dolores (Marcia Henderson) in *Back to God's Country*. Universal Pictures.

Uppy under arrest in *Back to God's Country*. Universal Pictures.

An Eskimo village in sledding distance of Juneau provides the background in *Ice Palace*. Warner Brothers.

Una (Dorcas Brower) warms a half-frozen Thor Strom in *Ice Palace*. Warner Brothers.

Strom's son tries to use an elk for shelter for his laboring wife in *Ice Palace*. Warner Brothers.

Real-life Dorcas Brower working as a secretary at the Barrow school. Bill Bacon.

Chester and Helen Seveck, one-time actors in *Ice Palace*, attending a whaling festival at home in Kotzebue in 1978. Bill Bacon.

half-Eskimo son driving his dog team through interior Alaska in an effort to reach civilization before his wife (in the sled) gives birth. Failing this, he shoots an elk that happens to be standing by the trail and starts to butcher it to provide a warm shelter for the impending birth. Meanwhile a bear—actually a man inside a bearskin—is attracted to the kill, and a battle ensues. The grandfathers miraculously show up in time to shoot the bear and save the baby, although not their own children. The entire scene was shot in the studio. Critics were not impressed and judged the movie, crammed with incidents rather than events, "just awful" (S. Johnson 1979:21–22).

The Iñupiaq couple Helen and Chester Seveck went on to a distinguished career in public relations. In 1960 they began working for Wien Airlines, promoting Alaska from coast to coast, as well as in Hawaii and Japan. Both worked for years as official "greeters" for Wien in Nome, performing traditional Eskimo dances in front of thousands of tourists and celebrities, including Walt Disney, Chuck Connors, Walter Cronkite, and Ronald Reagan. Over the years

the couple appeared on the Art Linkletter, Steve Allen, and Groucho Marx shows. After Chester's death in 1980, Helen continued working in tourism until 1985. The Alaska Visitors' Association in September 1989 honored her for her contribution and dedication to the tourist industry (*Tundra Times* 1993). And it all began with *Ice Palace*.

Dorcas Brower, who played Thor Strom's ill-fated wife, still lives in Barrow, where she works for the North Slope Borough. Her aunt, Sadie Brower Neakok, had been offered a bit part in a movie twenty-five years before, but Sadie's father, Charles Brower, forbade it. His niece, however, was a different generation, and her family encouraged her to pursue a career as a film star, however briefly.

Return to the Tundra

Alaska Eskimos continued to garner only small roles in the handful of Hollywood feature films dealing with arctic themes produced in Hollywood studios before 1960. Two minor features that proved exceptions to this general rule were *North of the Sun* and *North of the Yukon*. Both films were made in the "documentary" style popular following World War II. Documentaries had generally fallen in popularity as Hollywood feature films gained audiences. The war, however, had given new life to the documentary tradition, and commercial features made use of this documentary approach in popular entertainment.

Travel conditions had also improved considerably since Ewing Scott had flown to Barrow to make *Igloo* and Van Dyke's crew had sailed the *Nanuk* to Teller to shoot *Eskimo*. By the late 1950s film crews could fly in and out of remote Alaska villages with relative ease and safety, and for the first time in thirty years a handful of commercial filmmakers turned toward Alaska to get the dramatic effects notably absent in Hollywood studio creations.

North of the Sun was a feature-documentary that focused primarily on the natural drama of the Arctic and Eskimos only insofar as they added "human interest" to that drama. Filmed by the nature photographer Gordon Eastman in 1960, the eighty-minute film depicts the encounter of a modern-day adventurer with the people of Point Hope. If nothing else, Eastman brought experience to his task—thirty years during which he worked on more than one hundred films, including some for Walt Disney. Eastman is the undisputed hero in *North of the Sun*. A narrator first introduces us to our hero sitting in an armchair in his home in Jackson Hole, Wyoming, reading about Alaska in preparation for his journey to Point Hope: "There he hopes to live with and capture on film the ancient lifestyle and culture of the Eskimo ice hunters before it disappears under the impact of the machines of Western Civilization."

The opening scenes follow Eastman's seven-day,

cross-country trip in his Supercub from Wyoming to Point Hope. In informal, down-home language, Eastman describes the places he has filmed on other wildlife expeditions as he flies over them. The tone is set. Nothing is important in its own right but only in relation to Eastman. Eastman is coldly received in Point Hope. He attributes this to the Eskimos' "long history of unpleasant experiences with white men," a half-truth that would never have caused the Point Hope residents to ignore a visitor in the manner shown. But the Iñupiat reticence to befriend Eastman is important as the dramatic prerequisite to what follows. Several weeks later Eastman and a friend crash their plane, barely escaping with their lives. But Eastman will not give up. When his wounds are healed, he returns to Point Hope to a hero's welcome. Why this sudden transformation? "Once in a great while a hunter stranded on the ice will float back to shore and survive. The Eskimos say of him, 'He came back from the ice.' They hold him in reverence and believe him to be touched by the gods. Eastman came back."

The remainder of the film consists of the footage Eastman's acceptance in Point Hope allowed him to shoot. Although Eastman treats the viewer to many interesting scenes of Iñupiaq life, the tone is condescending and exploitative. For example, Eastman finally gets to go hunting with "the Eskimo." Only well into the trip do we learn the hunter's name. In another scene Eastman introduces us to an Iñupiaq woman, Nanu: "Old Nanu is famous for her boots, and she's making a pair for me…. It will take Nanu about a week to make my mukluks. She makes hundreds of stitches. And when they're done they'll be a work of art. I paid her $15 for my pair." In film advertising, Eastman billed himself as "one of the few men in history allowed to hunt the 120,000-pound bowhead whale with an all-Eskimo crew." As white whalers and Eskimos had been working together for over a century, this claim was a patent lie.

A second feature-length movie focusing on the natural drama of the Arctic, albeit more on its Eskimo inhabitants, is *North of the Yukon* (1967). The film is only slightly less patronizing than Eastman's film. Provocative advertising announced "strange Eskimo love rituals" and "primitive Eskimos boldly challenging the horror of the Arctic white death." In fact the film is tame, a modern version of an ancient Eskimo narrative theme—the trials of an orphan who, in the end, proves himself and wins a wife. The film is a marriage of Hollywood story and Iñupiaq setting not seen since *Eskimo*. But whereas *Eskimo* was a dramatic play employing actors and actresses to tell its tale, *North of the Yukon* juxtaposed scenes of Iñupiaq life with detailed narration in the documentary tradition.

The narrator (Lorne Green) begins by introducing "Eskimo country … the land of limitless nothingness." The viewer zeroes in on "an isolated three-thousand-year-old settlement" (probably Point Hope), with its "sod igloos" and ancient whalebone cemetery. The arrival of a bush pilot establishes the contemporary setting as he makes "the first small crack in this centuries-old wall of arctic isolation. He is Mercury, messenger of the Gods, and Santa Claus all in one." Yet even the candy the pilot throws cannot raise the spirits of a young man named Amaluk: "What Amaluk wants you can't buy from outside. He wants to marry Sivalu. But tribal custom says he has to prove his manhood as a mighty hunter. And the hunters say, 'He's too young, like those Husky pups, not grown up enough.'"

The film then follows the village men on both a seal hunt and a walrus hunt ("The steel nerves and determination of the Eskimo against the crushing forces of nature"). Although the narrative emphasizes the life-and-death character of the hunt ("Each man knows he's heading into mortal danger, yet they run to meet it. This is their life!"), the light musical score undercuts its impact. Amaluk has been excluded from these serious endeavors ("If Utak sounds cruel, remember this is a cruel world in the Arctic"), and we follow him on a simple fishing expedition ("But you'll find nothing simple in the life

of an Eskimo"). Further frustrated in his efforts to join the village hunters, Amaluk tries to hunt on his own and is swept away on an ice floe. The remainder of the film follows him on his journey south, his eventual rescue, his slow but steady return to his own village in the spring, and his acceptance by the hunters. Finally Amaluk "claims his bride in a wild and colorful Eskimo celebration," which turns out to be a community dance.

North of the Yukon is well filmed, and the native actors speak in Iñupiaq. These conversations are not directly translated but lightly commented on by Lorne Green, whose overabundant narration never allows the viewer enough mental space to learn anything visually. The presumption is that what is going on is so foreign as to require complete and constant description. On the contrary, the visual sequences tell their own story and are sufficiently detailed to require little verbal accompaniment. For example, we cannot view the seal hunt without being told that "to sustain life, this tough operation must be repeated time and again, day after day, 'til the arctic night sends weary men and dogs to their beds of snow." At every turn, the narration reinforces our image of the hardy Eskimo pitted against a harsh environment at the expense of any attempt to present the Iñupiaq view of the significance of their own acts. To the film's credit, however, we are at least viewing Iñupiat portraying Iñupiat.

Lost in Alaska

> "Bud and Lou Hit the Yukon Trail … and the Yukon Trail Hits Back … as They Mush Through the Slush … It's all New—and a Riot, Too." (Universal Pictures 1952)

A truly unique film creation was the absurd, slapstick concoction *Lost in Alaska* (1952), starring Bud Abbott and Lou Costello. Most films featuring Alaska Eskimos, from *Igloo* and *Eskimo* to *Ice Palace*

Abbott, Costello, and Mitzi Green mug for the camera in *Lost in Alaska*. Academy of Motion Picture Arts and Sciences.

and *North of the Sun,* are presented in a realistic style. In the name of entertainment, they provide audiences with stereotyped images of Eskimos that the audiences then take to their heart as the real thing. Whatever its flaws—and many critics panned the picture as one of the weakest and unfunniest of the Abbott and Costello comedies—no one can mistake the spoofing in *Lost in Alaska* for reality. Rather, it makes use of the Eskimo stereotype as just that—a stereotype to hang a gag on.

Critics considered *Lost in Alaska* typical of the "irrepressible inanities" that mark Abbott and Costello films. The pair is always lost somewhere; this time they're lost in Alaska (Bongard 1952). As firefighters Tom and George, they save the life of

Nugget Joe McDermott, who has made a will bequeathing his $2 million Alaska gold mine to fifty old friends, all of whom now want him dead. Following Joe back to Alaska we are introduced to his lady love, Rosette. Sporting authentic zebra skin parkas, the pair then journey to Joe's claim with a motley dog team that takes off after a cat, leaving our heros to be rescued by—you guessed it— Eskimos. Slapstick scenes in the Eskimo village of Mukaluk include George being squirted by a piece of whale blubber and the two taking part in—horrors—an Eskimo masked dance. Back on the trail, the duo pass the time fishing for trained sea lions through the ice. In the end, George accidently pushes the gold into the ocean, and, the divisive

Costello scares a bear in *Lost in Alaska*. Academy of Motion Picture Arts and Sciences.

Abbott and Costello lost in Alaska. Academy of Motion Picture Arts and Sciences.

Bud, urging his dog team to run: "Oatmeal!" Lou: "That's *mush!*" Bud: "Same thing." Academy of Motion Picture Arts and Sciences.

lucre lost, everyone lives happily ever after. The song "There'll be a Hot Time in the Igloo Tonight" was to be included, but it was censored as unacceptable because of its "sex suggestiveness." In the finished film, Rosette croons:

> Eskimo men are courageous when,
> they head out for the open sea.
> Eskimo she's just wait and freeze
> saying "Blubber come back to me!"
> The young and the old face the bitter cold
> knowing that they must not fail.
> Get a sharp harpoon and a serving spoon
> I want a piece of the whale.
>
> There'll be a hot time in the igloo tonight.
> You know a what time in the igloo tonight.
> Drape your carcass with your best parkas.
> Hitch the caribou, he'll be smilish·
> pulling your stylish
> icicle built for two.

Reviewers judged the plot "a riot of improbability." None of the Eskimos, of course, was played by an Eskimo, and the entire film was shot without leaving the studio. Despite the ready market for Abbott and Costello buffoonery, *Lost in Alaska* apparently had some "tough sledding" at the box office as its sequences of high comedics were few and far between. The producers obviously tossed the film off on a very limited budget with practically no story and nothing in the way of backgrounds.

Whereas Chee-ak and Mala are depicted as serious igloo-dwellers, the Styrofoam constructions in *Lost in Alaska* are so fake they are funny. At one point a storm blows them over, and they sit like turtles turned upside down on their shells. Abbott and Costello melt one igloo when they fall asleep beside a blazing wood fire they have lit inside to keep themselves warm, and they engage in a wild chase in and out the front and back doors of another igloo trying to escape their pursuers. Eskimos and igloos are inseparable in most peoples' minds, and Abbott and Costello take this association to new heights of ridiculousness. Yet Alaska Eskimos, unlike Canadian Inuit, do not even have snowhouses as part of their heritage. In a *Tundra Times* editorial Howard Rock once reported: "When Paul Tiulana of King Island was asked by a tourist if he had ever seen a snow igloo, he replied, 'Only once.'

'Where was that?' the tourist asked.

'In Florida,' was Tiulana's reply."

Abbott and Costello's comic use of the Eskimo image is reminiscent of a recent flap in the *Tundra Times,* in which a reader complained that the cartoon "Tumbleweed," which spoofs Eskimos, is racist and demeaning, "a throwback to ignorance and stupidity" which "no longer has a place in American newspapers and especially not in Alaska newspapers" (Bloom 1990). He asked newspaper editors around the state to throw out the offending strip. But all readers were not equally offended. Satire, they reminded Bloom, builds on stereotypes. Should we therefore ban satire?

Writing in the same vein, George Owletuck (1991) of Anchorage complained to the editors of *Newsweek* concerning their representation of Eskimos:

> I also found the illustration … offensive—an igloo in the background of three stereotyped Eskimos. I would find it very difficult to watch my MTV in the early '80s had I lived in an igloo. My father would have an equally difficult time watching Ali, the Heavyweight Champion Boxer, during the height of his career.
>
> Reinforcing stereotypes is destructive to the cohesiveness of American society…. The stereotypes portrayed in the media, i.e., *Newsweek,* do not help me any … as an Eskimo."

The year before an Anchorage columnist had commented on the demeaning Eskimo image in the popular comic strip "Mukluk" drawn by Philadel-

Eskimo village after a storm in *Lost in Alaska.* Academy of Motion Picture Arts and Sciences.

Our heros prepare to leave igloos and totem poles behind in *Lost in Alaska.* Academy of Motion Picture Arts and Sciences.

The Igloo Hotel in Igloo, Alaska

phia-area artist Robin Heller and running in about a dozen weeklies in the United States and Canada, including four in Alaska. "Mukluk," he reminds us, "is as much an Eskimo as Mickey is a mouse." When queried, Heller said of his strip, "I'm realizing that I've got to build it not on how Eskimos live but people's perception of how Eskimos might live. I'm not worried about whether Eskimos drive the dog sled into McDonald's… , but that makes for a cute joke. So it's really built on perception rather than the authentic" (Doogan 1990). Abbott and Costello accomplished no more and no less.

For years illustrators have used Eskimos, like Indians, as comic figures through both extreme stereotyping and through a complete reversal of the stereotype (Price 1973:162). Popular culture has repeatedly appropriated Eskimos to create humorous commentary on the human condition. Filmmakers, however, have been much more hesitant to capitalize on the comic potential of Eskimos, to show the Eskimo stereotype in a ridiculous light. Abbott and Costello's arctic antics provide the first funny Eskimos since the fishing scene in Buster Keaton's *Frozen North* thirty years before. The

Eskimo image, it appears, is not only frozen, but frozen in a serious pose.

THE FAR SIDE By GARY LARSON

Ralph Harrison, king of salespersons.

Savage Innocents: Anthony Quinn
as Primitive Child

> Eskimos are among the strangest people on earth, with a morality and way of life so different from ours that at first glance many things they do seem horrifying or ridiculous. To be hospitable to a stranger or a friend, an Eskimo will offer his wife; if his first-born child is a girl, he may kill her; he is so modest that the word "I" is not in his vocabulary. He is primitive, often violent, often strangely tender. His laws are not our laws, for our laws have no relevance in his wilderness. (*McCall's* 1960)

Following the release of *Eskimo* in 1934, a major commercial film would not feature Eskimos again until 1960 when Anthony Quinn took the starring role in Nicholas Ray's *The Savage Innocents.* Ray based his screenplay on Hans Ruesch's best-selling novel *Top of the World* (1950), published in fifteen languages with more than two million copies sold. Maleno Malenotti produced the picture, which Aldo Tonti filmed in Technicolor on location at Resolute Bay in northern Canada with interiors done in London and Rome. The result was an Italian/French/English coproduction released in the United States by Paramount Pictures to saturation bookings and splashy ad campaigns. Dubbed a novelty picture with "off-beat prestige," its potent mixture of sex, violence, and human interest made it eminently exploitable. Although portraying non-Alaska Eskimos, the film merits attention as the first major feature dealing with any Eskimos in almost thirty years.

Like *Eskimo, Savage Innocents* portrays the disastrous contact between pristine Eskimos, perfectly adapted to their harsh environment, and the outside world. The film shows the Inuit as simple (if not simple-minded) children, capable of violence only when ignorant whites violate their naive values. The story follows the childlike but invincible Inuk through courtship, marriage, and his first mystifying encounter with the civilized world. Following in the footsteps of both Nanook and Mala, Inuk is eulogized as "elemental man." But Inuk the hunter himself becomes hunted after he accidently kills a bumbling missionary who not only refused his best food (old caribou eyes, fermented bear brain, and a year-old piece of marrow swarming with maggots) but his offer of his wife as well. Just as in *Eskimo,* the arm of the white man's law reaches out to bring Inuk to justice, and just as in *Eskimo,* the white man sent to do the job sees the error of his ways and ultimately allows the bewildered Eskimos to slip through his fingers. But whereas Mala skillfully eludes his pursuers, the innocent Inuk has to be chased away at gunpoint. On the merits of the white man's pursuit, Inuk offers good advice: "When you come to a strange land, you should bring your wives and not your laws."

In the production of *Savage Innocents,* an international cast, including three Japanese actresses but no Inuit, put on furs, snow goggles, and mukluks to portray the most commonly held stereotypes about Eskimos: "Anyone wishing to study the private life of an Eskimo will learn … that the femme is subservient to the male, that one of their favorite dishes is raw seal-meat which on wide screen and in color can be quite a shock to a patron's stomach, and that it is courtesy for an Eskimo to offer his wife to a friend" (*Variety* 1960). All three of these "truths" had been dramatized in *Eskimo* thirty years before, and they represented the stock-in-trade of the popular Eskimo image. Recycling them on an irregular basis continued to be both financially and critically acceptable.

Anthony Quinn and company enact the quintessential primitives that Ruesch (1950:52) described in *Top of the World:* "They are like children, forthright, pitiless, and gay.… too artless to lie. So crude are they." In fact, Inuit sociality is far from crude but is circumscribed by countless prohibitions and proscriptions. From the time they become aware of their surroundings, children are taught to follow these rules or risk the consequences. Their attention

Inuk (Anthony Quinn) offers an Eskimo delicacy to a squeamish missionary in *The Savage Innocents*. Quinn had to shave his chest as well as his face for his role. Paramount Pictures.

Inuit maidens steam up the igloo in *The Savage Innocents. P*aramount Pictures.

A Mounty who didn't survive in *The Savage Innocents*. Paramount Pictures.

to an elaborate social etiquette throughout their lives may appear natural and artless, but this is far from the case.

Quinn's dominance over a bevy of Japanese actresses does not reflect the real-life division of labor. Rather, it reveals the ethnocentric Western viewpoint that Eskimo men dominate Eskimo women. Euro-American viewers take as self-evident that the combination of a demanding environment, a major reliance on hunting, and male dominance over women go hand-in-hand. On the contrary, Inuit peoples contend that women "draw" the animals that their husbands bring home. Appropriate activity on the part of a man's wife is as critical to his success as his own prowess. According to one Iñupiaq whaler in north Alaska, "I'm not the great hunter, my wife is" (Bodenhorn 1990).

Some who saw the film, including the *McCall's* reviewer quoted above, took the celluloid portrayal as the real thing. According to *Motion Picture World,* "The manners and mores of the uncivilized Polar Eskimos imposed upon him by the rigors of the frozen wasteland which he inhabits are realistically presented" (Rechetnik 1960). The film's off-screen narration and vivid reenactments helped to solidify this impression: "*The Savage Innocents* is undoubtably unique in filmmaking, exemplifying as it does heretofore unphotographed phases of the Eskimos most personal life" (*Hollywood Citizen News* 1961). Some even appraised the film's "sickening frankness" a near fatal flaw, potentially providing civilized viewers with more gruesome ethnographic detail than they could handle: "We see the world through Inuk's eyes, and it is a cold harsh world, indeed. Before the picture is over, Inuk's ways no longer seem so strange. We find him sympathetic, almost appealing; it is hard to imagine his behaving otherwise.… We recommend it to those willing to stand some bloodshed in the interests of learning about a strange people" (*McCall's* 1960).

The *New York Herald Tribune* reported: "Nicholas Ray went to great lengths to authenticate every aspect of the film before the cameras rolled. He toured Eskimo villages, interviewed anthropologists, read about Eskimo life, and finally flew the stars to Copenhagen to meet a colony of Greenland Eskimos, listen to their music and learn more about their customs before shooting on 'The Savage Innocents' began." Paramount alternately declared that Ray had "read everything published about Eskimo life" and that talking to Eskimos in Copenhagen and reading Ruesch's novel "gave him a pretty good insight into the unusual country he was greasepaint-pioneering."

While some judged the picture true-to-life, others roundly criticized it as crude melodrama: "It is hard to tell whether Nicholas Ray who directed and wrote the screenplay … intended it as honest documentary made commercial by some sex interludes or as a straight sexploitation film dignified by authentic shots of the Arctic wastes.… The documentary shots, far from authenticating, merely emphasize the artificiality of the studio-made story. Starring Anthony Quinn as the noble savage, it is an Arctic waste from start to finish" (Knight 1961).

Shrewd viewers and reviewers saw the film for what it was—fantasy not history. Although billed as scrupulously accurate anthropology, the film, with its carefully simulated "Eskimo English," the nose-rubbing, the festive gulping of raw, bleeding seal flesh, and the continual childlike giggling (Stinson 1961), once again used images Euro-Americans had come to associate with Eskimos to tell a story about the virtues and vices of civilization. No Eskimo was ever as noble or as innocent as Anthony Quinn's expressive portrayal. This cannot be leveled as a criticism, as Nicholas Ray was not directing a documentary but creating an artistic rendering. Regardless of how much "research" he engaged in before filming, his goal was not to realistically represent Eskimos but rather to use ideas about Eskimos to talk about knowledge and innocence, savagery and civilization. Like Flaherty and Van Dyke before him, he employed the Eskimo image to point out the simplicity and nobility he felt civilization had lost.

The title *Savage Innocents* is ironic, as the film leads the viewer to see that compared to so-called civilization, there is nothing savage about the laughing, gentle, truly innocent Eskimo. Bob Dylan, for one, saw the irony and took it one step further in his enigmatic song, "Quinn the Eskimo" (1968):

> Everybody's building ships and boats.
> Some are building monuments. Others are jotting down notes.
> Everybody's in despair. Every girl and boy.
> But when Quinn the Eskimo gets here, everybody's gonna jump for joy.
> Come all without, come on within.
> You'll not see nothing like the mighty Quinn.

Along with sensational and spurious ethnographic representations, Hollywood movies then as now use conventional symbols to portray certain underlying problems and solutions for each generation of viewers. Just as Indians in the movies originally figured not as human beings, but as emblems for the wild and savage forces of nature which civilization must overcome, Eskimos originally embodied the innocence lost in the process. By the 1960s, Hollywood was employing Indian motifs in movies such as *Billy Jack* to express frustration with the Vietnam war and to illustrate the world view embraced by young Anglo Americans (Deloria 1989). Eskimo motifs, however, remained frozen in time, their use unaltered by half a century of moviemaking.

Given his aim—theater not documentary—Ray's artistry profits from his casting of Quinn, Yoko Tani, and Anna May Wong in the major Eskimo roles.[2] The transparent whiteness of these Eskimos is a reminder that we see not Eskimos *per se* but a white man's projection of an Eskimo, an artist's deployment of an image in a poetic fiction. As Yacowar

Mikel Conrad and his Eskimo sweetheart, played by Carol Thurston, in *Arctic Manhunt.* Museum of Modern Art, Film Stills Archive.

(1974:134) points out, it is naive to complain about the casting of whites as Native Americans: "While the practical reason for these castings may have involved such unartistic considerations as Box Office appeal and the paucity of experienced minority actors, the artistic effects of this casting should not be ignored. First, one gets the stylized representation of the type. Second, what one gets is not the type, but a metaphoric use of that type. These … do not depict the humanity of the Indians … rather an index of the humanity of the white man." Quinn's Eskimo is not a real Eskimo, but a metaphor for the "innocent primitive extraordinaire." Similarly Ray's subject is not Eskimos encountering whites. Rather he uses

---

2. Anthony Quinn also played Indians in movies such as *They Died with Their Boots On* (1942).

Inuk (Anthony Quinn) and Asiak (Yoko Tani) admire their first-born in *The Savage Innocents*. Paramount Pictures.

stereotyped images of them to talk about the conflict between "primitive innocents" and corrupted/corrupting civilization.

Like the habitat groups in the African Hall of the American Museum of Natural History described by Haraway (1989:29), Eskimo family groups in the movies are actors on the stage of nature: "Gradually the viewer begins to articulate the content of the story. Most groups are made up of only a few animals, usually a large and vigilant male, a female or two, and one baby. Perhaps there are some other animals—a male adolescent maybe, never an aged or deformed beast. The animals in the group form a developmental series, such that the group can represent the essence of the species as a dynamic living whole." Whereas taxidermy "froze one frame of an … intense visual communion" (Haraway 1989:42),

moving pictures of the paradigmatic Eskimo hunter, wife, and child gave life and breath to the idea of "natural man," locating the myth in time and space.

What finally makes the oblique meaning of the image clear is the fact that most Euro-Americans know no Eskimos. Thus—as with vampires and aliens—we can accept their film images for their "metaphoric suggestiveness" (Yacowar 1974:139). Although the intensity of Technicolor tempts the viewer to accept screen images as accurate reflections of reality, Hollywood Eskimos—Nanook, Chee-ak, Mala, Inuk—are only figures of speech: They are terms in a fiction but never the topic (Yacowar 1974:135). Quinn's Inuk underlined this metaphoric quality in ways that Ray Wise's more "authentic" Chee-ak and Mala could not.

Disneyland Eskimos

Alaska Eskimos featured in few Hollywood fiction films in the 1950s and 1960s. They did, however, make a brief comeback in the early 1970s as players in a series of television shows filmed by Walt Disney focusing on animals of the north and their relations with their human neighbors. During the production of *Bambi* in 1941-42, the Disney studio housed a small zoo to which animators could adjourn to draw from life. Disney also employed nature photographers to shoot footage of animals in the wild. The results were often technically expert but dramatically weak and sentimental (S. Johnson 1979:20).

Snow Bear (1970) was the first Disney television production to deal with Eskimos. An Eskimo version of *Born Free,* the story revolves around the relationship between Paka, a polar bear cub, and Timko, an Iñupiaq boy who befriends her (S. Johnson 1979:21). Viewers watch the bear grow from a cute, cuddly cub to a powerful she-bear with cubs of her own at the same time Timko grows from a boy to a young man. Although their friendship inevitably causes problems for both, the ending is happy.

In *Snow Bear,* which first aired in two parts on NBC's Sunday-night "Wonderful World of Disney," the animal, not the Eskimo, is the star: "Walt felt that we could interest more people in nature and the threats against the wild by having a story people could follow built around a single creature, something we could root for, a hero" (Smith 1970). The film proceeds from the polar bear's point of view, with humans introduced as "the deadliest enemy for all polar bears." In the process the bear is "humanized," as when the soundtrack plays a lullaby while she sleeps. The bears in the film were raised in captivity and trained to perform at Klants Zoo Center in the Netherlands. They had never been near the Arctic until Disney flew them to Barrow by jet to make the movie and had a hard time at first adjusting to the cold. Barrow residents remember them for

their circus stunts, as they liked to stand on their hind legs and bow to passers-by.

The Eskimos, however, were the "real thing," intended to underscore the film's true-to-life character. According to one reviewer: "Another 'dividend' was the caliber of Eskimo actors in the film, notably Steve Kaleak as the teen-age friend of the bear, and Rossman Peetook, a commanding figure, as his father. There is a native dance, the visit of a trading plane and a meeting of village elders, all immensely effective in natural performance" (Smith 1970). These real-life Iñupiat, however, do some remarkably un-Iñupiaq things, as in the sequence in which the boy and his father build a snow-block igloo for their hunting headquarters: "Astonishing how quickly they do it—about 45 minutes to completion. Tytle [the film's producer] said the Eskimos had to be taught how" (Smith 1970). The reviewer concludes, "Polar bears who've never seen snow; Eskimos who can't build igloos. They're shattering all our Aleutians!" For the general public, however, the illusion was all too effectively reinforced.

Both the use of a continuous voice-over narration as well as the striking nature photography gave *Snow Bear* the appearance of documentary. On the contrary, *Snow Bear* was as much a Hollywood fabrication, created for entertainment not edification, as *Eskimo* and *Savage Innocents.* As always, the film presents the northern environment as the real adversary, motivating the need for both Timko and Paka to become competent hunters in due time: "This is the Arctic … where time stands still … a bleak and lonely place of lingering snow and ice, of frigid wastes and barren lands seemingly lifeless." In Timko, we encounter the conflict between a gentle nature and harsh reality, "a dreamer wanting to watch and carve, not kill." When he realizes that his failure to become a hunter is endangering others, he determines to leave for a year "to survive on his own or perish" in a cave along the arctic coast. In fact, no Iñupiaq boy would test his manhood in like manner, let alone in a coastal cave, as no such geological feature existed in the region.[3] But there is no doubt that Timko's self-imposed banishment works dramatically and adds interest to the story line.

The Eskimos appear as picturesque as possible, both in the film's visuals and in its moderately patronizing narration. The annual arrival of the benevolent trader is handled in an idealized fashion, as is the meeting of the village council of elders to decide Paka's fate, where Timko unabashedly pleads his furry friend's cause. Barrow residents found particularly amusing the supposed Eskimo names Disney gave to his characters: Timko, Akotak, Oogala, Ramaluk, and Paka, "the mischief-maker." Even the bears were constructed around human cultural stereotypes—Kanuk, the male cub was the leader, while his sister Paka played the part of the wayward tagalong. The result is a moving story of a young boy's coming of age, some fine wildlife sequences, and yet another film presentation of Eskimos—contemporary Iñupiat no less—as hardy, happy, resourceful primitive people.

Audiences liked *Snow Bear* so well that four years later the "World of Disney" returned to Barrow to film a second Eskimo television feature, *Two Against the Arctic* (1974), based on the Sally Carrighar novel *Icebound Summer* (1953). Again, the coastal tundra provided the setting—this time near Nome—and Iñupiat supplied the cast. Rossman Peetook performed so well as Timko's father in *Snow Bear* that Disney rehired him to play the part of the stalwart father and hunter Ningeok. Susie Silook and Marty Smith played the children, Lolly and Joseph, while Jerome Trigg and Vernon Silook took minor roles as their grandfather and uncle, respectively. Disney employed a realistic style and an incessant narration that overlays the Iñupiaq dialogue and almost overwhelms the visuals. When the narrator is not describing how the viewer should read the scene, the dramatic orchestral score is.

3. Steve Kaleak, who sports his "Timko" hat to this day, recalled that Disney filmed the cave scenes inside a Barrow warehouse.

Whereas the spotlight is on animals in *Snow Bear,* this time the Iñupiaq actors take center stage. A variety of animals come and go, but they are important only insofar as they affect the fate of the two children. The story opens with the children setting up a summer fishcamp and waving goodbye to their father and two companions as the men leave in search of walrus, promising to be back in twenty-four hours. Within a day, seals tear the children's fish net, a wolf steals their fish, and the men fail to return. They find themselves alone with little food, in danger of starvation. The remainder of the film follows them on their quest, first for eggs and berries to fill their stomachs, then, after they find pieces from their father's hunting outfit washed up on shore, on a 150-mile overland trek toward home. In the process they encounter a variety of wildlife, including lemmings, hawks, wolves, caribou, wolverine, and polar bear.

Although a more likely story than *Snow Bear, Two Against the Arctic* is constructed around familiar stereotypes. Certainly it portrays the "typical" arctic drama, frail but resourceful humanity fighting for survival against a forbidding environment: "Lolly and Joseph were Eskimo through and through, and it was their native intelligence and self-reliance that were to be put to the test." Little Joseph is described as having "hunting in his blood." When the hunters depart, they are "off to sea, to adventure and risk, pitting themselves against the unknown dangers of the Arctic deep." Lolly takes inventory "stoically" when the hunters fail to return. Their main problem is not keeping warm or protecting themselves from wild beasts, but finding food: "Strangely the main predator is not the wolf but starvation, the specter that cuts down man and beast alike. It is everpresent, and all creatures must learn to live in its shadow.... Eking out a living here is touch-and-go at best for bird or human. In this bleak scene there is little that is edible. Still tribal experience had taught Lolly's people how to look for things.... The wisdom of her race would be their only hope now."

The problem for both Walt Disney and the children is what to do when they eventually find food in the form of baby birds and a defenseless caribou fawn: "Their only wise move is to kill it. This seemed a cruel thought. Yet the Eskimo way is to face the hard facts of existence, and Lolly was trained in the Eskimo way." In both cases, however, the children relent: "She could see her brother was too soft-hearted to be a proper Eskimo. But could she herself kill a thing so helpless? … For all the seriousness of the situation, the children were not beyond a few lighter moments. For to smile is to survive in this harsh land." The stereotypical representation of Eskimos as relentless yet smiling survivors is the unwritten definition against which Lolly's lenience is presented. Having the children act with compassion toward helpless animals and eventually save themselves with meat from a wolf kill also got the Disney studio out of the uncomfortable situation of having its appealing young hero and heroine act in a way that might alienate them from the average American viewer.

In fact, Iñupiat view the relationship between humans and animals in a very different way than Euro-Americans. Although this difference is at the heart of their "survival," the film avoids it altogether. Many nonnatives, including the youngsters who watched *Two Against the Arctic* on "The Wonderful World of Disney," view living animals in the Disney tradition as humans in furry or feathered clothing. Violence toward them is as unthinkable as violence toward human babies playing in a sandbox. They see Eskimos as pushed toward such horrific acts by the rigors of their environment. Eskimos, on the contrary, view animals as nonhuman guests who give themselves to their human hosts in exchange for careful treatment and respect. For them there is not the same finality in killing an animal for food. If properly cared for an animal does not "die dead forever" but returns the following season in a never-ending cycle of birth and rebirth (Fienup-Riordan 1990:167-91).

The film manages to avoid all significant differences between real Eskimos and other people. The children, like ideal Eskimos, survive because they are fit: "Lolly and Joseph were aware of the ancient laws and began to feel their sharp edge since they too were competitors in the fight for life. They had become predators like the rest." Here again, concepts like competition and predation fit poorly with the Iñupiaq view of animals as nonhuman guests with whom they had an ongoing reciprocal relationship. Lolly and Joseph succeeded because "the Eskimo eye is a trained eye" and because Eskimo children learn early that "nothing was ever guaranteed to be safe and secure." Their reunion with their father was "quite joyous for Eskimos, usually so solemn and restrained. Emotion for these people is only an occasional luxury." The film does not teach audiences anything about Eskimos that storybook representations had not inculcated in their psyche years before. Disney did not deal with Eskimos again for close to ten years and then featured Canadian Inuit rather than Alaska Iñupiat.

In 1983 *Never Cry Wolf* opened to good reviews in theaters across the country. Carroll Ballard, director of *The Black Stallion* (1979), demonstrated again his mastery of pictorial technique and psychological nuance. Based on the book by Farley Mowat, *Never Cry Wolf* depicts the inexperienced biologist Tyler gradually coming to understand the nobility, even humanity, of a pack of wolves. The film was three-and-a-half years in the making—the crew nicknaming the project "Never Cry Wrap"—and cost the Disney studio $12 million, twice the original budget. The original story was set in the flat barren grounds (Keewatin) of the Canadian Arctic, whereas the film was made in the scenic mountains of the Yukon Territory and Alaska.

The Eskimo angle is peripheral to the film's central theme: civilization corrupts. A variation on the noble but doomed Eskimo, the film presents the Inuit as the possessors of secret knowledge and primal understanding. Ootek, the elder Eskimo played appealingly by Zachari Itimangnaq, keeps appearing when Tyler least expects him but most needs him, only to vanish again when his job is done. Moreover, he has a special affinity with wolves who are his "helping spirits"; he knows when the howling of the pack tells of the approach of a herd of caribou and takes Tyler to view the hunt. In an ironic twist, the wolf hero and heroine eventually are killed not by the malevolent white bush pilot, but by the young Eskimo hunter Samson Jorah—Noble Savage gone modern—to get money to buy himself a new set of teeth. In a sharp touch of irony, he turns the ubiquitous Eskimo smile into a badge of treachery. As Marsden and Nachbar (1988:616) point out, this film's focus on Native American spirituality brought their screen image full circle: "Just as Edison's one-minute movies in the 1890s were sold to audiences eager to view the strange otherness of Native peoples, so too do audiences in the 1980s go to the movies for the pleasure of seeing Indians whose mystical lore makes them fascinatingly different."

Although not appearing on screen, Alaska Eskimos had a hand in important aspects of the production of *Never Cry Wolf*—the climactic chase involving a herd of five hundred "caribou" and a pack of wolves. To shoot the ten-minute sequence, director Carroll Ballard traveled to Nome, housing his crew in the old high school just outside town. Poor Mr. Ballard: "We had to move a whole pack of wolves, the crew and a ton of gear to a place that really is the end of the world." Arriving in Nome, his troubles did not end:

> The first problem we had was finding the caribou. There are a couple of wild herds in Alaska, but no way you can get to them.… We had to negotiate to borrow the caribou from local reindeer barons, Eskimos who raise big herds of the animals for the fuzz on their antlers, which they can sell to the Koreans as an aphrodisiac.

Greenhorn biologist and his knowledgeable Inuit benefactor in *Never Cry Wolf*. Walt Disney Productions.

Inuit mentor Zachari Itimangnaq, standing by his tent in *Never Cry Wolf.* Walt Disney Productions.

It was unbelievable what these guys wanted. Some of them wouldn't even talk to us. One guy wanted us to buy him two helicopters in exchange for letting us borrow his reindeer.

We eventually made a deal but only had a few weeks to shoot the sequence. It rained for the first 10 days. On the eleventh day, Korean businessmen arrived on the scene with briefcases full of money for the fuzz. On top of that, the reindeer were always moving to where we couldn't find them.... The problems filming that scene were almost never ending. (Walt Disney Pictures 1983)

When the reindeer finally gathered outside Nome, Tyler's role was to sneak up on them by coming around a peninsula in a motorboat, climb up a hill, tear off his clothes, and leap into the surprised herd while the cameras rolled. Just as Tyler bounded

over the hill, however, the herd headed off in the other direction, and a handful of Iñupiat on horseback were unable to round them up. Although Ballard was finally able to get one day's shooting, the arrival of the Korean businessmen threatened to put an end to his work:

> Ballard ingeniously tried to extend his shooting time by negotiating to buy the antlers himself. "The plan was, when the shoot was finished, we'd sell the antlers which would make Walt Disney studio the middle man in an aphrodisiac business.... The guy who owned the reindeer wouldn't go for it, and Disney wouldn't go for it either."
>
> Thus Ballard was forced to leave Nome, go back to Canada to shoot other scenes, and return the following June to re-shoot the caribou sequence—this time successfully using helicopters to herd the animals. (Warren 1983)

How did Ballard direct the wolves and reindeer when he finally had his chance?

> I would shout "Get the wolves out there. Alright, now set the caribou that way. Okay, let 'em go! Woaaaaaaa!" That was it. (Walt Disney Pictures 1983)

White Dawn

Aside from Disney's flurry of activity in Alaska, Hollywood produced only one film involving Eskimos between 1960 and 1990. Although filmed in the Canadian Arctic, its innovative approach merits discussion. *White Dawn* (1974), based on the novel and screenplay by James Houston, is a moral study of three whalers marooned in the Central Arctic and their relationship with their Eskimo hosts, played by Baffin Island Inuit. Fine performances by Timothy Bottoms, Lou Gossett, Warren Oates, and a diverse cast of Inuit actors result in a visually compelling and dramatically successful movie. The film was made on location at Iqaluit (Frobisher Bay) on the southeastern tip of Baffin Island. There producer Martin Ransohoff, best known for his successful TV series, *Mister Ed* and *The Beverly Hillbillies,* set up production headquarters in a long unused Canadian Air Force compound, including space for two sound stages where interior sequences were filmed. Like Van Dyke setting up Camp Hollywood at Teller forty years before, he imported a chef from Montreal to feed the crew. Work in the Frozen North was ready to begin.

The story concerns three whalers stranded in the Canadian Arctic in the 1890s, and the film follows their interaction with the Inuit band that saves their lives. The tribe takes them in as part novelty, part family, but gradually comes to view their guests more as a curse than a blessing. One whaler in particular repeatedly takes advantage of his hosts, stealing what could have been his as a gift. In the end the Inuit, their patience with their dangerous charges exhausted, do the only sensible thing and execute them in proper Inuit fashion. One reviewer quipped that the film was "at once artful, [but] also an entertainment rich in organically justified blood, sex, violence, love, hate, comedy and tragedy. And most currently successful movies would settle for any one, justified or not" (Champlin 1974).

As in every arctic drama, the film portrays the conflict between man and a hostile environment. It eulogizes "these remarkable people whose very existence seems a testimony to man's incredible powers of endurance and to his ability to adapt to his environment" (Boyum 1974). The main theme, however, as in its predecessors, *Eskimo* and *Savage Innocents,* is the conflict between pristine Eskimos and corrupt civilization. It portrays the first skirmish in that battle, predicting the eventual destruction of a primal people, "the spoiling of something pure" (Champlin 1974). According to the Paramount press book, "The *White Dawn* is a penetrating study of civilization that is quickly vanishing, the proud and

noble Eskimos whose way of life is undergoing tremendous changes."

Houston had lived many years in the Arctic and been instrumental in starting the arts movement, particularly painting and carving, in the Baffin region. He based his book on a supposedly true story that had been passed down for several generations within a number of Inuit families on southern Baffin Island, and he wrote it from the native point of view. The film version—like every arctic movie before and since—foregrounded the whaler's perspective. Investigation of the Inuit vision of reality rarely transcends their hunting technology and domestic practices, especially their "exotic sexual mores" and "culinary aspects that most challenge the western appetite" (Dorr 1974). The film, *White Dawn,* makes only passing reference to the irony that fires Houston's novel: Whereas the whalers consider themselves civilized and Eskimos primitive, the Inuit see things the other way around, explaining their guest's white and black complexions as the result of the union of Eskimo women and dogs. Even this ironic contrast is a self-reflective one. In the end *White Dawn* does not reveal the humanity of the Inuit but "reiterates modern man's romantic view of primitive culture as a nearly ideal state of being, perfectly in tune with the earth" (Boyum 1974).

In Paramount's press book, director Philip Kaufman, as modern as the next person, expressed an ideal view of his subjects: "There are similarities between the American Indian and the Eskimo. And I think what we are saying in this film is very strong about what happens to a really pure culture when it is violated for the first time." Working with Inuit on Baffin Island only confirmed his bias: "You didn't raise your voice working with the Eskimos.… These are the world's most gentle people." Cameraman Mike Chapman described the Eskimos as "Zen masters—maybe the brightest people on earth." James Houston was of the same mind: "They are of course, remarkable people. And one worries for them. Wor-

Timothy Bottoms pursued by disgruntled Inuit in
White Dawn. Paramount Pictures.

Timothy Bottoms confronted by Joanasis Salomonie in
White Dawn. Paramount Pictures.

Timothy Bottoms relaxes with his Inuit hosts (left to
right) Pilitak, Meetook Mallee, and Seemee Nookiguak
in *White Dawn.* Paramount Pictures.

Inuit celebration, including the famous "mating dance," in *White Dawn.* Paramount Pictures.

ries deeply. This film will give some idea of the splendor of their way of life—how proud and noble it is.... How much longer it will remain, only God knows."

Reviewers likewise responded to the nobility and purity of the screen Eskimos that Kaufman and Ransohoff brought home from Frobisher Bay. As in the case of *Eskimo* and *Savage Innocents,* the majority approved *White Dawn's* "rare mixture of documentary re-creation and heavy melodrama" that recaptured "a harsh and timeless Eskimo life which has already almost entirely disappeared.... The great majority of Baffin Island Eskimos now live a civilized life" (Champlin 1974). Critics lauded its stunning photography and fascinating, "sometimes shocking" folkways. Judith Crist of the *New York Times* wrote: "The ambience is overwhelming: the

individual and communal living, the fetid yet erotic atmosphere of the igloos, the timelessness of Arctic days and nights, the primitive mores and moralities. There is, in fact, something old-fashioned in the best sense about the film in its presentation of an exotic culture, an exhilarating honesty in its survival theme, a heartbreaking truth to its tragic denouement, and a story as educational ... as it is absorbing."

As in *Nanook, Eskimo,* and *Savage Innocents,* critics applauded both the film's effective drama and its striking "documentation" of Eskimo reality. There is no doubt that the use of Inuit actors contributed substantially to this "fiction of realism." All told, Ransohoff hired fifty Inuit as technical advisors, interpreters, drivers, and hunters to procure the thirty seals, fifteen caribou, walruses, and bears needed for various scenes.

For the important role of tribal chief, Kaufman had auditioned dozens of Oriental professionals in Los Angeles before deciding on a Japanese actor. They brought him to Baffin Island, only to find out they had made a mistake. On their arrival at Frobisher Bay they broadcast a series of announcements over local radio for Inuit to audition for the other roles. Their request met with a cool response, and initially few Inuit showed up.

Meanwhile Houston set out on his own casting search. The first on his list was his old friend Simonie Kopapik, who was soon cast as Sarkak, the chief. Then Houston began to introduce other Inuit friends for key roles in the film. Joanasis Salomonie, a thirty-four-year-old Cape Dorset adult education teacher, plays Kangiak, and Pilitak, a twenty-four-year-old mother of four also active in local politics, plays Neevee. An Inuit girl, Neelak, raised by American foster parents, plays Gossett's ill-starred love (Paramount Pictures 1974).

Unlike Ewing Scott, who had judged the Iñupiat "wooden" performers, Kaufman later contended that the Inuit were the best natural actors he had ever seen: "It was the happiest choice I ever made. These are the most responsive and flexible actors in the world. No professional could have supplied the same truth and detail about Eskimo life that they did for us on camera.... They invented so much of what they did in the film that it got to the point where we relied on them to give life to each scene. They were revelations" (Paramount Pictures 1974). The "mating dance," a climactic sequence in the film wherein the Eskimos initiated the whalers to their more exotic courting rituals, took nearly four days to film, and once again Houston and Kaufman took their cues from the Inuit: "'It was the older people who remembered the dances and the games the tribe played during the endless winter months,' Houston said, 'I had a number of ideas and so did Phil, but much of what we had planned was changed by the Eskimos themselves and what you see on screen is largely the result of their improvisation. I think

some of the most interested members on the film set were the younger Eskimos, many of whom were being introduced to some of their customs for the first time'" (Paramount Pictures 1974).

The finished film presents smiling, igloo-dwelling, wife-sharing Inuit, who say to their guests things like, "When it grows dark, our souls must grow light" and "Let us build a huge igloo to dance away the cold." Yet the film deals with the Inuit of central Canada, that part of the Arctic where these stereotypes first developed and in which to some extent they apply. The Inuit speak their own language throughout, reinforcing the "fiction of realism." Moreover, they appear dressed in authentic caribou and sealskin outfits, all expertly sewn by a team of local women who were also responsible for manufacturing the tents and domestic paraphernalia.

The "realistic" portrayal of nineteenth-century Inuit life had unlooked-for repercussions when *White Dawn* first came out. Though educators praised its "careful documentation of Eskimo life"— some said that it was more important as education than as entertainment—the Motion Picture Association of America (MPAA) rating board gave *White Dawn* a restricted (R) rating. Its objections revolved around scenes of nudity and scenes depicting Inuit killing animals for food. No matter that the Inuit viewed this "killing" not as execution but as the animal's willing gift of its body to satisfy the hunter's need.

Ransohoff complained publicly that finances as much as cultural differences affected the rating. *Papillon* (1973), which cost $13 million to produce, had successfully appealed its rating, while *White Dawn,* costing only $2 million, had its appeal denied. Ransohoff had cut a sex scene between Timothy Bottoms and his Inuit sweetheart but retained several shots of exposed female breasts, which apparently was enough for the MPAA to deny his appeal. Ransohoff subsequently rallied support from both critics and church groups, including the Council of

Ray Mala in *Igloo*. Academy of Motion Picture Arts and Sciences.

Noble and Enduring, Still Waiting in the Wings

During the last seventy-five years, Hollywood has repeatedly looked north, producing more than two hundred films dealing with Alaska and the Yukon (Norris 1992:53). In these films, however, prospectors and Mounties outnumber Eskimos five to one. In the beginning most of what people knew about Alaska was based on the gold-rush period, and this was the period Hollywood most often recreated. In films harkening back to the gold rush, Eskimos appeared as little more than primitive backdrop, if at all.[4] When Alaska Eskimos took center stage, most often they portrayed precontact Canadian Inuit.

The scripts and reviews of Hollywood films dealing with Eskimos to date run like a broken record. Themes rarely range further than the hardy Eskimo versus the hard environment (*North of the Yukon, North of the Sun,* and the Disney movies) and the pure Eskimo corrupted by civilization (*Frozen Justice, Eskimo, Savage Innocents,* and *White Dawn*). All major Hollywood creations either explicitly or implicitly claim Flaherty as their inspiration and set out to do him one better as entertainment. A decade after Flaherty's triumph, the *New York American* praised *Eskimo* for its "vital primitive realism." Documentary had declined in stature as the popularity of fiction films had increased. But public interest in film coverage during World War II breathed new life into documentary, and the postwar period saw a return of *Eskimo*-like expeditions. *White Dawn* began shooting on the fiftieth anniversary of the release of *Nanook.* Lobby cards told viewers what to expect: "Where no civilized man has ever been before … based on a true story, with the descendants of the actual tribe, and filmed where it happened."

Churches, who had previously complained to the MPAA about lenient ratings but never that a rating was too strict. *Post* critic Gary Arnold wrote: "*White Dawn* is as likely to corrupt the young as a subscription to the *National Geographic.* Why penalize serious film makers from depicting a way of life accurately?" Ironically, the R rating resulting from Ransohoff's attempt at "accurate" reconstruction of traditional Inuit mores barred the very audiences most likely to want to see the picture. The message was "next time he should try a straight exploitation movie, with plenty of violence, plenty of sex, and no attempt to make alien cultures understand each other" (Arnold 1974). On its second appeal, the board changed the rating to PG.

4. For example, in the made-for-TV *Alaska: The Abbott and Costello Show* (1950s), the comedians never leave New York. The program begins with Costello announcing, "My uncle discovered gold in Alaska" and continues with the ins and outs of trying to get money to go up and mine the claim. Alaska evokes images of gold, not Eskimos.

Joy Boyum (1974) observed, "Today, many of the qualities which make up that idiom—the use of actual locales; the nonprofessional actors; of events drawn from real life with the usual disclaimer replaced by a claimer that any resemblance to persons living or dead is not at all coincidental—have more and more been adopted by the fiction film, helping to give it some of the same conviction they have given to the fact film."

Igloo, Eskimo, Snow Bear, Two Against the Arctic, Never Cry Wolf, and *White Dawn* were all filmed in the north using Inuit and Iñupiaq actors. All made good use of Inuit/Iñupiaq dialogue, explaining it either with onscreen narration or, more effectively, English subtitles. The stories emerge from the Arctic as Euro-Americans understand it. All these factors contribute to the films' apparent and appealing realism. Audiences come to be entertained, and they leave not only smiling, but with all their patent images of Eskimos confirmed.

Hollywood tends to produce one major Eskimo movie every ten years. Of all the Inuit and Iñupiat who have acted in Hollywood productions, Ray Mala and Rossman Peetok are the only two Alaska Eskimos who have taken major roles in more than a single feature. Many an Alaska Eskimo has played a bit part in a Hollywood production, however, and most recall their experiences as pleasant, harmless diversions. Sadie Neakok of Barrow remembered a frantic search for old clothing to supply authentic wardrobe for one production. Barrow children liked seeing themselves on "The Wonderful World of Disney," and Alaska Eskimos who remember seeing *Lost in Alaska* found Abbott and Costello's gags humorous rather than offensive. On a visit to Alaska several years ago Simonie Kopapik, who played chief Sarkak in *White Dawn,* was asked point-blank, "Didn't you feel exploited by those guys from Hollywood when they came up north to make their movie?" Kopapik paused for a long time. "No," he said. "It was fun!" (Francine Taylor, pers. comm.).

Hollywood production standards also worked to insure that viewers experienced Eskimo movies as good, clean fun. Nudity was a major concern. The Production Code Administration (PCA) insisted that the two Eskimo women in bed beside Thor Strom in *Ice Palace* be properly clothed, and their approval of *Red Snow* was contingent on covering things up, "specifically the breasts of the women" (Breen 1951). Similarly, they advised Paramount Pictures to reduce closeups of Inuk and Asiak in bed as well as delete shots of the heroine taking off her top garment in *Savage Innocents* (Shurlock 1959). By 1974 brief shots of Inuit girls revealing bared breasts remained intact in *White Dawn,* but not without a fight.

Hollywood applied their production standards as rigorously to language as to exposed flesh. In *Red Snow,* the line "always thinking of something to eat" had to be changed to "always thinking about food" because of its "sex suggestiveness" (Breen 1951). The PCA objected to the double meaning of the line "I'll come with you if you hurry" in *Savage Innocents* (Shurlock 1959). Lines "suggestive of sex starvation" had to be removed from *Petticoat Fever* as well as "vulgar movements" in the dance of the two Eskimo girls. Regarding this lighthearted farce, Breen (1935) wrote Louis B. Mayer that "neither should you emphasize the business of the Eskimo suggesting that he has brought an Eskimo woman for Dinsmore's convenience."

Hollywood also carefully monitored physical violence in Eskimo movies, as in the scene in *Back to God's Country* when the Great Dane Walpi kills the Eskimo guide. The PCA advised Universal Pictures to "kindly avoid excessive gruesomeness as to the action showing the dog at the Eskimo's throat" (Breen 1952). Not only should dogs not kill Eskimos too grimly, but in *Savage Innocents* Inuk could not be depicted kicking dogs (Shurlock 1959). Although these strict standards began to fade in the 1960s, the furious battle waged by the producers of *White Dawn* to dispel their R rating is but one indication of the difficulty Hollywood would have disengaging itself from the pure and noble Eskimo image. While sex and violence run unchecked across the silver screen, Eskimo movies are held to a different standard. Now and again they are arenas for the consideration of more serious topics, such as the comparison between civilized and primitive codes for living. Sex and violence are important insofar as they help to define these differences.

Other than Disney's back-to-back productions in Barrow, producers and directors tend to make Alaska and the Arctic in general a one-time commitment. They come, they experience, they film, and they never return. If they learn anything from their successes and mistakes, they apply these lessons to other films in other places. On their return home, they take on the aura of noble and intrepid filmmaker, worthy of admiration for effort in the face of daunting odds. Van Dyke took this pose, as did Kaufman forty years later: "'If you say anything at all about this picture,' director Philip Kaufman murmurs gently, eyes half closed, 'be sure to let them know how hard it's been to shoot, harder than any of them back there could possibly imagine'" (Paramount Pictures 1974).

Other than *Ice Palace* and the two more recent productions, *Never Cry Wolf* and *White Dawn*, none of these early Hollywood depictions of Eskimos are available on video, and the films live on only in archives, television retrospectives, and the memories of those who viewed them. The likelihood of an endless and repetitive use of Alaska Eskimos to represent the noble native, pure but doomed, seems all too real. In fact, as times change, the theme of noble natives has come full circle and is being applied to the Indians from whom it was originally stolen. To those who have seen *Eskimo, Dances with Wolves* (1990) came as no surprise. Many of Kevin Costner's supposed innovations—Lakota spoken on screen and explained with subtitles, his presentation of the Lakota as paragons of virtue in contrast to the corrupt U.S. cavalry—were part of the baggage Van Dyke had taken with him to Alaska sixty years

before. Both were created as entertainment, movies of epic quality not soon to be forgotten. When leaving the theater after seeing *Dances With Wolves,* I heard one viewer remark, "It makes me want to be an Indian." I had heard a comparable comment a year before at a small Anchorage theater showing of *Eskimo:* "Seeing Ray Mala makes me proud to be an Eskimo."

To date, the only film to make light of Eskimos is the Abbott and Costello spoof *Lost in Alaska,* still occasionally run on late-night television. Whereas the directors of *Eskimo* and *White Dawn* went north to capture the purity of real Eskimos, Abbott and Costello never left the studio and give us a humorous play and reversal of the standard Eskimo image. As in *Savage Innocents,* the all-too-obvious whiteness of the film's Eskimos tells the audience that they are not seeing real Eskimos but a white man's projection of an Eskimo, for better and for worse. While Abbott and Costello's gags were so slapstick many did not even value them as entertainment at the time, we can still hope that Eskimos are allowed the leeway to be funny in the future and to do so on their own terms.

Film historians note changes in the portrayal of Native Americans beginning in 1950 with Delmar Davis's financially successful western, *Broken Arrow,* in which the dominant theme of the admirable, though probably doomed Indian hero replaced the ignoble Indian savage. This romantic tendency solidified in the 1960s, and following the Vietnam War in the early 1970s the film industry released a series of pro-Indian films. As Bataille and Silet (1980:xxv) point out, however, Indian stereotypes remained. The films comprised an attempt by non-Indians to understand their own place in history: "American audiences zealously applauded the brutal exploitation of our collective guilt in movies dealing with their relationship with Native Americans" (Bataille and Silet 1980:xxv). Although the films of the 1970s purportedly paid more attention to "authentic" native life, they were still an often

Igloo antics in *Lost in Alaska.* Universal Pictures.

erroneous hodge-podge of tribes and customs and so say very little about the first Americans (Marsden and Nachbar 1984:607).

Some critics cite the handful of films dealing with Eskimos produced during this same period as exceptions to the treatment of Native Americans more generally (Price 1973). Compared to Indians, they say, Eskimos have escaped negative stereotyping and have been portrayed more realistically in Hollywood productions. The documentary precedent of Flaherty's *Nanook of the North* set standards still difficult to meet. Flaherty, in fact, touched on the major themes that later filmmakers took as representative of North Country life—survival, isolation, community, and the idea that a person is his own provider and his own law. Although *Nanook's* written titles, announcing the "fearless, lovable, happy-go-lucky Eskimo" may seem archaic now, these images persist. Their elaboration in *Nanook's* successors, however, did not comprise a realistic portrayal of Eskimos. Recent films in Technicolor present Eskimos differently but no more realistically than

Indians, although the "fiction of realism" would have the viewer believe this to be the case.

Hollywood's representation of Eskimos as hardy stoics persists, as opposed to the presentation of Indians before 1950 as warlike and after 1950 as admirable but doomed. The film representation of Eskimos, however, should not be confused with realism. Mass arts, by definition, tend to be allegorical, dealing in types rather than individuals. Although Eskimos may be portrayed more sympathetically and accurately in the future, they must continue to be recognizable as previously defined. Nor should the denizens of Hollywood bear full blame. As Marsden and Nachbar (1988:608) point out for the much-abused American Indian, "There is as much danger in obscuring the truth … through critical rantings about how Hollywood warped the American imagination on the topic of Native Americans as there is in relying on movies for total knowledge about the world." Hollywood, after all, did not create the image of the primitive Eskimo as hardy and pure, it merely perpetuated it in more potent form.

Children revel in the 'make-believe,' but only when the real is impossible.... But the question arises, should not the Indians of today be real?... While we still have the real Indians with us, why cannot thoroughly representative films be produced.... It is to be hoped that some of our Western manufacturers will yet produce a series of films of REAL Indian life, doing so with the distinct object in view that they are to be of educational value, both for present and future use. Such a certified series will be of great value." ("The Make-Believe Indian" from *Moving Picture World,* p. 473, March 4, 1911)

CHAPTER FIVE

Alaska Eskimos in Documentary and Ethnographic Films

URING THE FIRST FIFTY YEARS OF commercial productions the subtle and not-so-subtle differences between Yup'ik, Iñupiaq, and Inuit peoples received little attention. Alaska Eskimos, when they appeared at all in Hollywood, smiled broadly, built snowhouses, and lived in perpetual peace with their neighbors. *Igloo* and *Eskimo,* both filmed in Alaska with Alaska native casts, depicted the central Canadian Arctic of the previous century. Presentation of Alaska Eskimos as Alaska Eskimos did not originate in Hollywood, where the primary goals were entertainment and box-office success, but among those whose interest was in actual Eskimo life.

In the 1940s a diverse group of filmmakers attempted to document Alaska Eskimo culture. It included a Jesuit priest, an anthropologist collaborating with *Encyclopedia Britannica,* and a Ketchikan-based husband-wife team employed by Walt Disney. All three reflected, albeit each in a unique way, the desire to document "pure" cultures, and each depicted Eskimos living outside time, as yet largely unchanged by the march of "civilization." The tradition of the "pure representation" had been instrumental in shaping Flaherty's vision. As the turmoil of war rocked the world, the desire to view humanity before the fall, unencumbered by interna-

tional power struggles, retained broad audience appeal.

The first of this trio of filmmakers was Father Bernard Hubbard, a California-born explorer, photographer, and popular lecturer. Prior to his ordination as a priest, Hubbard studied theology in Austria where he received the name "Der Gletcher Pfarrer" or "Glacier Priest" because of his liking for climbing in the Alps. Hubbard first went to Alaska in 1927, and his summer expeditions of exploration and photography became an annual event. During the winters he traveled around the United States giving lectures and showing his films, with the proceeds going to support the Jesuit missions in Alaska. "Half the year the highest paid lecturer in the world, the other half a wanderer among treacherous craters and glaciers"; thus *The Literary Digest* described him in 1937 (Hubbard Collection 1991). In 1935 he purportedly set the world's record for lecturing, talking to 215 audiences in 185 consecutive days, a total of 230,000 persons (Burton 1937).

During his career Hubbard produced dozens of short travel films issued through Twentieth Century Fox. Of the eleven that feature Alaska, three deal with Eskimos: *Eskimo Trails,* reporting a six-week expedition by umiak (skinboat) along the Arctic coast; *Eskimo Springtime,* revealing the life of the

Father Hubbard and his camera. Santa Clara University Archives.

Father Hubbard sets sail on a two-thousand-mile umiak trip in *Eskimo Trails*. King Island, 1938. Santa Clara University Archives.

Eskimo when the ice and snow have gone; and *Eskimo Winter,* showing Eskimo life in winter—hunting, carving, playing football, and boxing.

Eskimo Trails (1940) is typical of Hubbard's engaging film style. In the opening frames we observe the precariously placed homes of the King Island Iñupiat on steep rocky slopes. We watch men finish construction of the wooden frame of an umiak and cover it with walrus skin. Lowell Thomas, the famous broadcasting personality whose voice resonated authority for an entire generation, narrates the film, and he tells us what we see. Several minutes into the film, Father Hubbard chimes in with "Well, Lowell" in a conversational tone. He then explains that Eskimos are building the umiak for a two-thousand-mile expedition "to solve the riddle of the Eskimo … to prove that [they] are recent arrivals by comparing my King Island Eskimos to Eskimos two thousand miles away."

The expedition that follows, including six men, two dogs, and four tons of equipment, is a success. On his arrival at Point Lay, Father Hubbard notes that "my King Island Eskimos could understand them perfectly…. Indians have many languages, but Eskimos only one." Thus Father Hubbard completes the "longest voyage ever made by umiak" and solves "the riddle of the Eskimos." The final scenes return the audience to King Island where villagers hold a masked dance ("not religious, just for fun") in the men's house to celebrate the expedition's success. On his "return to civilization," Hubbard described the Iñupiaq people as "the most moral and happiest of any in the world" (*Spokesman Review* 1939).

A definite film philosophy underlay both Hubbard's visual and verbal lectures extolling the virtues of the Eskimos. He believed that films shown in schools should be as technically good as Hollywood films or should not be shown at all. Also, they should be entertaining, just as a good teacher is entertaining: "Even if the visual film is mostly entertainment and yet in the course of a ten minute showing, merely puts over one sound correct point,

it has been a worthwhile educational showing." Hubbard's emphasis was on "proper" films: "It is said that one picture is worth ten thousand words. Then if one picture can imprint something on the mind that would take ten thousand words, imagine the damage that could be done by showing pictures that were not proper or lacked true facts." All his films had his personal seal of approval "so that they may be shown before any type audience without fear of anything unwanted, untrue or otherwise objectionable creeping in" (Hubbard Collection 1991).

Eskimo Children (1941), an eleven-minute black-and-white film produced by Smithsonian anthropologist Henry Collins for *Encyclopedia Britannica,* depicted the lives of Alaska Eskimos in equally proper fashion. The film combined footage from remote Nunivak Island that Collins had taken in 1929 with a didactic narration. Like Hubbard's Eskimo films, it was intended for classroom use to instruct elementary and junior high school students in the ways of a group of "primitive" Alaska Eskimos. A teacher's handbook accompanied the film, which was intended, among other things, as "illustrative case material in broad social studies units on such subjects as food, shelter, clothing, [and] primitive peoples." Together, the film and guide functioned as the basis for significant generalizations about Eskimos. Although they effectively debunked some common ideas, such as the misconception that most Eskimos live in snow igloos, they left intact the two most common ideas associated with Eskimos—their primitiveness and their adaptability. After viewing the film, students were expected to conclude that "the Eskimos are a primitive people; that is, they have no written language and lead a simple existence" and "the Eskimos have shown great ingenuity in adapting themselves to a cold and barren environment" (Griffiths and Ramsey 1942:11).

Comparable to other culture-area films of the day, *Eskimo Children* did not depict an actual family. Collins hired local residents to play the parts of family members acting out typical scenes from daily life

Silook and his friends practice with their bows and arrows in *Eskimo Children. Encyclopaedia Britannica.*

on Nunivak, including sleeping, eating, playing, hunting, and, at the end of the day, dancing. The film is a valuable record of the material culture of Nunivak in the 1920s, including both interior and exterior views of semisubterranean sod houses. We see a woman trim her lamp, a hunter use his spear-thrower, and children pack their boots with grass for warmth. The familiar stereotype is also present: "Yes they laugh, the Eskimos—a warm and friendly laughter, on the remote Island of Nunivak." Although a school, church, and reindeer industry had been introduced onto Nunivak between the time Collins shot his footage and the time the film was released, the film mentions none of these alterations. On Nunivak, as on King Island, the hardy, happy, primitive Eskimo image remained.

Ana enjoying the trader's gift of peppermint candy in *Eskimo Children. Encyclopedia Britannica.*

Walt Disney at Hooper Bay

Probably the most widely viewed Eskimo documentary from this period was the Academy Award–winning short film *Alaskan Eskimo,* produced by Walt Disney in 1949. Disney billed the twenty-seven-minute film as "highly entertaining documentary."

> And it will come as a delightful surprise to many persons to learn … that the Eskimos are not a glum, frozen-faced people but actually a warm bunch of human beings full of smiles and innocent wiles, especially where the younger element is concerned. (*Hollywood Reporter* 1953)

The film was the first in Disney's Peoples and Places series of "factual productions," following the precedent set by the award-winning True-Life Adventure presentations. Just as the True-Life series delved into the private lives of animals, insects, birds, and reptiles, the People and Places series set out to portray "intimate family life" in countries all over the world. Some naturalists criticized Disney's nature films for anthropomorphizing animal life, as both his editing and musical accompaniments repeatedly portrayed animals as burlesque humans (Barnouw 1983:210). Conversely, the Peoples and Places series often explained away human cultural diversity as variable environmental adaptations and reduced cultural activity to an animal-like struggle for survival.

Walt Disney on location for a True-Life series feature. Bill Bacon.

The goal of the Peoples and Places series was "complete photographic honesty, without bias, and to study people as they have been influenced in nature and custom by environment." The documentation of "authentic" acts is once again invoked: "Accuracy, authenticity, careful reporting with the camera to catch the significance as well as the picturesque, will guide these adventures." The series dealt with near neighbors as well as "more primitive people, like the Eskimos." The image of the Noble Primitive pitted against the environment persists, as the film shows "in fascinating … detail … the way in which the survivors of the stone-age days adapted themselves to a harsh world with indomitable spirit" (*Hollywood Reporter* 1953).

Alaskan Eskimo grew out of the True-Life series in fact as well as in theory. An Alaska husband-wife team, Alfred and Elma Milotte, shot the film's footage while gathering material for the True-Life series. The first film to come out of their 1946 tour of Alaska was Academy Award–winning *Seal Island* (1949), depicting the life of the northern fur seals of the Pribilof Islands. The Milottes, however, viewed their "Eskimo material" as more valuable: "We believe that Disney has a much greater picture in the Eskimos than in the seals. The people photographed very well and we are sure you will be pleased with the outcome" (Milotte 1949).

The Milottes filmed *Alaskan Eskimo* in the village of Hooper Bay during March-April and September-October 1946. Before flying out to Hooper Bay, they asked the Bureau of Indian Affairs for permission to film. They did not consult the people of Hooper Bay. In Hooper Bay the couple moved into the old and drafty teachers' quarters. Although they felt that they were "roughing it," they found the people friendly and genuinely seemed to enjoy their stay: "This has been a hard 7 weeks in this Eskimo village—we haven't had a bath for 2 months.… Have tried two kinds of seal meat—one good, one not so good—but it's fun trying. Seal oil is wonderful food, for these people have *beautiful* teeth"

Alfred and Elma Milotte in Hooper Bay, 1946. Milotte Collection, Alaska and Polar Regions Department, University of Alaska Fairbanks.

(Milotte Journal, May 4, 1946).

Shortly after their arrival the local Catholic priest, Father John Fox, gave the villagers permission to have a masked dance for the benefit of the picture, the first such dance in twenty years:

There seemed to be an undercurrent of unseen activity. We learned that the older men were busy in the Kasga [*qasgiq* men's house] carving masks and learning songs. In the evening from 8 to 10 they taught the dancers the motions to interpret the songs. Everyone seemed happy and excited over the coming event. (Milotte Journal, March 1946)

Filming these masked dances proved the high point of their trip. When the dances were done, the men started to burn the masks. The Milottes intervened, bought all the masks that were not damaged, and shipped them back to California. Later, they donated the masks, along with the ivory Donald Duck that local carver Jonathan Johnson made for them, to the Alaska State Museum in Juneau.

When the plane finally came to take the Milottes home, they were both happy and sad to leave. They found themselves "fond" of the Eskimos whom they felt sorry for: "Life is hard and 43 is considered old." Yet they saw no sign that the people of Hooper Bay longed for the outside world: "They really know nothing about it" (Milotte Journal, May 6, 1946).

Disney gave the Milottes' Hooper Bay footage a structure comparable to Flaherty's *Nanook,* although never so intimate. The film focuses on the hunter Koganak and his family. Like the empathetic portrait of Nanook, the film is grounded in the belief in a common humanity and lets us identify with the lives of a family from another culture. From the first, the didactic and often patronizing narrative points to the same themes that mark so many previous film

Donald Duck doing an Eskimo dance. Milotte Collection, Alaska and Polar Regions Department, University of Alaska Fairbanks.

Alfred Milotte filming women sewing skinboat cover. Milotte Collection, Alaska and Polar Regions Department, University of Alaska Fairbanks.

Girls telling stories in the snow. Milotte Collection, Alaska and Polar Regions Department, University of Alaska Fairbanks.

depictions of Eskimos invariably "struggling against the elements." The narrator introduces the people of Hooper Bay as "a hardy, courageous people. Of all the primitive Americans, they have never felt the yoke of conquest."

The pattern of Koganak's life, we are told, is "an endless struggle—his tools crude, his weapons primitive." We watch him at work: "When he builds a house, he buries it.… He uses no plans, but works by instinct." In fact Koganak's lack of a blueprint reflected his detailed comprehension of all points of construction, not any "instinctive" understanding of what a house required. Another sequence shows Koganak's wife making *akutaq,* known as "Eskimo ice cream." Again, the film emphasizes the "primitive" character of Eskimo habits: "Add blubber and reindeer tallow to this savory sauce. Mix thoroughly and by hand. Add blueberries. Finally clean utensils thoroughly. This mess, ah, mixture is called *akutaq*—blueberry ice cream with a fish flavor. It is

appreciated by young and old alike, but only if you're Eskimo." Condescending as the narration is, the film has the distinction of showing the process of making *akutaq* for the first time.

One review emphasized the film's depiction of "the methods of survival taught young Eskimos … [who] rely on hand-made weapons more than store-bought rifles.… It is an art they must master, for a wasted arrow or bullet can mean an empty stomach.… Children's games are as rugged as the people themselves." Actually most adult hunters used guns by the mid-1940s, but their early training was with sling-shot and bow.

The film closes with masked dancing in the men's house to "thank their gods.… By midevening all the gods have received their due.… These are a happy people.… Although he has no goods that anyone wants, he has treasures beyond price—peace, happiness, and contentment." Although Yup'ik dancing continues to this day to be more than mere recreation and to have an important spiritual component, Hooper Bay residents in the 1940s were far from pagans "thanking their gods" as the narration implies. Catholic priests had been active in the area since before the turn of the century, and the current resident priest, Father Fox, was a stern taskmaster.

How different the film narrative would have been had the Milottes included their part in making the dance possible. They might have framed the dance sequence with footage documenting the process of getting permission from Father Fox to hold the dance, the dance practices, and their purchasing and packing up the masks after the dancing was done. But the Milottes created their film in the then taken-for-granted "realist" tradition and made no reference to its situated character. They completely hid the dialogue that produced the film.

The soundtrack that accompanies the film is typical Disney. Crusader music accompanies a sled trip to get water and wood, and a battle theme plays in the background while the men try to corral a herd of reindeer. The blanket toss is accompanied by a steady "boing, boing, boing." Disney Studios anticipated a problem in selecting a musical score to go with the masked dances. In August, the film's associate producer, Ben Sharpsteen, wrote the Milottes:

> It has occurred to some of us here that the material you photographed on the Eskimo ceremonial dances … should be accompanied by a sound track which is enough like the original intonations so as to appear authentic. Therefore, we would like to inquire whether or not it would be possible for you to make a recording of their chanting and such music as is used for their ceremonials so that we could have the record here to study and possibly duplicate. (Sharpsteen to Milotte, August 13, 1946)

Apparently the Milottes were unable to procure a recording with the requisite "appearance of authenticity." The final accompaniment to the masked dances reminds one of movie Indians attacking Fort Apache.

A contemporary review summed up the film's point of view:

> [The Milottes] take their cameras right into the Koganak igloo … and show the family and their fellow citizens at work and at play, fighting the rugged elements of their bleak surroundings, building their homes, making their clothes, gathering food for the long winter, and finally taking part in their fantastic ritual dances in fancy multi-colored costumes.
>
> Of particular fascination is the industriousness, enterprise, and resourcefulness of the Eskimos in coping with their raw and largely barren surroundings, and the way they live in absolute freedom and in harmony with each other. (*Hollywood Review* 1953)

In fact, the coastal environment on which the Yup'ik residents of Hooper Bay relied was far from barren, providing them with a variety of plants and animals. The film makes no reference to this natural abundance and the cultural elaboration it supported. In the same way it ignores the violent bow-and-arrow wars that coastal Yupiit engaged in through the early 1800s in favor of the "harmony" outsiders had come to associate with Eskimo life. Finally, the emphasis on "absolute freedom" was as inaccurate in the Disney documentary as it had been in previous fictional films. Few peoples have ordered their lives so rigorously, circumscribing action both within the human world and between humans and animals with rules detailing what was and was not appropriate. People viewed these rules as critical to their well-being. If a hunter or his wife failed to treat an animal guest appropriately it would not return in future, and the community would suffer.

Although films no longer depicted Alaska Eskimos living in conical snowhouses, expectations about "typical" Eskimos continued to mask what was unique to the way of life of the people of Hooper Bay. The Milotte's film made no mention of the tuberculosis epidemic that was running unchecked in western Alaska at the time of their visit, nor of the frustrating problems villagers experienced trying to get aid from the outside. Father Fox waxed eloquent on these and other current issues in his mimeographed church newsletter, *The Hooper Bay Gossip*, but these hard truths were not what the Milottes had come to film. Documentary had not yet become a tool of dialogue and empowerment, and the Milotte's retained the focus on a fictionalized past that had characterized so many previous films.

In 1988 Hooper Bay residents had a chance to view *Alaskan Eskimo*, and they enjoyed what they saw. They could laugh at the narration and appreciate the photographs of friends and relatives taken more than forty years before. Many in the audience remembered the filming and as school children had written letters to the Milottes to practice their English. Some hoped the film could be made available on video so that they could see it more often.

One villager commented, "This home life is exactly … the way my home life was when I was young" (Alaska State Film Library 1989). At the same time Disney produced a period piece that can tell us a great deal about how Americans viewed Eskimos in the 1940s, he bequeathed a record that the people of Hooper Bay can appreciate.

Documenting Eskimo Lives

Eskimo Trails, Eskimo Children, and *Alaskan Eskimo* reflect the times in which they were made. The authoritative narrative and constant visual emphasis on the exotic "primitivism" of the Eskimos filmed typify documentaries of the era. Their variety of "visionary exhortation" was grounded in the social documentary film of the 1920s and 1930s, a "mass education medium sensitive to the needs of government policy" (de Brigard 1975:23). Whereas Flaherty had given us close-up portraits of remotely located people familiar in their humanity (Barnouw 1983:99), the documentary of this period typically contained narrative commentary that to a large extent controlled what sense the viewer would make of the film images presented. The authoritative tone of the abstract male narrative voice carried the metamessage "Believe me, I speak Truth." Opinion and bias were what the films in fact presented: "Scientific data are to be found amidst the actuality, but they are clothed in argument more subtle than fiction" (de Brigard 1975:23).

Until the recent debate on representation, documentary was most often understood as a transparent vision of reality (Ginsburg 1992). Viewers believed it had the potential to show them what strange peoples in strange places were really like. The constructed character of documentary film is only now beginning to be widely recognized. Looked at from the vantage of the 1990s, we can see that the filmed images of Hooper Bay and Nunivak and King Island were the product of a complex process of negotia-

tion between filmmaker, subjects, and the viewing public.

Whatever their limitations, the documentaries featuring Alaska Eskimos in the 1940s are groundbreaking in one important respect. Except for the early expeditionary films of men such as Van Valin, they are the first films to depict Yup'ik and Iñupiaq men and women living in the present. The choice of images still reflects the desire to see Eskimos living outside time, incapable of change, and a preconceived narrative describes the films' subjects as "happy primitives," undercutting their purported realism. Yet the visual images are largely true to life as it was lived when the films were made. There is much that viewers are not shown, but what they do see adds to what they know.

The documentary film chronicle gained tremendously in subject range and viewing audience during the two postwar decades as television was introduced, and filmmakers began to realize its potential as a "window on the world" (Barnouw 1983:211). The censorship that was born of McCarthyism bridled studios and made many recording ventures perilous. Films that looked affectionately back at our presumed "simpler" past provided both a safe harbor in stormy seas and a respite from the trauma of present altercations.

Independent filmmakers produced an additional dozen documentaries dealing with Alaska Eskimos from the mid-1940s through the 1960s. These include: *Return of the Musk Oxen* (1943), documenting the transplant of a group of musk oxen from Nunivak Island to their former habitat along Alaska's arctic coast; *Eskimo Hunters of Northwest Alaska* (1949), a twenty-minute black-and-white film shot at Point Hope by Louis de Rochemont; *Alaskan Sled Dog* (1956), filmed in Unalakleet by Fred and Sara Machetanz for Walt Disney and following a boy Nip-Chik and his dog Nan-Nook as the latter grows from a puppy to leader of Nip-Chik's team; *Eskimo River Village* (1957), a twelve-minute look at the Kuskokwim village of Sleetmute, filmed by local BIA teachers and including shots of children studying Africa in school, Russian Orthodox Christmas, and harvesting activities; and *The Children of Eek and Their Art* (1966), a closeup view of the remarkable results of an innovative after-school art program in a small Yup'ik village at the mouth of the Kuskokwim. Narration describing the "typical" character of Alaska Eskimos accompanies all of these films. *Return of the Musk Oxen* extols the "Eskimo knack for improvising," *Eskimo River Village* their "hard work, faith, and self-reliance," *Alaskan Sled Dog* their "expertise depending on taking calculated risks," *Children of Eek* their character as "a shy and gentle people for whom life is generally hard," and *Eskimo Hunters of Northwest Alaska* their "constant battle for survival in a rigorous climate." Yet even the shortest of these films visually expands the viewer's understanding of what it means to be a twentieth-century Alaska Eskimo, whether Yup'ik or Iñupiat, a distinction the films ignore. We see men using snow machines as well as kayaks, children pledging allegiance to the flag and working with acrylic paints, the *Selaviq* star circulating among frame houses during Russian Orthodox Christmas, and pot-hunting for prehistoric artifacts at Point Hope to add to the family income. For the first time Alaska Eskimos begin to appear in three dimensions, men and women sharing our humanity but living in a unique time and place. Whereas twenty years before the Eek schoolteacher might have attributed student success to their special character as "primitive Eskimos," in *Children of Eek* he states that "their natural talent is not more than anyone, but just has never been developed."

One reason for the increased intimacy and contemporary detail of these short documentary portraits is the fact that men and women who lived and worked in Alaska made them. For example, Fred and Sara Machetanz, producers of *Alaskan Sled Dog*, were married in Unalakleet in 1947. The couple traveled the lecture circuit for fourteen years, showing films and talking about their experiences in

Alaska. From September through April they lectured, returning to Alaska in the spring to gather new material, taking every third year off to make a new film. During their itinerant years they produced a number of movies, including one on the Alaska Highway, a documentary on the territory of Alaska, a film on Alaska statehood, and a half-dozen films on Alaska Eskimos, including: *Eskimo Summer* and *Eskimo Winter* produced specifically for their lecture series and showing the seasonal changes in Alaska Eskimo communities; *The Modern Frontier* and *Eskimos* produced for *Encyclopedia Britannica;* and *Alaskan Sled Dog.* The latter project actually involved two films: one finished film, which Walt Disney included in his True-Life Adventure series, and a second reflexive film, showing themselves making the movie, which they took with them on tour. In fact, the Machetanzes appear in all the movies they made to show Outside. As in the case of Van Valin, audiences were as interested in the filmmakers' exotic adventures as in the way of life of people they adventured among.

Sara Machetanz recalls that *Alaskan Sled Dog* was one of the more difficult films they ever produced. It required close coordination with the Disney Studio, whereas they normally worked independently. Such a collaboration had its advantages, however, as Disney provided them with a cinemascope lens with which to shoot their picture. They also received credit for the filming, something Disney rarely allowed. Not only is the finished film technically good, but the Machetanzes' familiarity with the people and place they were filming allowed them to capture intimate moments in community life absent in the early documentaries on Alaska Eskimos.[1]

1. Moviemaking and lecturing marked the beginning rather than the end of the Machetanzes' careers in Alaska. After the birth of their son, the lecture circuit proved too hectic, and they returned to Alaska for a year to see if Fred could make a living as a painter, an iffy proposition. His showing of forty-three paintings at the end of his first winter's work proved an instant success, and he and Sara have been painting and writing in and about Alaska ever since.

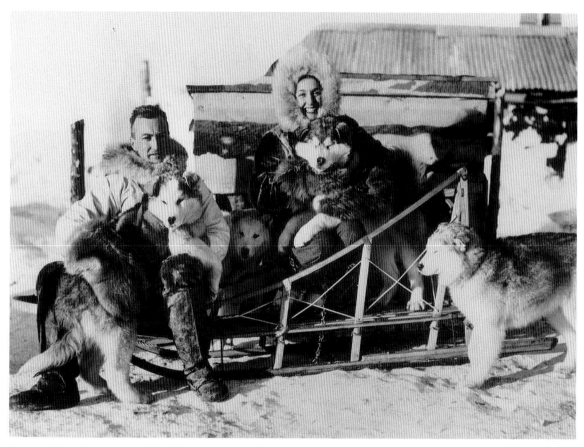

Fred and Sara Machetanz in Unalakleet during the shooting of *Alaskan Sled Dog.* Fred and Sara Machetanz.

In the 1960s Alaska Eskimos also made cameo appearances in a handful of documentary films extolling the wonders of their new state. *Alaska: America's Brightest Star* (1959), produced by the Alaska Chamber of Commerce, unabashedly advertised for tourists. Narrated by Lowell Thomas and accompanied by the drumming and singing of the Kotzebue dancers, its images range from giant king crabs to Chilkat dancers to Anchorage symphony concerts. In this glowing booster film Eskimos represent perpetual "primitives" in contrast to the new "civilization": "Alaska—where old industries like Eskimo ivory carving merge alongside oil and timber." Like the king crabs, Eskimos were an Alaskan resource, and the Chamber of Commerce hoped to encourage their "harvest." Dancers dressed in furs provide an "Alaska Aloha" for the passengers arriv-

ing by commercial jet in Nome: "The Eskimos—one reason Alaska's visitor business is growing so rapidly."

Alaska Movie Trails (1965), a sixty-minute advertisement for Kodak, treats Eskimos more incidentally, as an ornament of the new state, part of its local color. The film follows Jim Steeb and Charlie Kingsley as they spend two-and-a-half weeks traveling all over Alaska, commenting on and taking pictures of everything within range. Like many other rosy-hued corporation-sponsored productions made during this period (Barnouw 1983:219), it promoted the good life, complete with leisure to take snapshots of picturesque Alaskana. Dog sledding is "good fun for people who brought their cameras," and caribou "are real hams when they see a camera." Eskimos only occupy the last minutes of the film, and their treatment is extremely patronizing. At a whaling celebration we are told that "Eskimo kids think muktuk delicious. We tried some. Tastes like white-walled tire." Likewise it "seems funny" to our hosts to see a young Eskimo mother in pin curls putting up whale oil. We learn that "the average Eskimo family has over a dozen children" and that "Barrow isn't a pretty place because people spend too much time just staying alive." The nonnative priests "have given up almost every civilized comfort to serve their fellow man." Unhappily, this film advertisement aired on television and was among the most widely viewed footage of Alaska Eskimos of the period.

In the 1970s an emphasis on change gradually replaced the early documentary emphasis on unspoiled, "primitive" Eskimos. Although courage, endurance, and resourcefulness were still the primary adjectives applied to Alaska Eskimos, now the narrator used these traits to describe their "adaptation to Western civilization" as well as to the environment. The advent of television had expanded the audiences that would view these films, and topics never covered before received film treatment.

One of the first yet one of the best of this group of films was *Eskimos: A Changing Culture* (1971), an eleven-minute short produced by Wayne Mitchell for BFA Educational Media. The film returns to Nunivak Island forty years after Collins made his movie. It opens with the question: "How does technology change peoples' values? To find out, let's look at a region where technology is a newcomer." Per usual, opening scenes depict Nunivak's harsh environment and the residents' struggle to find food: "Summer is the hardest time. The land is soft, no seals.… Only a few feet below the surface, the ground stays frozen.… In the old times, Eskimos spent hours spearing one fish at a time."

The film then focuses on recent changes on Nunivak, including the new school, reindeer industry, wage labor, and teenagers leaving to attend high school off the island. In no case are these presented

as unmitigated improvements. Describing the reindeer industry, the narrator says, "People get paid by the hour instead of sharing like in the old days. We don't eat much, we sell it." Of the new educational system, students "go to school but they don't learn Eskimo ways." In one poignant scene, the camera focuses for thirty seconds on students saying goodbye to their families and boarding a plane to leave for school. The voice of one of the departing students comments, "We'll miss our little brothers and sisters, also our snow machines. We'll be gone four years. I wonder how we'll feel after being in the city?" Of changes in general he adds, "My folks think the old things were better but they buy new things." Twenty years later these observations still ring true.

Another short film, *Alaska: End of the Last Frontier* (1970), takes a different slant on development. Billed as "a visual and verbal plea to preserve Alaska," it is a case study (complete with educational guide) of whether "the human race can civilize a great region without destroying the environment that nurtures it." The film opens with contrasting views of untouched snowscapes and the machinery of the newly introduced oil industry. Although less than eleven minutes long, the film presents a number of different perspectives on development. Iñupiat are pictured decrying the loss of their language at the same time they wonder if they will reap any of the advantages of the new oil industry. Industry personnel counter that their work will not harm the land and will provide jobs for the Eskimos. A third perspective, and one that is unique in film discussions of Eskimos, is that "it's not industry but the natives with their shanties that are a threat to the environment." Never before or since have Alaska Eskimos been filmically depicted as in less-than-perfect fit with their environment. Even here, the mismatch is attributed to introduced technology, not the "natural character" of the Eskimos.

Much more typical is the twenty-minute newsreel, *The Emerging Eskimo* (1972), focusing again on the sudden changes experienced by Alaska Eskimos as a result of oil development. The question this time was not what would happen to the land but what would happen to its aboriginal inhabitants moving "from stone age to machine age without warning … a trial for any people." As usual, the film begins with the premise that the land is harsh but Eskimos "have made an asset of this hostile environment." The simple traditional economy ("none are rich but none are poor") is juxtaposed to the new mixed economy in which the Eskimos are "robbed of old resources and tempted to new ones." As the breach between rich and poor widens, "Eskimos are organizing to gain control."

The film is the first to point out, however briefly, the conflict between commercial and subsistence interests and the desire of northern people for greater control over how their resources are developed. To a stirring, heroic accompaniment, the narrator concludes, "The ambivalent Eskimos struggle with a choice.… Yet when he speaks he wonders, 'Is anyone listening?'" Although word-regimented and visually heavy-handed (when Eskimos are said never to let sleeping dogs lie, the screen shows dogs sleeping), the questions the film poses are as relevant now as when the film was made.

Two other films made in Alaska in the 1980s continue to document contemporary Eskimo lives, but in a more intimate way. Barbara Lipton wrote and produced *Village of No River* (1981) for the Newark Museum in New Jersey. The sixty-minute film follows the annual cycle of the seasons in the coastal Yup'ik community of Kwigillingok. Fast-paced, the film touches myriad topics, including hunting and fishing, wage employment, education, religion, family life, children's games, and much more. It also juxtaposes original footage shot in Kwigillingok by Moravian missionaries in the 1930s and 1940s with contemporary scenes to show change as well as continuity in the villagers' activities. For instance, it alternates shots of contemporary houses with footage of a semisubterranean sod house. The visual and narrative discussion of the

Moravian Church, which forms an important focus of community life today, precedes old footage of the dances and raised graves that the Moravians replaced.

Village of No River pays close attention to historical detail as it focuses on a single community. Also, unlike many of the shorter newsreel documentaries, it made nominal use of anthropologists as consultants to contribute to an accurate presentation. As the viewer follows the visual sequences and listens to Elsie Jimmie of Kwigillingok talk about her community, the film rings true. This native narration, however, is misleading. In fact, Lipton wrote the text and flew Elsie Jimmie to New Jersey to read it into a tape recorder. Although much of what she says is factually correct, Jimmie's narration is as staged as the acting in Collins' film fifty years before. The control Lipton exerted over her material is no more than that of other documentary filmmakers working in Alaska during the same period. But with its scripted narration, it is no less.

The politics of the production of *Village of No River* shed light on its content. An experienced museum administrator, Lipton was well aware that in the political and emotional climate of the 1980s Alaska Eskimos would not want to be involved in a film project unless they had a say in its content. She also needed the participation of qualified anthropologists to obtain the National Endowment for the Arts funding she sought.[2] After NEA granted her funding, she made minimal use of these experts, and the study guide proposed to accompany the film was never produced. Although she continued to work closely with the residents of Kwigillingok, the Yup'ik filmmaker originally involved in the project was let go in favor of a New York-based cinematographer.

Village of No River is a sampler box of the sights and sounds associated with life in village Alaska,

2. Jay Ruby (1993b) has aptly labeled this practice of hiring scholars to fulfill funding agency requirements but giving them no real power to shape the film, the "rent a scholar" approach.

flitting from scene to scene and treating nothing in depth. Although Lipton had lived with the Jimmie family during her brief stay in Kwigillingok and knew them well, the film's interior shots are wooden and contrived, and they fail to communicate the bustle and intimacy that characterize so many Yup'ik households. Elsie's husband worked for the village school, and the family was well-off by village standards. They put on their Sunday best for the film crew. The same formality applies to many of the shots taken around the village. Rather than a vital portrait of village life, the film provides a series of posed pictures. It presents audiences with a village scrapbook, containing a little bit of everything but nothing in detail (see also Briggs 1983).

The same year that Lipton produced *Village of No River,* the Alaska Department of Education filmed the thirty-minute instructional video *Agnes of Tununak* detailing a day in the life of a "typical" fifth-grade Yup'ik girl in a small village less than one hundred miles up the coast from Kwigillingok. Although lacking the polish of Lipton's production, the video provides one of the best introductions to village life for urban viewers, especially young ones, produced during this period. The narration, read by a young nonnative girl, notes both obvious differences and similarities between Agnes's world and her own. We see and hear that Agnes lives seven hundred miles from the nearest highway, that she speaks Yup'ik as well as English, and that most of the food she eats comes from the land and sea. The video provides a simple, straightforward definition of subsistence: "Even though Agnes's parents could buy most of their food, they don't. Living off the land is called subsistence. It is the way people have lived as long as people can remember." It goes on to show how Agnes is just like any other young Alaskan— she goes to school, practices cheerleading with her friends, and although she isn't chosen, roots for her teammates at the big game. *Agnes* is a combination of action shots and staged appearances. The young star is remarkably poised and friendly throughout,

as if giving a tour of her community to a sympathetic guest, which she is. The video draws a sensitive portrait of life in a modern Yup'ik village and gives the viewer a lot to think about in a short amount of time.

Three years after the release of *Village of No River* and *Agnes of Tununak,* Larry Lansburgh and Gail Evanari produced a shorter educational video, *Alaska: The Yup'ik Eskimos* (1985), for Chevron U.S.A. This overview of contemporary Yup'ik culture highlights many of the same contrasts Lipton's film touched on between past and present patterns in the changing face of western Alaska. Although dealing with four communities—Bethel, Eek, Chevak, and Toksook Bay—the film is ultimately more satisfying than *Village of No River.* This is largely due to the filmmakers' clearer handling of the narration. Listeners know when they are hearing a native voice. Much of the narration consists of statements by Yup'ik elders translated into English and read as accompaniment to pictures of delta life. These statements are often eloquent, such as the description of the Yup'ik attitude toward plants and animals: "All things were like us people having a sense of awareness.... We regarded them like people." They tell the audience as much about the Yup'ik view of the world as about the routines of daily life.

At the same time Chevron was filming Yup'ik Eskimos in western Alaska, a film crew from the University of Alaska traveled to Barrow to produce *The People of Ukpiagvik* (1985), a video documenting the discovery and excavation of a prehistoric Iñupiaq family preserved where they died when ice crushed their house four hundred years ago. The hourlong program places the discovery of the site and the subsequent archaeological investigation in the context of contemporary life on the North Slope. It combines interviews with visiting archaeologists and Iñupiaq residents to highlight the different meanings the discovery had for different people. James Nageak, then working for the North Slope

Borough's Office of History and Culture, comments that archaeologists were more excited about the discovery than village elders because the site had confirmed what the Iñupiat already knew. At the same time elders were concerned that outsiders treat the bodies of their ancestors with respect. The video does a good job of showing the initial village distrust of the archaeologists gradually replaced by a closer working relationship between the community and the crew, including the establishment of a field school with Iñupiaq students involved in the excavation process.

The video concludes with a brief but effective presentation of some of the dilemmas associated with rapid social change. James Nageak remarks, "That was the main activity of a person's life—hunting and gathering. But we have to find other ways. Getting enough money to buy a speedboat so we can quickly go out seal hunting, and come back with a seal, and put it in our cellar and go back to the office, and sit behind the desk and write letters to people from the film company who want to do an interview! All these things are important." Comments like these make it clear that today the struggle is no longer for sheer physical survival, but for the survival of a way of life. *The People of Ukpiagvik* is not only an effective teaching tool for anthropology classes in Anchorage and Fairbanks, but remains popular in Barrow, as people feel it fairly represents their point of view.

From the 1940s through the 1980s, the tradition of the narrator persists—the outsider who tells us what we see with more or less sensitivity or distance. All too often this narration disengages the viewer, who has little left to attend to. The result—especially in the early films of the 1940s and 1950s—is "information overload" with the visuals treated like incidental illustrations. Even in the best documentaries, such as *The People of Ukpiagvik* and *Alaska: The Yup'ik Eskimos,* where Iñupiaq and Yup'ik people speak for themselves, verbiage simultaneously informs viewers yet distances them from what they

see. The majority create a gulf rather than a bridge between the viewer and the subject. We do not listen to or even watch the Eskimos themselves but observe them like animals in cages (Preloran 1975:104-5).

This view of documentary narration must, however, be taken in context. Good documentary is, after all, more like journalism than ethnography. It attempts to introduce the viewer to a new and interesting aspect of the world which it is not capable of examining in detail. It may be fair to criticize documentary for what it does wrong but not for what it cannot do. By the standards of social science it is bound to be inadequate (Ruby 1990). To satisfy ethnographic ends, another kind of filmmaking is required.

Alaska Eskimos and Ethnographic Film

While the tradition of documentary realism continued to flourish in Alaska, in the early 1970s Sarah Elder and Leonard Kamerling began to experiment with alternatives. Compared to their unnarrated films of contemporary life in rural Alaska, even the best-scripted documentary appears less satisfying. Although still framed by its creators, the windows they opened shed light on Alaska Eskimos in unprecedented ways.

The work of Elder and Kamerling grew from the recent marriage between film and ethnography. Although both cinema and anthropology were born in the nineteenth century and came of age together in the 1920s, some feel they did not join forces until after World War II (Heider 1976:16). Following the war, social scientists renewed efforts to mobilize their knowledge and skills to better understand foreign peoples through the written and visual study of single culture areas. Film became a valuable tool in this endeavor. Moreover, by the mid-1960s synchronous sound equipment was portable enough to go all over the world, allowing filmmakers to replace heavy narration and orchestral accompaniment with the sounds of the place and the voices of the people being filmed (Heider 1976:17).

Both this new attitude towards the scientific importance of film in the service of ethnography and the development of equipment that made such service practicable provided the impetus for the flowering of what came to be known as ethnographic film. Ethnographic film differs from documentary film in its focus on ethnographic understanding—film is at the service of ethnography. Ethnographer and filmmaker work together to achieve such understanding, and their collaboration in the filmmaking process is essential (Heider 1976:8).

Heider's classic definition of ethnographic film emphasizes its focus on "whole acts, whole bodies, and whole people." Although most contemporary filmmakers reject the naive empiricism underlying such a claim, ethnographic film continues to favor sequences of shots detailing a particular human activity from beginning to end with naturally occurring sound, as opposed to the documentary snapshot illustrating a narrative lecture. As film length limits complexity, ethnographic film presentations also typically include written material to help viewers understand both what they have seen and how it was recorded. This is especially important to enhance the use of the film as a research tool and in the classroom. Finally, although all films—including ethnographic ones—involve selectivity and all are constructions, ethnographic films aim for the appearance of more direct apprehension.

The Netsilik Series

One of the first and most ambitious attempts at ethnographic filming in the Arctic occurred between 1963 and 1966 among the Netsilik Eskimos of Pelly Bay on the Central Arctic Coast of Canada's Northwest Territories. Like *Nanook of the North,* the Netsilik project would impact filmmaking not only in the Arctic but worldwide. The project was part of a bigger program developed in response to the U.S. government concern about Soviet technical superiority following the launch of Sputnik (Heider 1976:41). In the nine-part series, totaling ten hours of unnarrated finished film, the Netsilik Eskimos of the 1960s reenacted the annual migration cycle as their parents and grandparents had lived it before the introduction of firearms in 1920. According to series advertising: "These films are for all who wish to see how life used to be among the Netsilik when they still lived apart and depended entirely on the land and their own ingenuity to sustain life through the rigors of the Arctic year" (Education Development Center 1968). As in earlier documentaries, the focus remained on the Eskimo adaptation to a hard land.

Each of the nine films revolves around a harvest theme (caribou hunting, seal hunting, jigging for lake trout) and includes related family activities. As in *Nanook,* the films focus on a nuclear family—father, mother, and young son. Also, like Flaherty, for whom a primary goal was to make Nanook and his kin comprehensible as humans, the pedagogical goal of the Netsilik series is to make strange and exotic Eskimos appear close and familiar and, thus, comprehensible. If indigenous people could be appreciated as full human beings with intelligible behavior, ideally this would promote tolerance for other cultures—both foreign and domestic (Balikci 1989:5). Heider (1976:94) points out that it was no accident that producers chose a fully clothed people like the Eskimos for this didactic purpose.

The Netsilik series (1968), aimed at upper elementary students as part of a curriculum program called "Man: A Course of Study" (MACOS), had the twin goals of introducing students to anthropology and developing in them a concern for the human condition. The viewer observes Eskimos in long sequences of intimate acts, noting their uniqueness at the same time empathizing with them. In the heavily narrated documentary *Eskimo Summer*

(1944), for which Flaherty acted as a consultant, fishing at a stone weir comprises a sixty-second screen sequence. The Netsilik series' treatment of the same activity took more than an hour of unnarrated footage.

The Netsilik series made a substantial contribution to documentary film. By carefully dubbing natural sound without distracting, generalizing narration or subtitles, the films achieved the same appearance of direct apprehension as the silent version of *Nanook.* As Flaherty had pushed the visual potential of film, creating and resolving puzzles without recourse to words, so, too, the Netsilik films heightened the viewers' interest in specific activities, rewarding them with the outcome. According to the films' promotional material, "The effect of this film series is that of a field trip where the student can observe Eskimo ways at his leisure and form his own impressions. The pace is unhurried … [and there is] a pleasing feeling of being there and seeing for oneself" (Education Development Center 1968). As in *Nanook,* viewers have time to consider what they are seeing and to ascertain some things themselves. The Netsilik series also covered familiar ground— Eskimo adaptation to an extreme environment. Anthropologists involved in the project, Asen Balikci and Guy Marie de Roussellet, drew inspiration from culture-ecology theory, especially the work of Julian Steward (1938), in relating camp events to basic subsistence strategies (Balikci 1989:6).

Asen Balikci and Zachari Itimangnaq take time to eat. Fifteen years later Itimangnaq starred in Walt Disney's *Never Cry Wolf.* Asen Balikci.

Although admiring the way the films allow viewers to observe Eskimos in uninterrupted fashion, some anthropologists criticized the Netsilik films for the content put before the viewer's eyes. The color films had the appearance of reality, yet for all practical purposes they were no less a play than Flaherty's *Nanook*. Balikci had chosen families willing to reconstruct the old ways for purposes of the film. Although such a reconstruction certainly has precedent in films about Eskimos and is not reprehensible in itself, in ethnographic film it is essential that the audience be made aware of how this recreation is accomplished. Some anthropologists (Heider 1976:55; Rouch 1975: 91) contended that to show past patterns as ethnographic present did more harm than good. Rather, they said, it is essential to show the meaning of the past for the present. Stefansson had raised the same issue in his critique of Flaherty's directed reconstructions. His point—unpublished and therefore never widely debated at the time—was left for ethnographic filmmakers to belabor forty years later.

Ironically, some educators and parents also objected to the apparent realism of the Netsilik series but for different reasons. When the films made their debut in U.S. elementary schools, criticism quickly mounted over the films' "unsettling realism" ("Every day it is violence and death") as well as the way in which Eskimo values and living patterns were presented as equally acceptable albeit different from middle-class American values (Balikci 1989:6). While some ethnographers criticized the films' "ethnographic impurity" because their appearance of reality masked their reconstructed character, the educational gatekeepers saw them as dangerous windows to a reality unfit for young viewers.

Anthropologists had other grounds for complaint as well. Mostly because of its realistic appearance, the Netsilik series tended to reinforce the general public's comprehension of Eskimos as prehistoric, preoccupied with adaptation to a harsh environment. In fact, during the 1960s the Netsilik

were involved in a complex encounter with political and social forces beyond their control. Yet the films show isolated Eskimo families, still happy, still surviving in snowhouses, still untouched by civilization. Ironically, the illusion of reality created by the detailed ethnographic reconstruction added weight to this vision of the pure primitive. The image was all the more effective authentically clothed in the garb of central Canadian Eskimos about whom the stereotype had originated.

Balikci (1986:43-44; 1989) noted the films' realistic depiction of Eskimos killing animals as counteracting the Eskimo stereotype. He believed this contributed to the public outcry against the Netsilik films in the 1970s, not to mention the withdrawing of funding from MACOS. Whereas Disney presented Paka and Timko as best friends, the Netsilik repeatedly killed and consumed Paka's relatives. Yet both Nanook and Mala were also at war with animals, if never so vividly. The image of Eskimos as nonaggressive is one part of the Eskimo stereotype that the Netsilik films successfully undercut.

Despite these controversies the Netsilik films appear widely on television and in classrooms both in the United States and abroad. Video copies of the series are today among the half-dozen most popular films viewed by the Iñupiaq residents of Anaktuvuk Pass (Margaret Blackman, pers. comm.). A group of Yup'ik schoolchildren watching the Netsilik on film insisted that those were the "real Eskimos," a particular irony since the Yup'ik self-designation means "real people" (Morrow and Hensel 1992:40). Once again the central Canadian Arctic provided Americans with a standard by which they could judge Alaska Eskimos. Ironically, it also provided some Alaska Eskimos with a standard against which they could judge themselves.

The Alaska Native Heritage Film Project

Collaboration between anthropologists and a cinematographer acting as director/cameraman produced the Netsilik films. Ten years later, filmmakers Sarah Elder and Leonard Kamerling began working together and co-founded the University of Alaska's Alaska Native Heritage Film Project—now the Alaska Native Heritage Film Center—in Fairbanks. Although not anthropologists, this prolific team has worked to go beyond the journalistic style of the documentary and has repeatedly demonstrated their ability to visually interpret anthropological concerns. Whereas the Netsilik series employed contemporary Inuit to recreate their past for the camera, Elder and Kamerling collaborate with Iñupiaq and Yup'ik community members to document what is going on in Alaska native villages today.

Responding to developments in documentary and ethnographic film, Elder and Kamerling's films also reflect their own personal histories. Kamerling's father was an immigrant Jew who raised his son in the ethnic diversity of New York City. His job as a film distributor gave his son access to movies at an early age, and Kamerling remembers watching John Marshall's ethnographic film portrayal of Kalahari bushmen, *The Hunters* (1958), over and over again. After high school Kamerling joined VISTA (Volunteers in Service to America), and in 1965, at age nineteen, began a two-year assignment in the village of Kasigluk, thirty miles west of Bethel. Combined with his ease with different cultures and a general literacy in films from his childhood, this stint in rural Alaska formed the embryonic experience for much that would follow.

After he left Kasigluk, Kamerling studied documentary film at the London Film School, where he made a ten-minute film featuring a school for the blind. Armed with this credential, he returned briefly to New York and then back to Alaska. His hope was to make his own films, and in 1972 he got his chance when Frank Darnell, the head of the Edu-

Filmmakers Sarah Elder and Leonard Kamerling, co-directors of the Alaska Native Heritage Film Project. Leonard Kamerling and Sarah Elder.

cation Department of the University of Alaska Fairbanks, was instrumental in getting him a $20,000 grant to film life in rural Alaska. The result was *Tununermiut: The People of Tununak* (1973), a series of vignettes in the lives of the people of Nelson Island. Kamerling made the film in collaboration with his brother, Norman Kamerling, and Andrew Chikoyak, a Yup'ik Eskimo born and raised in Tununak, who was at the time working at the Eskimo Language Workshop in Fairbanks.

Just as he was beginning work on *People of Tununak,* Kamerling met Sarah Elder, then finishing her training in ethnographic filmmaking at MIT. As an undergraduate at Sarah Lawrence College in the 1960s, Elder sat in anthropology classes and viewed films like Robert Gardner's *Dead Birds* (1963) and Marshall's *The Hunters.* She was simultaneously impressed by these films' communicative power and disturbed by the filmmakers' attribution of thoughts to the natives on screen and the huge assumptions of the films' narrations. Although sympathetically presented, the films' subjects remained powerless and were not allowed to speak for themselves. Fired by both a passion for film and a desire to give it a more "authentic" voice, Elder went on to study under Timothy Asch, John Marshall, and Richard Leacock. All three were pioneers in the field of ethnographic film, concerned with issues of epistemology well before the "crisis of representation" that occurred in the social sciences more generally in the 1980s.

Elder helped edit *People of Tununak* long distance while finishing school on the East Coast. She joined forces with Kamerling in Alaska in 1972, beginning a collaboration that would span more than fifteen years. As the team as yet had no funding, Elder spent her first year in Alaska as the only high school teacher in the Yup'ik village of Emmonak, population 250. This experience was comparable to Kamerling's year in Kasigluk and gave her invaluable firsthand understanding of the character and tempo of contemporary village life. Along with teaching, she fished, took steam baths, learned Eskimo dancing, and forged friendships that remain to this day. She left Emmonak determined to make a film that communicated the texture of village life in western Alaska, something that had never been done.

Kamerling submitted *People of Tununak* to the American Film Festival. In part because of the film's long sequences and light editing, it was rejected for inclusion. Critics judged the film, like the stereotypical Eskimo, to be "primitive," simple, and naive. Yet it held the seeds of a style and point of view. An informal showing at the festival's close drew the attention of Alan Lomax, who subsequently introduced Kamerling to Edmund Carpenter and Margaret Mead. With their support, the Ford Foundation funded a larger project for filming in rural Alaska,

and the Alaska Native Heritage Film Project was born.

Both Elder and Kamerling were fired with the desire to document life in village Alaska from the point of view of the people who lived there. In their efforts to accomplish this goal, Elder and Kamerling pioneered what they initially called community-determined filmmaking, in which the subjects become partners with the filmmakers in determining the content and direction of the film (Gilbert 1989:14; Sarah Elder, pers. comm.). In all previous ethnographic and documentary filmmaking, even the nondirected shooting style of *cinema vérité*,[3] the structure of the film was imposed by the filmmaker who chose what it was that would be filmed. Elder and Kamerling made the artistic as well as political decision to give their "film subjects" the power to choose whom they would interview and what activities they would film.

Unlike the Milottes, who arrived in Hooper Bay unannounced, Elder and Kamerling seek permission from the community before they begin a project. They spend as much time living in the community before they begin filming as many documentary crews spend on the entire shoot. Typically, nothing is filmed during the first month of a four-month visit, although they open camera cases and let village residents explore their contents. They visit and talk with village residents, answering questions and building trust. They take the time to screen their past films and so give people an idea of what they have in mind, and they provide opportunities for viewing and comment during various production stages. As a film is no more than a record of the relationship between the filmmaker and the people being filmed, this initial stage is critical to the depth of interaction the finished film can ultimately convey.

---

3. The French ethnographic filmmaker Jean Rouch originated the tradition of observational documentary without narration, which came to be called *cinema vérité,* in the 1950s in works such as *Les Maîtres Fous* (1954), *Jaguar* (1955), and *Chronicle of a Summer* (1960).

...they harpooned the whale right here on each cheek.

Frames from *At the Time of Whaling*. Leonard Kamerling and Sarah Elder.

Most important, the team solicits opinions from community members about what they will film. For example, when they worked in Gambell, it was the community, not the filmmakers, who chose the focus on whaling. Certainly Elder and Kamerling arrive with preconceptions, but they try to let the people speak for themselves.

Since Elder and Kamerling began their collaboration, both with each other and with Alaska natives, the Alaska Native Heritage Film Project has produced eleven films, ten of which are about Alaska Eskimos: *People of Tununak* (1973) depicts daily life on Nelson Island; *At the Time of Whaling* (1974) follows a whale hunt, including preparation and aftermath, on St. Lawrence Island; *From the First People* (1976) shows the fall and winter activities (including dressing up for Halloween) of the people of Shungnak; *On the Spring Ice* (1976) features wal-

rus hunting at Gambell and hunters who are lost on the ice; *Overture on Ice* (1983) follows the Anchorage Symphony on tour in Savoonga; *Every Day Choices: Alcohol and an Alaskan Town* (1985) deals with the problem of alcoholism among Yup'ik Eskimos in western Alaska; *From the Elders* (1987) presents interviews with Iñupiaq and Siberian Yup'ik elders in three short films; and *Uksuum Cauyai: Drums of Winter* (1989) shows the vitality of Yup'ik dancing in the village of Emmonak.

The total cost of all eleven of their finished films is less than that of one B-rated Hollywood movie. But the one million dollars Elder and Kamerling have raised in their careers represents good funding in the world of documentary film. The original Ford Foundation grant of $160,000 paid the bulk of the costs for the three films produced between 1974 and 1978, with smaller grants including one from

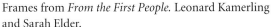

Frames from *From the First People.* Leonard Kamerling and Sarah Elder.

Atlantic Richfield and another from the Folk Arts Division of the National Endowment for the Arts helping to fund more recent work. *At the Time of Whaling* and *On the Spring Ice* were produced as part of a single film project. After shooting in Gambell, they realized that they would lose too much material trying to edit their footage into a single film. New to the film business, they were concerned that the Ford Foundation would reject an expanded project. On the contrary, the foundation was delighted, and the result was two fine films for the price of one.

Elder and Kamerling have simultaneously expanded upon what was valuable in the Netsilik series and avoided what was problematic. Like the Netsilik films, the films they produced during the 1970s were devoid of narration, a radical departure from classic documentary style. In their early films Elder and

Kamerling primarily used synchronous sound. Soundtracks consisted of conversations of the local people with English subtitles as well as natural sounds. Information titles gave the date and location of filming. The films had no music, no plot, and no contrived situations. A good example of this is the dance sequence in *People of Tununak* with its focus on the faces of and the relations between the dancers. The result for the viewer is a feeling of being present in the community hall. At the same time, the film's stringing together of events refuses to give the illusion of complete knowledge. The picture is always partial. One of my favorite sequences shows men leaving the village on snowmachines to check their fish traps. After driving a ways, all the machines stop, and we watch the men dismount, look around, and take time to reconnoiter. At many points the filmmakers allow viewers to do the same thing.

The format of Elder and Kamerling's films encourages the viewer to look at the people and what they do. Although harvesting activities predominate, as they do in contemporary Alaska native life, the films also give insight into everyday life. For example, in *At the Time of Whaling* the camera lingers for long minutes on a group of older men sitting on a roof, quietly talking and watching the ice. One comments, "It looks like there are maybe some whales today." Another climbs up to join them, "I would have come earlier but I was carving." It is small acts of consideration such as these that make up the lives of any group of people, and viewers learn a great deal in going through this process with the people being filmed. No previous Hollywood or documentary filmmaker working in Alaska had found such acts relevant. Elder and Kamerling would perhaps not have considered this and comparable scenes worth the attention they gave them were it not for their experiences living in rural Alaska, establishing friendships, and learning the texture of village life and the meaning people make of it.

Elder and Kamerling's approach grew directly out of a general renegotiation during the 1970s of the conventions governing the roles of filmmaker, subject, and audience. During this period the filmmaker appeared to be the transmitter of "truth," with subjects judged by their own words and actions (de Brigard 1975:37). As a result, interpretation weighed heavily on the viewer who the filmmaker attempted to involve as a participant rather than simply an audience for interesting information. Although recognizing that an entirely unmediated film image is impossible, filmmakers attempted to amplify the native voice.

In their early years together, Elder and Kamerling thought of themselves as giving Alaska natives a voice in determining who would be interviewed and what they would film. While they provided a context for Alaska natives to speak, they still "authored" the films, as they controlled the editing phase during which they sculpted the shape and form of the finished productions. The myth is that the filmmaker simply records reality. In fact, it is the final editing, which is not community determined, that creates the film's meaning. Elder and Kamerling changed the name of their method from "community determined" to "community collaboration" as experience helped them recognize their own role in the filmmaking process.

To increase the audience's sense of participation, Elder and Kamerling characteristically lengthened the time in which images remained on screen from seconds to minutes. They got the audience response they were aiming for when people commented of their finished film: "When I saw it I felt I was really there." Their editing style also displays an increased understanding of story structure over the years—from the loose series of events presented in *People of Tununak* to the much more complex *Drums of Winter*. *On the Spring Ice* begins with villagers watching and waiting for the return of hunters caught out on the ice, providing a dramatic entré into the perils of the hunters' world. It also provides depth to the film's subsequent details, such as a hunter's statement while butchering a walrus, "The ice is closing in. We've got to go before we get caught."

Elder and Kamerling's films also contain casual yet far from spurious references to the filmmakers' presence, such as when a Gambell hunter holds up a tin can, saying "And that's for the commercial." *At the Time of Whaling's* dance sequence is a performance for the camera. After one man takes his turn on the dance floor, he faces us and says in Siberian Yup'ik, "Well, now I'm in the movies."

However one may judge the viability of their attempt to collaborate with Alaska natives in the filmmaking process, Elder and Kamerling's work demonstrates both affection and respect for the people they film. They do not display Eskimo lives merely for the viewer's entertainment or edification. They expect viewers to learn something from the Eskimos, not simply about them. If the significance of the Hollywood Indian was largely negative, show-

Watching the sea and butchering walrus in *On the Spring Ice.* Leonard Kamerling and Sarah Elder.

ing Americans what they were not, the significance of filmed Eskimos remains positive, showing what we as humans can be at our best.

Since 1980, ethnographic filmmakers in Alaska have explored both the potentials and the limitations of a number of different approaches to accurately represent the lives and beliefs of Alaska native people. In 1987 Elder and Kamerling were executive producers of a series of three short films (*In Iirgu's Time, Reindeer Thief, Joe Sun*), focusing on the remembrances of three elderly Alaska natives. They had filmed the interviews in the 1970s, and Katrina Waters worked with them to produce the finished films. In editing their raw footage, Waters alternated "head shots" of the men being interviewed with old photographs and modern scenes of village life. The elders' words provide the only narrative accompaniment. The impact of the three-part series, *From the*

Elders, comes as much from the contrast between the three speakers as in the words of any one of them in isolation.

In 1982 Elder directed *Every Day Choices: Alcohol and an Alaskan Town* (1985). Elder and an all-woman crew made the film in the Yup'ik community of Bethel during four months in 1982, returning in 1983 for followup interviews. She chose Bethel in part because of the people's willingness to speak about the issue, and the community's close involvement in the film project is evident throughout. The film provides both an overall portrait of the problem and an intimate view of its human consequences. It first introduces the viewer to Bethel residents whose lives have been devastated by alcoholism. Nastasia Peterson, a recovering alcoholic, sits at her kitchen table and in moving terms describes her daily fight to stay sober. Later we meet Ephram Alexie in the treatment center where he is trying to turn his life around. Very briefly, we see drunks roaming the streets at sunrise and moaning on the floor of the local treatment center. Unlike the intimate portraits of Nastasia and Ephram, the drunks are intentionally unidentifiable. We then follow a policeman through an attempted bust and listen to local officials talk about the violence and heartache that come with heavy drinking in a small town. At the end of the film, we meet Nastasia again, one year later, still sober and still recovering. But Ephram is in the local jail where he has been booked for shoplifting Lysol. "Why did you take it?" asks Elder behind the camera. "It was the cheapest way of drinking strong stuff," Alexie answers.

The film runs more than an hour and a half, too long for many venues, and it is a small tragedy that it has not been more widely distributed. The film is, however, regularly used in alcohol treatment programs throughout the state. Not only is it a unique film treatment of Alaska Eskimos in an urban setting, it is also a portrait of a complicated issue that could go a long way towards removing the scales from the eyes of many nonnative Alaskans who alternately idealize the Eskimos of the past and disdain the stereotyped Eskimo drunken bum.

In their most recent film, *Uksuum Cauyai: Drums of Winter*, Elder and Kamerling attempt a more structured and highly edited treatment of their subject. They built the film from footage of the midwinter dances (*kevgiq*) filmed in the Yup'ik village of Emmonak in 1977, where Elder had spent the winter four years earlier. It includes preparation for the event, the dances themselves, and the aftermath of the celebration. The dance sequences are framed by an historical discussion of dance in southwest Alaska—the Yup'ik origin story of dance, their view of its significance, how missionaries originally suppressed dancing in the region, and later how villagers revitalized dance and reintroduced it as a keystone of community life. At one point in the film, Ivan Hamilton uses the metaphor of a modern

movie to describe the power of the old dance performances: "Long ago they made the dance house a happy and exciting place. They hung a hoop from the ceiling and hung feathers from it which they called snowflakes.… It was breathtaking to see, like a movie. It lifted one's spirits.… It was something to behold."

The complex process of cultural revitalization is visually communicated through the use of film clips and historic photographs, supported by an elaborate verbal accompaniment. The words that support the visual images, however, do not take the form of a single objective voice. Rather, the film interweaves interviews with Yup'ik elders talking about dancing, letters written in the late nineteenth and early twentieth century by missionaries opposed to dancing, and an extended interview with Father Rene Astruc, a Jesuit priest who has served in Yup'ik parishes in western Alaska since 1956, who is himself a dancer, and who was instrumental in the revival of dancing. The result is an example of the best that ethnographic film can offer. Nothing that has been written about Yup'ik dancing comes close to the power of the Yup'ik commentary contained in the film. Nor does any previous film treatment of Yup'ik dancing communicate so well the historical and contemporary context of dance. The combination is extraordinary, accomplishing much more than either the written word or the unnarrated visual image in isolation. The film also appeals to residents of Emmonak, not so much for the information it carries as for the vibrant picture it provides of their community. Recently, the village bought one-hundred video copies of the film for local use, as residents enjoy seeing their friends and relatives on film, especially respected elders who have since passed away.

Villagers are not the only ones who admire Elder and Kamerling's work. Their films have received impressive public recognition, especially considering their relatively small budget. At the national and international levels, they have won numerous awards, including four first prizes at the American Film Festival, two awards from the Society for Visual Anthropology, and awards at both the 1989 International Arctic Film Festival in Italy and the 1990 International Ethnographic Film Festival in Manchester, England. Their films are as popular at home as abroad and have enjoyed wide distribution within the state. Every school district in Alaska has copies of them. When Elder and Kamerling travel to villages in Alaska today, all they need do is describe a scene from one of their movies—"Remember the film where the whale spouts blood?"—and people know who they are.

CHAPTER SIX

Movies by and for Alaska Eskimos

URING THE PAST TWENTY YEARS indigenous peoples everywhere have reasserted their sovereignty. The notion of shared interests among Inuit peoples has taken firm root (Clifton 1989:25-26). In the special-interest politics of the last half of the twentieth century, Alaska Eskimos have become active locally, regionally, nationally, and internationally. Organizations such as the Inuit Circumpolar Conference draw representatives from around the Arctic from Greenland to Siberia. Contrary to previous assumptions of cultural assimilation underlying early documentaries—that Alaska Eskimos could and would "adapt" to the intruding civilization—Yup'ik and Iñupiaq groups have increasingly used film and video to parlay ethnicity into nationhood.

Beginning in the late 1960s with the struggle for passage of the 1971 Alaska Native Claims Settlement Act (ANCSA), film became one of the many tools Alaska Eskimos, as well as Alaska natives more generally, employed both to gain recognition and to create a new identity. No longer are films produced only about Eskimos, they are produced by and for them to express their views of the world. For the first time, Alaska Eskimos, like a handful of indigenous people throughout the world, are using film both as a mechanism of self-expression and as a tool in the process of cultural revitalization and political recognition.[1] While some audiences continue nostalgic for snapshots of "pure primitives" stopped in time, Iñupiaq and Yup'ik organizations and individuals are increasingly using film and video in dynamic acts of self-representation.

One of the first films produced at the behest of Alaska Eskimos was *The Alaskan Eskimo: A Way of Life* (1973), commissioned by the Alaska Federation of Natives. As in so many previous film incarnations, Eskimos appear as a struggling people. This time, however, they are not only fighting against the environment ("Eskimos live in the cruelest country in the world"), but also against unwanted development from outside: "This film presents the struggle of the Alaskan Eskimos to maintain their traditions and, at the same time, adapt to technological developments that may completely destroy their old way of life." The tone of the film is one of resignation. We see children playing, old men carving, sled-dog racing, a whaling feast, a blanket toss, and snatches of the Eskimo Olympics. The film ends with a view of the

1. Films created in collaboration with other Alaska native groups include Curt Madisen's *Songs of Minto Life* (1985) and Richard Nelson and Mark Badger's *Make Prayers to Raven* (1988). See Faye Ginsburg's article, "Indigenous Media: Faustian Contract or Global Village?" for a discussion of this phenomenon worldwide.

setting sun: "Children experience life between a disappearing past and uncertain future."

The Alaskan Eskimo is consciously constructed around an effective variation on the theme of Eskimo as stereotypical child. It presents a politically current theme showing "the changes in the Eskimo's life-style from that of complete self-sufficiency to dependency" through the eyes of Eskimo children:

> Using Eskimo children as the link to the past as well as the key to the future, this motion picture on Eskimo life will begin with children at play. In the opening sequence, we will see Eskimo children of all ages "doing their thing." … It will also show the Eskimo children engaged in those activities which are peculiar to the Eskimo society. As the film progresses, it will be the children who introduce the audience to each new aspect of Eskimo life…. As the children are a part of the Eskimo society, so are they our view of the Eskimo in Alaska today…. The Eskimo child, living in a changing society, is seen as the continuing link in the chain which stretches between the self-sufficient ways of the Eskimos of the past and the encroachment of the new technology being fostered upon the Eskimo by the modern world. (Films North 1973)

Andrew Chikoyak with "Wild Kingdom's" Marlin Perkins on assignment to cover the musk-oxen transfer from Nunivak Island to Russia in the 1970s. Lael Morgan.

At the time it was produced, some judged it "the most sensitive film on Eskimos ever seen" (Films North 1973).

The Alaska Federation of Natives produced another short film, *Early Days Ago,* in 1975. In less than thirty minutes, the film introduces the viewer to the changes that have occurred in Alaska natives' hunting, land use, food gathering, and transportation. The film focuses on contrasts. It juxtaposes the noisy heavy equipment accompanying development with an old man saying how quiet it used to be. Another man remembers, "They tried to keep us down, early days ago." Those days may be gone, but their influence remains.

At the same time that Alaska native groups employed nonnative cinematographers to document their lives for political purposes, one Yup'ik Eskimo became interested enough in filmmaking to give it a try. Andrew Chikoyak, born and raised in Tununak on Nelson Island, was introduced to moviemaking by Leonard Kamerling in the early 1970s but had been intrigued by film from a young age. When he was eleven years old, Chikoyak was hospitalized in Bethel for tuberculosis. After the hospital burned down, he was transferred to Mount Edgecumbe, where he remained away from home and family for five years. Chikoyak spent his time in confinement reading what was at hand, including camera catalogues. He learned everything he could about the equipment. He remembered pretending he owned cameras like those pictured in the magazines.

Chikoyak was working in Fairbanks when he met Lenny Kamerling and agreed to help him with his film. After working on *People of Tununak*, Chikoyak took a semester's training in filmmaking at the San Francisco Art Institute, and on his return to Alaska he did camera work on a number of other film projects, including Art Davidson's *Our Land, Our Life* and Lipton's *Village of No River*. He also made his own film, *Once Our Way* (1982), about the construction in Tununak of a *qasgiq* (communal men's house) made from driftlogs and sod. Through the film the viewer enters people's homes and at the end takes part in the dancing and drumming that celebrate the building's completion. The finished film, including a musical accompaniment, bears the mark of the Los Angeles editor who helped him cut and edit his footage. Even so, it retains a unique directness that is as remarkable as the best of Elder and Kamerling's work. The people of Tununak either removed or never put on the face they reserved for white people and allowed Chikoyak an intimate view of their lives.

The public cannot see *Once Our Way* today because it never went into distribution. Like a number of other native filmmakers from the 1970s, Chikoyak was encouraged to learn enough about filmmaking to get started in the fiercely competitive business but not enough for him to survive financially. No Alaska Eskimo is seriously pursuing ethnographic filmmaking in the state today.

Another all-but-forgotten yet very influential experiment, known as the Sky River Project, occurred in the late 1960s and early 1970s. Tim Kennedy (1971, 1982) adapted the idea from a film project called "Challenge for Change," originally developed in Canada. "Challenge for Change," begun in 1967, "aimed to promote citizen participation in the solution of social problems," especially minority dissatisfaction. Indian film crews were trained and equipped to document their own problems (Barnouw 1983:258).

Kennedy also believed in the use of film as a vehicle to effect social change. The target of the films produced by Kennedy's small dedicated team was neither television nor university classes on Eskimo life. Rather, the filmmakers took their finished products to Juneau, where they hoped their images would influence the state legislature. One such film, made in Emmonak in the late 1960s before the passage of the Molly Hootch decision mandating village high schools, showed children getting ready to leave home for school. Legislators in Juneau could see firsthand the implications of their actions. Other short films made in Emmonak as part of the Sky River series included a ten-minute, black-and-white film entitled *White Man and Missionaries;* two interviews with Yup'ik elder Charlie Lee, *Eskimo Life on the Yukon Delta* and *Eskimo Medicine Man;* and a film on the same annual intervillage dance exchange that Elder and Kamerling presented in more polished form in *Drums of Winter* almost twenty years later.

The Sky River films made in western Alaska were recorded in the Yup'ik language with no translation and minimal editing of the footage. A notable exception was *River Is Boss* (1971), a thirty-minute film following the drama of spring breakup at the mouth of the Yukon River. Both a folksy musical score and translations of comments of the Yup'ik villagers accompany the finished film. The film came about accidently when Phil Cook, the Sky River cameraman, found himself stuck in Emmonak during breakup and decided to film what was going on. Although the result did not fit within the original guidelines of filming for social change, it did a good job of communicating the pace and flavor of village life and was perhaps the most widely viewed of the Sky River films.

A very different but equally aggressive treatment of issues of native identity and power appears in four films produced by Bo Boudart in the late 1970s and early 1980s in cooperation with a variety of Eskimo groups. The Alaska Eskimo Whaling Commission sponsored *Hunger Knows No Law* (1978) to explain objections against whaling quotas to the outside world. The film opens to the sound of Iñupiaq singing and shots of whale bones marking hunters' graves. The viewer follows a whaling crew on its annual trip to the ice edge, where camp is set up and the men begin to watch for the arrival of the whales. Iñupiaq voices describe recent attempts by the government to limit their harvest. They also describe their part in research begun to determine the numbers and habits of the bowhead. The Iñupiaq magistrate of Barrow, Sadie Neakok, speaks before the camera: "We knew 350 whales was a mistake.… We wanted an actual account to make it official that our word was good."

Back on the ice the whale is sighted, hunted, and successfully landed, to dramatic orchestral accompaniment. The hunters distribute the meat and celebrate the catch. The scene then shifts to a meeting room in which Iñupiat are testifying before the International Whaling Commission. Although the commissioners compliment the whalers on their respect for the quota, a disgruntled Iñupiat responds, "I have to live by your counts … but hunger knows no law!" Sadie Neakok picks up his refrain, "He may be breaking the law … but the whole community will back him.… He's not the only one concerned, but the whole community. It is really apparent that we will prevail.… Our people have never conceded and we won't concede now."

Contributing to the effectiveness of *Hunger Knows No Law* is the fine camera work of Bill Bacon, a long-time Alaskan cinematographer. Bacon had spent several years in the early 1950s living in Barrow, renting a small frame house next to Sadie Neakok, before moving south to do wildlife filming for Walt Disney as part of his True-Life series. Having hunted with the fathers and grandfathers of the men he was filming twenty years later made the presence of this remarkably generous and friendly individual easy to accept. Bacon and Boudart stayed

Bill Bacon and Bo Boudart stayed with a Barrow family while they shot *Hunger Knows No Law*. Here Bill lends a helping hand, fastening a child's diaper with the only thing he could think of—four-inch strapping tape. Bill Bacon.

with Iñupiaq friends during their stint in Barrow, helping the family out when they could. Contrast their presence with the segregated "Camp Hollywood" Van Dyke set up for his nonnative crew fifty years earlier.

In 1979 Boudart produced a second film, *The Sea Is Our Life (Tagiuq Inuggutigigk)*, in cooperation with the people of the North Slope. With local sovereignty advocate Charlie Edwardsen (Etuk) serving as consultant, the film is a strong, articulate endorsement of Iñupiaq rights: "It is said that all men are one. But we are a race apart. To the rest of mankind we are Eskimos. But we call ourselves Iñupiat." The nonnative image of Eskimos surviving in a hostile land is turned back on itself, replaced by the image of Eskimos living in perfect harmony with their environment: "Outsiders think the land is harsh but … like the animals, we live in harmony with our environment.… I am an endangered species also."

As in *Hunger Knows No Law,* the scene shifts to a meeting room where testimony is in progress opposing oil development in the Beaufort Sea: "Today we Iñupiat are treated like a minority in our own land.… While other men hunt for sport, we hunt to eat.… We become animals.… The only alternative is to starve or become criminals." Visual images underscore the drama of the testimony. A photograph shows the pipeline blocking caribou: "These things were done without our consent and with little concern." We see heavy machinery in operation: "No one can be sure machines will not result in massive blowout." A smug, suited oil man assures the Eskimo gathering that oil development is safe, followed by shots of San Francisco Bay and the Gulf of Mexico after oil spills.

The film ends with the query: "What will happen to Iñupiat when oil is gone and men move south? Will there still be seals and whales? Will people still know how to hunt?" The film is still widely circulated. In March 1993 the Alaska Whaling Commission met in Anchorage, and after individual commission members had spoken, they showed the video to their nonnative audience to add weight to what they said.

Viewers can make an interesting comparison between *The Sea Is Our Life* and the contemporaneous SOHIO production *The End of the Road,* a public relations film intended to convince U.S. citizens of the necessity, even nobility, of the Alaska pipeline. Eskimos are not mentioned once in the film, which focuses exclusively on Prudhoe Bay, "rafts of technology in islands of snow." The emphasis is on the emptiness of the North Slope and the isolation of the oil field. A somber voice intones, "The edge of town is the edge of the world." No mention is made of SOHIO's Iñupiaq neighbors. In contrast to the

love of the land expressed by Barrow residents, SOHIO describes the Brooks Range as an unnamed, uninhabited wilderness. Technology, not the Eskimo, is the undisputed hero in this arctic drama. The prose is purple: "The pipeline is an industrial Olympiad, but it is from this cold corner that the flame must first be carried."

Boudart also produced two films for the Inuit Circumpolar Conference: *Inuit* (1977) focuses on the first ICC meeting in Alaska and *Rope to Our Roots* (1980) on the second ICC meeting in Greenland. These films are more celebratory than accusatory. Both document milestone events in the creation of Inuit identity. We see Inuit from across the Arctic gathered in deliberation on the meeting floor and singing and dancing after the speeches are done. Individual Inuit discuss the ICC and the voice they hope it can give their people, both to protect their way of life and to insure that they can influence future developments in their homeland: "It is important to have a rope to our roots but we have to look forward too."

In all four Boudart films, Eskimos defend their right to continue to live as hunters—fighting a battle that American Indians lost a century ago. Film has ennobled Eskimos as the ultimate survivors, while in fact their rights to hunt and fish in their homelands have been sharply curtailed. Ironically, Eskimos have begun using their movie image as survivors to fight back.

Throughout the world, representational media (photography, audio recording, film, and video) continue to play a critical role in the process of self-objectification of indigenous peoples (Turner 1990:10). Representing themselves through film has become for the Inuit a means of conferring value on their lives both in their own eyes and in those of the outside world. Acquiring the technology to produce their own films allows them a measure of control in how the outside world will view them and, ultimately, the ways in which they will come to view themselves (Turner 1990:10).

The nineteenth century enshrined the idea of the inevitable progress from savagism to civilization, from hunting to farming culture, and the virtues of civilized systems of private land tenure. Both Indians and Eskimos were deemed "wandering hordes," devoid of a sense of property, laws, and government (Pearce 1953:71). Americans were convinced of the Manifest Destiny of civilized life: Indians as hunters had to die (Pearce 1953:73). Perhaps with the help of the movies, with their vivid, dramatic presentation of the viability and fiercely defended value of the hunting way of life, Eskimos can avoid the same fate.

From Show Hall to Home Video: Hollywood Comes in from the Cold

As vital as films have been to issues of Inuit identity and power, the increased involvement by Alaska Eskimos in television and radio production, broadcasting, and programming cannot be overestimated. The 1970s brought an explosion of telecommunications in Alaska. Television today has replaced films in terms of shaping images and perpetuating stereotypes. It influences not only how Eskimos are seen, but also how they see the outside world and their place within it.

Although villagers had been watching occasional films since the 1920s, it was not until the 1980s and the satellite disk that television became a daily feature of life in rural Alaska. Since 1950, the Anchorage-based firm Pictures, Inc. had shipped 16mm prints of Hollywood movies to villages all over the state, where they were shown from once to five times a week in community halls or specially built "Show Halls." The fare ranged from westerns to kung fu to horror. Whether the Iñupiaq and Yup'ik audiences understood the dialogue apparently made no difference to how much they liked what they saw. The community of Wales made it a point to rent *Eskimo* at least twice a year, and villagers especially enjoyed pointing out their relatives. The circulating copy got

shorter and shorter as repeated showings resulted in innumerable breaks and repairs.

Missionaries and public servants alike often took a dour view of the early Eskimo attraction to the silver screen. Reverend Ferdinand Drebert (1959:162) gave movies no quarter:

> What good have the people received from the movies? Oh yes, occasionally they see an educational film and perhaps a religious picture. But for the most part it is the exciting Wild West type of picture, with its shooting and killings. Life is made cheap. The criminal is idolized. Chastity and other Christian virtues are often ridiculed. For some of the people the movies get so entertaining and exciting that they think they must attend five or six times a week. To do so they literally take the bread out of their children's mouths and let them run around scantily clothed.

Sadie Neakok of Barrow, however, recalled people's enjoyment of the movies, even the most blatant misrepresentations. She said they found them humorous rather than offensive. When *Lost in Alaska* made its debut on the North Slope, adults and children alike piled into the theater to laugh over Abbott and Costello's antics. Theresa Demientieff Devlin (1989) recalled how savage the Hollywood Indians looked compared to their civilized selves during the weekly movie at Holy Cross Mission on the Yukon:

> On Sunday nights we always had a movie. We would file into the movie house and sit on the long wooden benches. The mission kids usually all sat in front, and we would drift off into movie-land with all the famous faces, cowboys and Indians. I could never identify with them Indians! Why they were *savage.* They had almost no clothes. They were mean, killing and all. They certainly were not civilized like us, not at all.
>
> Anyway, the big girls all sighed over Alan Ladd, and thrilled over Ma and Pa Kettle.

Children anticipate the showing of *Lost in Alaska* in Barrow in the 1950s. Bill Bacon.

Farther east in Canada's Frobisher Bay, Warren Oates' presence during the filming of *White Dawn* had caused quite a stir among his many faithful fans who knew his work from the three-times-a week showings at the local 155-seat movie emporium. In honor of his stay the theater presented an Oates film festival, beginning with *The Wild Bunch* (1969) and including *The Hired Hand* (1971) and *Two-Lane Blacktop* (1971).

Whatever their relative merits and flaws, the lively village gatherings that made even the viewing of a bad movie a memorable event ceased in the 1980s with the wide diffusion of television sets in individual households. Beginning in 1977, Alaska's state government switched on television in rural Alaska. RATNET (Rural Alaska Television Network) initially reached only about twenty villages but by 1990 carried more than eighteen hours a day of commercial entertainment and news to more than two-hundred small communities. Families now stayed at home in the evenings, and villagers converted local movie houses into more mundane uses. Pictures Inc. continued to distribute 16mm films while rapidly converting their stock to the videos most in demand. In 1990, the company let go their franchise on the majority of films it had circulated around the state for more than forty years. Classic Alaska features from Disney and MGM, including *Snow Bear* and *Eskimo,* were quietly shredded in the back room of the Anchorage distribution office. Studio policy prohibited either donating the films to public archives or allowing them to remain intact after the franchises lapsed.

Thanks to VCRs, HBO, and the Movie Channel, however, villagers today are as current, if not more so, than the general American viewing public. Yupiit and Iñupiat, who at the onset of the movie industry were the objects of daring and extravagant filming expeditions, are now avid consumers of the latest Hollywood productions.

The impact of mainstream American entertainment on native communities is still being debated.

Edmund Carpenter (1972:65-66) has judged television, including the movies that it airs, a "potent trip" for consumers. Echoing missionary concerns, linguist Michael Krauss (1980:82) gives television a grimmer characterization, dubbing it "a cultural nerve gas—insidious, painless, and fatal" for the devastating effect it is having on the continued vitality of Alaska native languages. He is not alone in his concern over the central place of television fantasies in American popular culture, not to mention the transformation the mere presence of television has brought into Eskimo homes, regardless of the programs viewed. In the dozen years since television has been in the Bush, it has been implicated in everything from the decline of language and literacy to the lapse of sexual morality, the rise of violent crime, and the general cultural decline. Some Alaska policymakers cite these problems as arguments against state funding for commercial television. They question spending millions of dollars for satellite delivery of programs that glamorize crime, violence, and alcohol when funding for rural alcohol and drug treatment programs is always in short supply (Alexander 1992).

Rural legislators, however, call RATNET a "window on the world" and Bush Alaska's major source of information about society at large. Not only do they resist efforts to exclude rural residents, but many native leaders want to preserve the television system while making it more responsive to native needs. Yup'ik broadcaster Peter Twitchell (1992) of Bethel, a RATNET council member, recently wrote on the important role RATNET plays in linking circumpolar people in a common cause—"programming that will benefit the people": "Before we lose RATNET, let's take it off of the State of Alaska's hands and put it in our own.… Television is a powerful tool, and we can have a powerful voice in the world."

The verdict is not in on the impact of television in rural Alaska. Storytelling by elders, not to mention general household conversation, has in many villages been replaced by TV viewing. Some observers have noted, however, that viewing habits are changing. Television is still turned on from early morning until late at night in many homes. But whereas television initially held its audience captive, people are more likely to ignore it today, treating it as background noise. And, with the advent of video, villagers can choose their own programs. Favorite shows include PBS nature programs and sports events. In northern Alaska, the North Slope Borough film office records the annual *Kivgiq* celebration and distributes these tapes to each borough community, providing another favorite program. In 1993 this amounted to thirty-three hours of programming, most of which was in Iñupiaq. Yet even if all programs aired in Eskimo communities were somehow magically translated into the Iñupiaq or Yup'ik language, so reducing the threat TV presently poses to the continued vitality of these languages, television's very presence would continue to affect the organization of time and social life in the homes it has so successfully invaded (Graburn 1982:15). Along with the school system, television continues to be one of the most potent transformers of Eskimo society operating today.

"Alaska Native Magazine": "Talk-back" TV in Bush Alaska

One of the earliest experiments in the involvement of Alaska Eskimos in television programming was "Alaska Native Magazine," aired in 1975. At the same time that Elder and Kamerling were working closely with communities to produce high-quality ethnographic portraits of life in village Alaska, the coincidence of technology and oil money in the early 1970s made it possible for Yup'ik reporter Moses Wassilie and cameraman Mark Badger to travel to villages in rural Alaska, film what they saw, and produce programs that were subsequently aired in the communities in which they were made.

"Alaska Native Magazine" (ANM) was a satellite production of KUAC-TV in Fairbanks, funded through the Governor's Office of Telecommunications, the Corporation for Public Broadcasting, and the National Institute of Education. It originated because an ATS-6 satellite was available launched as a test to India. The satellite's "footprint" (the shape of the signal patterns it gave off to earth) as it crossed Alaska included eighteen Eskimo, Tlingit, and Athapascan communities in rural Alaska, fourteen of which had an average population of fewer than 250. The ATS-6 experiment explored the use of advanced communications systems to lessen the isolation of living in rural villages in Alaska. The idea was to give native residents experience with television before installing it in the Bush. Beyond basic experience in the uses of a satellite receiver, the goal was to provide the villagers who used the program with the means to express their priorities (Office of Telecommunications 1975a:3-4). No one else, regardless of experience or authority, could accurately predict what users would want; and until users got experience with television's potential, how could they define their needs?

Over an eighteen-month period "Alaska Native Magazine's" four-person team produced a total of thirty-one hour-long programs, consisting of fifteen minutes of prepared program and forty-five minutes of "talk-back" interaction between villagers and a panel of invited experts in the studio. One television was installed in each of the "footprint" villages, with a microphone hookup to the Fairbanks studio. Although a mere blip on the screen of Alaska communications history, "Alaska Native Magazine" remains unique in its involvement of Alaska natives in the production process.

Moses Wassilie, a twenty-eight-year-old Yup'ik Eskimo born in Nunapitchuk, was the program's studio moderator and village interviewer. Originally hired as the on-camera talent and reporter, he later worked as producer and writer as well. Wassilie's job was both difficult and demanding, in many cases

Moses Wassilie filming a whale hunt for *Law of Our Fathers.* Ten years later, Wassilie took a minor role in Steven Seagal's *On Deadly Ground,* giving the film's only realistic portrayal of a contemporary Alaska native. Moses Wassilie.

made harder rather than easier by being an Alaska native. This was especially true when he interviewed in Athapascan and Tlingit communities where communication styles differed as much from Yup'ik as they did from nonnative patterns. Going into a village and gathering material for multiple stories on rural issues in a short time period was also challenging and sometimes stressful.

Wassilie worked closely with Mark Badger, who had trained as a newspaper photographer in California. In Alaska, Badger got his first experience with a video camera. He and Wassilie became a familiar sight in the "footprint" villages.

A key feature of "Alaska Native Magazine" was its commitment to what those involved referred to as "viewer-defined programming," conceptually comparable to Elder and Kamerling's community-determined filmmaking during the same period. The show's production plan called for an oversight com-

mittee with responsibility well beyond that given to village collaborators in filming projects before or since. Native regional corporations selected the committee, which both determined program content and set priorities for handling topic suggestions received from the villagers during the program's interaction segment. In the beginning some of these "consumer committee" members were skeptical of the process. During their first meeting one stated, "Not until I see the implementation of the goals and objectives and am able to see advice we give being properly carried out over the TV satellite screen will I believe we are involved in a productive workshop committee" (Office of Telecommunications 1975b:82).

Though the ANM production staff suggested possible programs to the native consumer committee, the committee was responsible for final topic selection, which the staff then developed for broadcast. One of the committee's first decisions was to broadcast programs in the languages of the footprint communities, including Yup'ik Eskimo, Kutchin Athapascan, and Tlingit, as well as English. They also chose the format of an on-camera host combined with guests, on-location footage, rural Alaska news, and time for interaction with the viewing villages.

Throughout the planning for "Alaska Native Magazine," the committee was concerned that the program be relevant and understandable to village residents, avoiding an overly "slick" format and bureaucratic language. Later they decided to slow the program's pace and insisted that the ANM film crew not decide beforehand how to treat subjects filmed on location. The committee believed that programs should show what could be done in communities, not just what was happening. They stressed that the film crew go into the villages with a flexible attitude about how program topics should be treated. They also insisted that profiles include "common people," not only the "successful." "Alaska Native Magazine" staff in large measure met these requirements (Office of Telecommunications 1975b:83, 129, 164).

The ANM film crew made more than twenty field trips to "footprint" villages. Three programs covered villagers' responses to what they would like to see discussed on television. Badger then filmed according to the comments received (Office of Telecommunications 1975b:166). Although some conflict occurred between the slower-paced native approach and the deadlines ANM production required, input from villagers during the video crew's visits to their communities frequently provided the staff with their most direct viewer response as well as much of the direction for on-location filming.

"Alaska Native Magazine" was broadcast on Tuesday nights, and young and old gathered around the television in the village school to watch. According to one Aniak participant in the project:

Each time we see a show it seems to improve. It's fun for me to be a part of an experiment that proves

people can work together. The Tuesday night show is the best thing that's ever happened to us here. The Native people feel involved. They see their problems on the air, ask questions directly then, and speak to the people. The older Natives smile as they hear a tongue they can understand, speak to them. I feel as though we're building history.

Later he added: "It has been very, very cold. As cold as 56 degrees below. That seems to make the TV act better. We also hope you will cut the opera Christmas shows. The Natives said that was just bum. (Old Eskimo saying.) I've never had a bit of trouble, never had to adjust the [satellite] dish since this fall. It's been the best job I've ever had" (Office of Telecommunications 1975b:88-89).

Interaction was the most experimental aspect of the program design, allowing for viewer reaction and input by way of satellite hookup with the broadcasting studio. At the end of the project, village aides discussed the problems of interaction, specifically that the guests often moved on too quickly to new subjects before people had time to ask questions. Also, villagers disliked pressing the button to talk with the studio, and the technology of the talk-back system prevented villagers from hearing their own questions. By repeating questions and preparing guests for village responses, some of these problems were ameliorated over time.

Villagers also commented that they preferred local filming over interviews, that they thought the studio set was too formal, and that sometimes they had trouble following the fast-paced English interviews. Whatever the program's faults, in less than one full year of planning, "Alaska Native Magazine" designed a hundred hours of original television programming. Moreover, it made viewer-defined programming accessible to thousands of Alaska village residents and proved that fast turnaround was possible in rural Alaska.

Moving Images in the 1980s and 1990s:
The Good, the Bad, and the Same Old Stereotype

In 1974 and 1975 when "Alaska Native Magazine" was in production, it stood out as a rare opportunity not only for Alaska Eskimos to have a voice in what they watched on television, but for them to see television in the first place. By the 1980s, television was ubiquitous in Bush Alaska, and watching everything from "Wheel of Fortune" to "All My Children" had become routine in village life. At the same time television entered Eskimo homes with such controversial impact, work was under way to improve the TV documentation about Yupiit and Iñupiat available to Alaskans in general.

With the removal of the ATS-6 satellite, the award-winning program "Alaska Native Review" replaced "Alaska Native Magazine" as television's most significant effort to feature Alaska natives. Again thanks to the oil boom, from 1976 through 1986 public station KAKM in Anchorage had available $250,000 of state-of-the-art video equipment to shoot and produce the program, which consisted of forty-five thirty-minute shows, sixteen one-hour shows, and one three-hour broadcast. ANM veteran Mark Badger worked as a cameraman and producer on the project for six of the ten years it was in operation, along with Eric Eckholm and Ed Bennett. Their collaboration resulted in the first statewide television documentary series produced in Alaska.

Whereas "Alaska Native Magazine" was tailored for native residents in rural Alaska, "Alaska Native Review" was designed for urban viewers. KAKM produced the program in English, but documentation and commentary on Alaska native lives were still most important. Not only was high-quality recording and production equipment available for the project, but a substantial travel budget—$40,000 a year compared to the $15,000 available in 1991 to Fairbank's station KUAC—allowed for regular filming in native communities. As in the production of "Alaska Native Magazine," the film crew continually

Deering students and Mark Badger, camera in hand, while filming Alaska Review's "Reading, Writing, and Rural Education." Alaska Moving Image Preservation Association/Alaska Independent Television.

jumped in and out of native communities, filming events that villagers would see on their TV screens soon after. This fast turnaround kept reporters on their toes. According to Badger, for many Alaska natives it was the first opportunity they had to see themselves presented on screen in nonstereotyped ways.

Typical of the documentaries made during the program's decade of production was "Living on the Land: Two Stories" (1983). This twenty-three-minute feature juxtaposed Alaska natives engaged in a variety of harvesting activities with shots of a group of setnetters from the East Coast now living in rural Alaska. Contrasting subsistence as an inherited way of life to subsistence as an adopted life-style, the film then posed the public policy question: Will resources continue to be available as competition among these two user groups continues? Documenting a conflict that continues to plague resource management in Alaska today, the film is still worth viewing.

"Broadcasting: Public Enterprise or Public Trust?" was a more reflexive program, commenting on the influence of television itself. The half-hour program first took viewers to the village of Emmonak where a nonnative teacher made the on-screen comment: "TV is just like traveling off into other parts of the world. You don't see kids playing around. I think it's a great thing in these outlying areas." Another teacher commented on television's influence on children's play, which appeared more violent. The homogenizing influence of television—replacing unique things with the same thing—also received attention. Both urban and rural viewers could simultaneously watch television and ponder the broader implications of their actions.

"Alaska Native Magazine" and "Alaska Native Review" have not been alone in documenting Yup'ik and Iñupiaq lives during the 1970s and 1980s. Literally hundreds of television programs aimed at both rural and urban viewers have been produced about Alaska Eskimos, ranging from third-rate to excellent. On the positive side are programs such as "The Reindeer Queen" (1991), produced by Marie Brooks for Alaska Public Television under a grant from the Alaska Humanities Forum. In the video more than 125 archival photographs, rare motion picture footage, and a dramatic narration depict the life and

Hovercraft designer Michael Proctor takes Alaska Review producer Mark Badger for a ride in the world's smallest air cushion vehicle during the shooting of "Hovercrafts: A Solution in Search of a Problem." Alaska Moving Image Preservation Association/Alaska Independent Television.

Sinrock Mary, the "reindeer queen," at Klikiktarek, Alaska. Lomen Family Collection, Alaska and Polar Regions Department, University of Alaska Fairbanks.

times of Sinrock Mary, northern Alaska's legendary reindeer queen. Not only is the documentary the first to highlight the life of an Iñupiaq woman, but her granddaughters' description of her as a woman who shared her wealth is a notable attempt to look at her from the Iñupiaq point of view.

With the widespread and relatively inexpensive use of video, not only can old film images be mined for what they can tell us about Eskimo lives, but new film images can be more widely seen. "Alaska Native Spirit Profiles," written in part by Alaska native news columnist John Tetpon and produced by Syntax Productions in Anchorage, also was released in 1991. Talking about the film, Tetpon described it as "the flip side of the 'People in Peril' Series," a Pulitzer-Prize-winning collection of newspaper articles (*Anchorage Daily News* 1988) detailing the social problems, especially those related to alcohol, facing Alaska natives. The profiles feature three recovering individuals from Barrow—North Slope Borough Mayor Jeslie Kaleak, Arctic Slope Regional Corporation President Jake Adams, and Barrow High School Iñupiaq language teacher Maasak Akpik. According to Tetpon (1991:3), "We have among us, those who have been through hell and have turned their lives around. The negative is now positive.... We hope more films like this one will be done in the near future. These are the positive portrayals that young people need to see."

The TV menu is also encouraging an increasing number of native broadcasters. For example, during 1991 KIMO's "Northern Lives," featuring Anchorage personality Jeanie Greene, aired twice weekly on RATNET, Alaska's statewide rural television network. Her show, which began October 1990, fast became a favorite among Alaska natives, certainly in part because Greene is Iñupiat. Greene also created a weekly TV news program, "Heartbeat Alaska," a native version of 20/20 that aired only in Alaska, but by 1994 had listeners in 300 stations nationwide, as well as in Canada and Greenland. Each thirty-minute show features segments on native news and life-styles throughout the state. Greene narrates the segments, which are made out of home videos sent in by viewers. Greene contends that she likes to air "fringe news, the kind of news that's important to villages. If an elders' conference comes to a village, that's news (in the Bush)" (Agos 1993). "My programming complements the lives and the lifestyles of our people out in Bush Alaska—it mirrors their lives. It's native hands holding those cameras. It's native eyes looking through those lenses."

Greene works twelve-hour days, acting as the show's producer, salesperson, office manager, and editor. "One of the things that motivates me is that I'm really pretty sick and tired of the media-generated stereotype of the Alaska native. It's similar to the 'noble brave' image of the American Indian. The Alaska native seems to be portrayed as either a colorful, traditional, dancing, smiling people or out on the street. I like to think I'm breaking stereotypes" (Agos 1993). Native people involved in television in Alaska are enthusiastic about Greene's "Heartbeat." According to Peter Twitchell, "She's connecting our communities. Rural Alaska is like a neighborhoold now." Viewers are also giving "Heartbeat" a warm reception. Greene is not surprised. "We've got a story to tell, but it has to be told by native voices" (Hill 1994).

The important question arises as to whether or not these television documentaries can change the view of Alaska natives, and, if so, how. Whatever their content, made-for-TV films are shaped by the broadcast industries' need to communicate to a broad nonspecialized public (Singer 1991). Given that imperative, do programs simply reflect public understandings of Yup'ik and Iñupiaq peoples, or can they change popular attitudes? If simply putting a native face like that of Jeanie Greene on screen has value, how much more empowering is the recent effort to showcase successful native lives?

Eskimos are, in fact, experiencing a renewed visibility on television in the 1990s as a result of a growing popular concern with the global environ-

"Heartbeat Alaska" host Jeanie Greene.

ment. The American public has never been as receptive to the observational style of TV ethnography as the British, perhaps due to Britain's colonial history. However, Americans and Britons alike have always been intrigued by Eskimos and seem ripe to have their preconceptions gently challenged. Some old stereotypes seem to be in danger of being replaced by new ones. The "great whale rescue" in Barrow in the winter of 1989 broadcast to the whole world the Alaska Eskimo relationship with the bowhead. "Sesame Street" recently filmed five sequences portraying the Iñupiat of Kotzebue. Children across the nation saw present-day Iñupiat fishing through the ice, carving ivory, making clothing, and receiving visits from a fly-in doctor. Through live broadcasts such as these, as well as an abundance of well-photographed publications aimed at all ages, the whale-hunting Alaska Eskimo has in many places replaced the Canadian igloo-dweller as the "typical" Eskimo. Although their external appearance and habits change, however, for better and for worse the Eskimo image remains in many respects happy, peaceful, primitive, and pure.

At the same time that Iñupiaq anchorwomen such as Greene and KUAC's Nellie Moore in Fairbanks appear in TV news broadcasts and Kotzebue children in *Sesame Street,* Alaska Eskimos can also be seen in an unending succession of television commercials playing on their character as fur-clad primitives. The new kid on the block in terms of location filming, Alaska has recently come to the attention of a number of advertising agencies which have sent casting crews as far as Kotzebue and Point Hope to audition Iñupiaq men and women for parts.

In 1991 Virginia-based Eskimo Pie featured Vincent Tocktoo of Shishmaref on the Bering Sea coast in a series of four ads. Tocktoo beat out 120 contenders at an audition in Nome with his "innocent looks." According to J. R. Hippie of Eskimo Pie's public relation firm, "He is just as real as they come, very innocent in a compelling way. Not naive, just very honest and very forthright. That's something the company feels it stands for" (Pytte 1991:1). In his latest spot, he sits atop an igloo clad in fur and says, "Hey, a polar bear with a sweet tooth ate all my regular Eskimo Pies. Bum me out." The audience hears a growl and the camera shot widens to reveal a studio version of a polar bear breaking into Tocktoo's igloo. Shown to audiences across the country, the ad both plays on and reinforces the image of Eskimos as simple, if not simple-minded, primitives. Once again, an Iñupiat is seen playing the part of an igloo-dwelling Canadian.

In August 1991 Gabe Muktoyuk, Sr., and John Pullock of Nome and Albert Porter of Kotzebue flew to Los Angeles to film a commercial for Luden's Cough Drops. Commenting on the job, Muktoyuk said they will be paid royalties each time the commercial is aired, so even if it is a "silly commercial," as he put it, he hopes it will run a lot so he can buy a new truck, a boat, and motor (*Anchorage Daily News* Staff 1991:6). Farther south, a car commercial was recently shot in Petersburg. To create the Alaska mystique, the producers had locals dress up in three

Snapshots taken while filming a Japanese McDonald's commercial near Palmer, summer of 1993. Bob Crockett.

layers of heavy clothing that were too hot for southeast weather. Quipped one participant, "I think they got us mixed up with Eskimos" (Thomson 1991:6).

In December 1991 Cappos Film Company of Los Angeles came to Alaska to find an Eskimo to show fishing through the ice in search of "flavor filled ridges." In Kotzebue the crew videotaped a parade of more than one hundred men for possible selection to appear in this national television commercial pitching new "light" Ruffles potato chips. The would-be commercial stars stood against a wall in the Nullagvik Hotel and answered a series of questions on camera. The original idea was to shoot the spot in Iñupiaq with English subtitles, but to the question, "Do you speak Eskimo?" only two said yes. In the end, all the Eskimos were rejected, and the company hired two Indian actors from Los Angeles and flew them to Alaska for filming. To make matters worse, the finished ad has its pretend-Eskimos perform one of the most un-Eskimo acts ever filmed—they refuse to share their potato chips. When one Eskimo asks his partner for a bite, the other answers, "Well, if I give one to you, I have to give one to everybody." The camera zooms back revealing a bleak, empty landscape and the words, "Better get your own bag." Silly, yes; Eskimo, no.

In November 1992 an international film crew went to Barrow to shoot a fifteen-second Swedish chainsaw commercial. The ad plays on the Iñupiaq use of chainsaws to cut ice. It shows a local Iñupiaq couple and child sitting in front of an igloo: "And the father carves a Christmas tree out of ice with the chainsaw … a very heartwarming type of story" according to the director (Hunter 1992). It was broadcast primarily in Europe but was also shown in the United States. The agency originally wanted to shoot the commercial on a glacier and make it look like the Arctic, but later decided to go to Barrow and "instead of replicating those conditions on a glacier, to come out here and do it for real with real Eskimos and the actual landscape." The fact that Barrow has no igloos or Christmas trees posed no problem, as

both were constructed by Richard Zerr, an award-winning ice sculptor from Anchorage. In December, after the film team headed south, locals found the setting a perfect backdrop for Christmas card photos (Hunter 1992).

Broadcasting from the Bush

Although the goal of both "Alaska Native Magazine" and "Alaska Native Review" was involvement of Alaska native viewers in the production process, both programs were produced in urban centers, and the staff of "Alaska Native Review" produced their show primarily for a nonnative audience. In regional centers such as Barrow, Kotzebue, and Bethel, Iñupiaq and Yup'ik newscasters and technical assistants produce and screen their own programs both for local and national, not to mention international, audiences. For example, in spring 1993 the North Slope Borough Film Office produced a program on traditional belukha whale hunting to show in Japan at meetings of the International Whaling Commission. They are also in charge of filming the annual *Kivgiq* celebration. Although the Borough Film Office produces a variety of video material, they do not broadcast. The Borough School District, however, has its own interactive two-way video channel and produces programming for local consumption.

The best single ongoing example of Alaska Eskimo involvement in TV and radio production in Alaska is KYUK, one of the first native-operated television and radio stations in the country. Today, KYUK provides a model for indigenous stations worldwide. It is unique in the United States in that it is the only public broadcasting station allowed to air commercial shows. Established in 1971 in Bethel as part of the Public Broadcasting System, KYUK's signal reaches more than twenty villages in southwest Alaska. Television broadcasts include programs in English available statewide as well as daily news breaks in both English and Yup'ik, a popular weekly

Tony Vaska, Carl Berger, and Bill Bowens square off in the season opener of "Ask an Alaskan," hosted by Chuck Bradley. KYUK-TV, Bethel, Alaska.

game show, "Ask an Alaskan," in which Yup'ik and non-Yup'ik contestants answer questions about the history and traditions of the region, and a Sunday documentary series.

Canadian organizations such as the Inuit Broadcasting Corporation in Iqaluit have emphasized broadcasting in their own language since the early 1980s. Yup'ik-language programming also forms an important part of KYUK's schedule and occupies up to two hours a day on radio and one hour a week on television. This programming is critical to the majority of southwest Alaska residents who speak Yup'ik as their first language, especially the estimated one in four who speaks little or no English.

KYUK's most popular Yup'ik-language production has been their "Waves of Wisdom" series, featuring interviews with Yup'ik elders talking about everything from arctic survival to shamanism to the medicinal uses of urine. The series' title comes from

the fact that those who shared their stories with program producer Alexie Isaac would in turn share them with hundreds of other Yup'ik men and women through the air waves. Another popular production is the daily Yup'ik News Service broadcast. With two full-time Yup'ik-language newscasters, KYUK is the first station to broadcast in Yup'ik[2] and the only Eskimo TV news service in America. Broadcasting in a region in which the native language is alive and well, Yup'ik anchorman John Active feels his programs help keep it that way: "There are so many people in this region who can understand what we're saying.... I feel it makes them proud to hear their language being spoken over the airwaves and on television" (*Tundra Times* 1991:8).

2. In 1989, a second Yup'ik/English station, KCUK, began broadcasting from Chevak. Just as the "Yuk" in KYUK is short for Yup'ik, the "Cuk" in KCUK is short for Cup'ik, the self-designation of the people of that area.

(Left) Yup'ik anchorman John Active. KYUK-TV, Bethel, Alaska.

(Below) Alexie Isaac at work. KYUK-TV, Bethel, Alaska.

(Bottom left) Yup'ik newscaster Adolf Lewis anchoring "Yup'ik News." KYUK-TV, Bethel, Alaska.

(Bottom right) Yup'ik reporter Lillian Michael. KYUK-TV, Bethel, Alaska.

For Yup'ik newscaster Adolf Lewis, one of the most important roles of Yup'ik programming is to bring Yup'ik people together—to get them to put aside some of their provincialism and celebrate what is Yup'ik: "Eskimos, especially Yup'iks, have suffered by stereotypes perpetuated by Western culture. And while Yup'iks loathe to be portrayed as nose-rubbing igloo dwellers, they really don't know much about the diversity of their own culture. Local prejudices remain" (KYUK 1991:17).

Working closely with the community has both advantages and disadvantages. Both Lewis and Active find the direct inquiry style of interviewing disconcerting, as it runs counter to typical Yup'ik conversational style, which relies on examples and allegory to make a point. "[Newscasting] is natural in the sense of telling stories, but it's unnatural in that we're talking about other people. I often feel awkward when I'm interviewing elders. [Yup'ik people] don't usually talk about other people." At the same time, both newsmen depend on their audience for help. Elders especially still take their role as teachers and advisers very seriously: "If ever I mispronounce a word or use a wrong word for a certain thing that we need to say, they'll call and correct us. And it makes them part of that…. It makes me proud when we're corrected" (Bliss 1992).

Yup'ik programming also gives people a unique opportunity to use the station to meet their personal needs. News director Rhonda McBride recalled one elderly man who had been interviewed a number of times in the past coming into the station one day and requesting an interview. He used his air time for some quiet talk and a song. That was the last interview he did for KYUK, as he died later that year: "It was then it hit me. What other television or radio station in the world could you just show up at and get air time to say goodbye to your friends? Perhaps nowhere else but KYUK. And why shouldn't you be able to? After all, the 'yuk' in KYUK translates into the Yup'ik word for person. And KYUK was and is the people's station" (McBride 1991:21).

Not only does KYUK programming reach into Yup'ik homes, it also occasionally makes the Yup'ik way of life come alive outside Alaska. In September 1991 National Public Radio's "All Things Considered" broadcast to the nation a mostly English version of a humorous six-minute radio piece on berrypicking by John Active. Fan mail from all over the United States flooded the station. One man wrote, "That work of yours has probably done more for understanding the world of subsistence than any other single thing" (Bliss 1992). KYUK General Manager John McDonald said that was the first time NPR had carried a report originating from Bethel: "We're more accustomed to reporters from outside our region coming in and doing stories. It's about time America hears about Native life from the Native perspective" (*Tundra Drums* 1991:5). John Active's voice is both Yup'ik and unique, and NPR has continued to feature him on an irregular basis.

As important as its programming for Yup'ik-speaking listeners, KYUK has also made an important contribution by its prolific production of video programs detailing the way of life, both past and present, of the Yup'ik people of southwest Alaska. Since 1981 KYUK's native and nonnative staff has worked together to produce more than forty programs, several of which have won national awards. *We of the River* (1985) won the Corporation for Public Broadcasting Award, and *Eyes of the Spirit* (1984) has been shown widely at both national and international film festivals. Program topics range from the broad sweep of regional history to the careful detailing of traditional technological processes. In a series of profiles of Bethel native artists, *From Hand to Hand* (1985), viewers observe the construction of a fishtrap, the carving of a dance stick, and the traditional Yup'ik girls' activity of story-knifing. *Eyes of the Spirit* documents the revival of masked dancing in Bethel in 1982, from the making of the masks through a lively performance. *Traditional Migration* (1983) discusses the decline in the populations of geese and brant that annually migrate to the wetlands of the Bering Sea coast to nest and raise their young. The video presents the Yup'ik view of the problem alongside the position of outside sports hunters and federal agencies responsible for enforcing regulations affecting bird hunting in the region. *Russian Mission: Yukon* (1981) interweaves elements of Russian, American, and Yup'ik tradition, not so much contrasting with as complementing each other. *Just a Small Fishery* (1984) presents the pros and cons of the newly opened commercial herring fishery. *Yup'ik Schoolroom* (1983) takes viewers into the classroom to observe differences in native and nonnative learning styles. The list goes on and on.

The range of video productions that KYUK has produced during the last decade is impressive. Although many deal with traditional Yup'ik skills and activities, many more cover such contemporary issues as alcoholism, child abuse, domestic violence, and suicide. Programs on bilingual education, subsistence controversies, and native sovereignty issues have also been on KYUK's agenda. Moreover, this agenda originates in the community KYUK serves. Many of the programs spring from the desire of local residents to record things they see as particularly important and valuable in the Yup'ik way of life, such as Yup'ik dance and oral tradition. Others spring from the need to circulate information on issues like rape and alcoholism.

In 1991 the Corporation for Public Broadcasting recognized KYUK for outstanding community service, awarding the station's "Respect the River" campaign second place in its national community outreach and public service competition. This was no small accomplishment as there were four hundred entries, and only forty won awards. Said KYUK General Manager John McDonald, "Out of the 40 stations we were by far the smallest. It's quite an honor to be lumped in with giant stations like KQED in San Francisco. CPB awards are the most prestigious in public broadcasting.... There was a lot of talk about the importance of community outreach. In many ways, I feel KYUK has been ahead of

its time" (*Tundra Times* 1991:6). The centerpiece of the "Respect the River" campaign was a one-hour television program, *Drowning: Can We Turn the Tide?* aired in December 1990. The program featured a mixture of video segments and live panel discussions examining why drowning is the leading cause of death in the Yukon-Kuskokwim delta.

KYUK's station manager noted that the award comes at a time when Alaska's public broadcasting stations are fighting not only state budget cuts, but also a plan to create a "superstation" system that would eliminate rural stations and convert them to translators that would rebroadcast a signal transmitted from either Anchorage or some other urban area: "Our drowning special is an example of the kind of programming you can't have from a superstation out of Anchorage. This is real one-on-one contact with the people in our community which affects people directly. It's not something piped in on a satellite. We're doing more than throwing electronic pictures on the airwaves. We're interacting with the community and other agencies to provide a public service" (*Tundra Times* 1991:6).

Along with community outreach, a common KYUK theme is the use of video as a tool in the process of cultural renewal and revitalization and as a means of self-expression. KYUK's video documentaries as well as its regular Yup'ik newscasts are important means of ethnic self-assertion. Productions connect with the local people in three ways: they are made by Yup'ik people, they depict Yup'ik activity, and they aim to remake Yup'ik lives (Weakland 1975:245). KYUK newscaster Adolf Lewis described his own experience:

When I first started working in the studio, I got into it because I was desperate for money, and the IRS was behind my tail ... and I was just hanging on a thread then. I've changed, I guess, and I became committed to what I've been doing. I was getting a lot of impact, positive feedback from my elders and from the community here in Bethel.

KYUK staff in 1985: The early years. KYUK-TV, Bethel, Alaska.

And even in the communities surrounding Bethel, I ran into elders telling me that I was doing a good job, I was making them understand. And that's what I always wanted to do, make them understand what's going on out there in the political world, what's going on in the economic world, socially what's going on in our country, what's happening to their longevity program. Is it being cut? (Bliss 1992)

By promoting Yup'ik understanding of their past and present, these programs have the power to alter their future. According to Alexie Isaac, a Yup'ik pro-ducer at KYUK, the station's efforts have encouraged new attitudes in younger Yup'ik community members. At a time when the subsistence way of life is under heavy attack from outside, KYUK provides both a Yup'ik voice and an instrument for self-realization. Yup'ik Eskimos, like other indigenous people the world over, are involved in a complex historical process of transformation, appropriation, and revival (Clifford 1988:338), and their increased control over their representation in the media is an important part of the process.

Although control of what they air and what they see is considered critical by KYUK staff and viewers alike, this is by no means always a straight-faced endeavor. The "authentic" productions engendered by local control are often unorthodox in the extreme. Take, for example, the battle waged over the KYUK production "Tundra Terror Theater," started in the fall of 1987 and featuring old horror movies introduced by a kooky bunch of studio monsters. KYUK's Jerry Brigham (1991:8) recalled the uproar that followed:

> A couple of RATNET [Rural Alaska Television Network] Council members had received complaints from viewers in the village which found Tundra Terror Theater "tasteless, a waste of time, and just plain dumb." Well, we couldn't argue with that analysis.…It described most TV programs.… Rather than passively accept the demise of Tundra Terror Theater on state television, KYUK decided that they would fight to keep monsters and creatures available to all Bush Alaskans.
>
> When they gave viewers the sad news, TTT fans throughout the state responded. RATNET Council members were buried in a flood of calls and letters.… The village of Tenakee Springs sent a petition of 100 names in support of keeping Old Clyde and the monsters. (It was remarked that this was the first time Tenakee Springs residents had ever agreed on anything). A number of viewers wrote in support of TTT, not because they particularly liked the show, but because it was locally produced and designed for folks in the Bush … not shot in Hollywood or Chicago.

"Tundra Terror Theater" stayed on the air.

By use of sophisticated communications technology to present Yup'ik lives to the outside world, KYUK creates as well as reflects reality. What kind of image does their programming project about Yup'ik people and their way of life? The Yup'ik relationship to the land and its resources is as central in their productions as it is in their daily life. KYUK productions also emphasize the successful, innovative,

sometimes goof-ball mix of modern and traditional elements in contemporary life.

KYUK's programming does not undermine the image of the happy, peaceful Eskimo survivor directly or polemically; rather it does so indirectly and persistently by providing viewers with the details of life in southwest Alaska today so that they can reach their own conclusions. In fact, this is a typically Yup'ik means of waking someone up to important issues in their lives. It seems only right that Yup'ik Eskimos should appropriate the new communication technology to aid in this process.

KYUK is also unique in that control starts in the local community and feeds into statewide and national systems. This reverses the process that produced *Village of No River* in which both the director and filmmaker came from elsewhere to document life in rural Alaska. In *Village of No River,* as in so many documentaries on Eskimos done before and since, control ultimately rested in the hands of non-native producers who wielded the power to hire and

Clyde and his monsters, "Tundra Terror Theatre." KYUK-TV, Bethel.

fire, edit and splice. Choices reflected what would appeal to the nonnative audience for whom the film was intended. In KYUK's productions, Yup'ik technicians and producers work with community members to make documentaries for and about Yup'ik people. The results are distributed widely within the state as well as beyond, and for that reason they are primarily in English. Local productions, however, often spotlight aspects of the Yup'ik way of life that residents want outsiders to understand. If viewed as a series, KYUK documentaries impart much about the region, both ethnographically and politically.

Although KYUK is one of the smallest public television stations in the United States, many of its video productions highlighting the culture and people of the Yukon/Kuskokwim delta region have been screened in various corners of the world, giving the little station an international reputation. In 1991 KYUK signed a distribution contract with the Native American Public Broadcasting Consortium for two documentaries on Yup'ik culture, *They Never Asked Our Fathers* (1982) and *Eyes of the Spirit* (1983). Although funding cutbacks in the 1990s have temporarily slowed KYUK's prodigious documentary output, video production will no doubt continue in the future. KYUK could undertake a modern version of the Netsilik series if community members supported the project. It is more than capable of such a production, and harvesting processes around which Yup'ik people continue to organize their lives are as vital in southwest Alaska today as they were in Pelly Bay in the early 1900s.

Alaska natives are not alone in taking up the camera that has repeatedly been turned on them. Beginning in the 1960s a general reevaluation of the conventions of representation has combined with new technologies to allow diverse groups to produce what has come to be known as "indigenous media." This term denotes both the shared political circumstances of indigenous people worldwide and the global communications networks which these small-scale, locally based organizations are entering. All

over the world, people viewed as "without history," let alone voice, are beginning to use film and video to talk about both their unique pasts and hoped-for futures. An early experiment began in 1966 when Sol Worth and anthropologist John Adair (1972) put cameras in Navajo hands to see how they might express distinctly Navajo things in a Navajo way. This collaborative approach to ethnographic filmmaking, like Kamerling's work with Andrew Chikoyak, both foreshadowed and encouraged the development of indigenous productions. Since Worth and Adair's experiment, indigenous filmmakers have begun transforming the process as well as the product of film and video production (Ginsburg 1991:93).

Today active centers of production of indigenous media include Canada's Inuit Broadcasting Corporation formed in 1980; the televisual work of Australian Aborigines, including the Warlpiri Media Association and Imparja Television, which began broadcasting in 1988; and recent co-production projects in Brazil, including Terrance Turner's work with the Kayapo and the Video in the Villages Project directed by Vincent Carelli (Ginsburg 1991:93; Michaels 1985a, 1985b; Turner 1990; Weatherford 1990:60). This diverse group shares with KYUK both common problems (limited and uncertain support) and a common mission (to communicate their unique cultural positioning in the modern world). Working in a medium whose dynamic is largely determined by commercial interests and consumer concerns, indigenous people in Alaska and beyond are using film and video to present themselves as simultaneously visible, modern, and "complex" in a world that has alternately deemed them invisible, "primitive," simple, and pure. Although their primary audience is local, what they have to say has relevance beyond the communities that produce them. Film and video are not instant panaceas for the problems posed by their encounter with the postmodern world, but in native hands they have become powerful tools in the creative construction of new ways of seeing and being seen.

CHAPTER SEVEN

North to the Past, North to the Future

A T THE SAME TIME THAT ALASKA NATIVE involvement in film and video is on the increase, outside television and feature film crews have focused in on Alaska—and Alaska Eskimos—in unprecedented numbers. More commercial footage in and about the state was shot in the three years between May 1990 and May 1993 than in the entire preceding decade, including films by Warner Brothers and the Disney channel. Many in Alaska welcome this flurry of activity, as the film industry brings more than $2 million into the state in a typical year (Loy 1992), and in 1993 twenty-eight projects left behind revenues estimated at nearly $14 million. Shots of picturesque Alaska also boost tourism, one of the state's top three industries. No wonder the state pumps $200,000 annually into its film office, which does everything from hosting lavish receptions (complete with artificial icebergs) to erecting a gigantic 3-D billboard of an Alaska grizzly bear on Hollywood's Sunset Boulevard. William MacCallum, a past president of the Association of Film Commissioners International, called Alaska's marketing effort second to none: "You've got the best advertising campaign in the entire country. Nobody comes close" (Loy 1992:11). The 1992 trade journal *Film and Video* named Alaska one of the nation's "hot spots" for filmmakers.

The making of *Eskimo* was the last great film expedition for more than a half-century. Now, in the 1990s, feature films with "authentic" Native American casts and scenery are again gaining popularity, made attractive by the success of movies such as *Dances with Wolves* (1990). But a new awareness of Native American issues does not necessarily accompany the desire to exploit the authentic "look" to sell films, and the results of this new interest in Eskimos are a mixed bag of playful innovation and cloying repetition.

Northern Exposure

Alaska's unprecedented media popularity is taking many forms. One of the least expected has been the runaway CBS hit "Northern Exposure," the first network TV show to focus on Alaska. The story revolves around Joel Fleischman, a persnickety doctor from New York forced to begin his career in the backwater town of Cicely, Alaska, to repay his medical school expenses.[1] The oddball characters

1. The Alaska Department of Health and Social Services continues to field calls from doctors and nurses searching for a "Northern Exposure" experience. The single-minded persist, and the department sends them on to the Alaska Area Native Health Service. In fact, there are one hundred and

who inhabit the town and their off-center view of the world have attracted an enormous loyal following and critical acclaim.

When the show began as a low-budget summer series in 1990, producers Joshua Brand and John Falsey scouted Alaska to find a suitable shooting site, but Alaska's lack of film facilities and crew made it too expensive. Instead they chose Roslyn, Washington, a one-street town about sixty miles east of Seattle at the foot of the Cascade Mountains. Alaskans immediately spotted the misfit between real Alaska towns and the quaint Washington state hamlet chosen to represent them. They pointed out flaws as soon as "Northern Exposure's" first episode aired— road signs unblemished by bullet holes, the wrong kinds of trees, dark summer nights, snakes. Although an occasional beer label or license plate has been added for window dressing, the show is still anything but realistic. Said Joe Senungetuk, Iñupiaq artist and writer, "It was not surprising to me since this is something which has been perpetrated upon native and nonnative peoples of Alaska throughout its complex and varied history. TV is a potentially strong tool to set the record straight. Instead, Hollywood has chosen to keep moving in the direction set by other notable movie productions such as *North to Alaska, Ice Palace,* and *Runaway Train*" (Freedman 1990b).

Some Alaskans take a less dour view of the producers' idiosyncratic re-creation. Cliff Fousell of the Fairbanks Convention Bureau said it well: "'Northern Exposure' may not be accurate, but it does project an image, and that image is bringing Alaska into the minds of people like never before. Some of the things are way off, but at least it gets us in people's faces" (Cross 1992).

The representation of Alaska natives in the series is as fancifully skewed as everything else. No Alaska

natives act in the show, Yup'ik, Iñupiat, or otherwise. Instead, Indian actors from the Lower Forty-eight carry the native angle. Why only Indians? They used Indians because they looked more like what the producers thought people expected Eskimos to look like. The show's two generic natives are Fleischman's enigmatic receptionist, Marilyn Whirlwind, and the sweet-natured young handyman, Ed Chigliak. Marilyn says little, moves deliberately, and has a down-to-earth clarity that hints at a sixth sense. Ed in many ways acts the part of the naive native, but his great love is movies, and he constantly compares film plots with what goes on in Cicely. At the close of the 1993 season, Ed successfully dubbed *Prisoner of Zenda* (1937) in Tlingit, and after Peter Bogdanovich visited Cicely, Ed finally set to work writing his own filmscript.

Native themes abound in Cicely. In one episode Holling, the owner of the town's tavern, says to Joel, who is experiencing sleep deprivation, "Ukatak Eskimos fasted for weeks to attain this kind of clarity." In another Maggie finds Indian artifacts, including a cradleboard, buried in her front yard and fends off an all-male excavation of these sacred "women's things." A third episode featured rivalry between the Raven and the Bear clans, which almost made sense, until Maurice, the windbag retired astronaut, began talking about the Walrus clan in Sleetmute. Moreover, natives regularly win in conflicts with the dominant culture. Leonard, the native healer, repeatedly demonstrates wisdom surpassing his nonnative counterpart, Dr. Fleischman, and when Maurice is beaten at his own game by an Indian in a land deal, he complains he has been "bamboozled by Nanook of the North."

References to Yup'ik and Iñupiaq villages are plentiful, especially the villages of the Yukon/ Kuskokwim Delta and the Bering Sea coast. Chris, the philosophical disc jockey, goes to Kipnuk to hear a new band, and the parents of Dave the cook come down to visit from Barrow. Holling planned to have an exotic dancer from Sleetmute at his bachelor

(note 1 cont'd) seventy doctors working around the state under the federal program to pay back student loans that average about $55,000, and every year about forty vacancies have to be filled (Phillips 1992).

party, but her five-year-old came down with the croup, and she had to cancel. Sleetmute is supposedly Cicely's closest neighbor, but the real Sleetmute (population 125) occupies the upper reaches of the Kuskokwim River in interior Alaska.[2] Producers admit there are some geographic incongruities with Cicely, but like the unspecified natives, they are intentional. According to producer Mart Nodella, "We want to utilize all the different elements of Alaska, and if we were to specify the town in one region we'd be limiting ourselves. Doing that would mean we couldn't have a lot of Eskimos in the show, which we want. We didn't want to restrict ourselves, so we went for the state-of-mind theory. We're not portraying Alaska as accurate always. We're portraying what a lot of people think it is, while trying to maintain what is true about it" (Cross 1992). Associate producer Alan Connell pointed out an example of the "production dilemma," as the filmmakers see it: "We wanted to have an ice igloo, but it turns out Eskimos don't live in igloos. It's only fishermen who use igloos as shelters; it's not the Eskimos." This piece of information, however, did not deter them. In a recent episode, Connell continued, "We wanted the visual look of the igloo so we made it fly by making it a dream" (Cross 1992).

Although Alaskans continue to be alternately irritated and amused by the misfit between the Alaska they know and the one that millions of Americans view each week on network television, most were mistaken on one major point. The majority quoted in an Anchorage newspaper survey when the show first aired predicted a short life for the improbable antics of Cicely's quirky residents. Instead, the show's high ratings have kept it on the air for four years, with no signs of its popularity waning. This unexpected success has not been lost on members of the film industry, and the Alaska location rush is well under way.

2. Recent Mark Air Airline ads read, "We fly almost anywhere in Alaska. Anywhere but Cicely."

Salmonberries

In October 1990, four months after "Northern Exposure" made its debut, the film *Salmonberries* began shooting in the northwest Alaska community of Kotzebue, the first major commercial production filmed in Alaska in almost twenty years. The film is a production of the German writer-director Percy Adlon, known for such offbeat gambits as *Baghdad Cafe* (1988) and *Rosalie Goes Shopping* (1989), aimed more for the art than the commercial market. Set in Kotzebue and Berlin, *Salmonberries* revolves around the relationship between an elderly German librarian, Roswitha, who moved to Alaska to escape her past, and a withdrawn half-Eskimo in search of her identity. The former role is played by the German actress Rosel Zech. Canadian country singer k.d. lang, a short-haired, boyish woman for whom androgyny is a trademark, stars as the young half-Iñupiaq, half-white woman named Kotzebue.

The only two white characters in the film are Roswitha and the operator of the local bingo parlor, played by Chuck "The Rifleman" Conners. The rest of the cast is Alaska native, including Aleut actress Jane Lind, the well-known Yup'ik public figure Oscar Kawagley, and Eugene Omiak of Nome. Adlon cast supporting players from among the native residents of Kotzebue, although not without difficulty. The $50 per day offered for bit parts was insufficient incentive for many Kotzebue residents, who were dubious about the film's intent and far from starstruck. They wanted no part of just another igloo picture.

Confirming their worst fears, k.d. lang tried the Iñupiaq community's patience with her outspoken views on hunting. In an interview published in the *Anchorage Times*, she condemned as a "sin" the killing of animals for subsistence by the people of Kotzebue: "I do think I have to be very tolerant of tradition and culture. I just find it difficult to understand why they still need these things when they can get microwaveable Cheese Whiz sent up in a day....

Jane Lind and Chuck Conners in *Salmonberries*. Jim Magdanz, *Arctic Sounder*, Kotzebue, Alaska.

doesn't really know anything about her culture, her parents, her family. She's a little bit angry because of it. She has a good soul. She's determined, fiery and sensitive, but guarded" (Lee 1990b). Except for the "good soul," a less typical Hollywood Eskimo is hard to imagine.

Although his colleagues advised him to build a faux Kotzebue in Minnesota or Idaho, Adlon chose to come to Alaska. His film, though fictional, required Kotzebue's authenticity: "I very voluntarily chose this season [October] because it is so dramatic.... Everything is very much entangled in the blowing snow and the silvery sky.... I need the magic of the real place.... It has to be here, and it has to be the beauty of the truth. Sure it's fiction, but it has the shine of the truth" (Freedman 1990a:2).

I think [subsistence] is less of a sin than factory farming, but it's still a sin.... I don't feel I have the right to take the life of any living thing. We're just another animal ourselves and we're almost extinct" (Lee 1990a).

Lang's statements offended the Iñupiaq residents of Kotzebue, to say the least. Not only did they take exception to her opinion, they felt it was inappropriate for an actress in her position to make her views public. NANA Regional Corporation president Roswell Schaeffer said that lang should have kept "her own personal views to herself," adding that the greater sin was lang's judgment on the Alaska native way of life (Lee 1990a). Although Adlon and his crew weathered the controversy, lang's very outspoken, very un-Eskimo point of view left residents wondering what kind of Iñupiat her film character would represent.

Adlon contends that in *Salmonberries* he wanted to do more than replicate the standard Eskimo stereotype. Therefore, he dealt with contemporary issues, including suicide and drinking. Lang described her character—an atypical tinsel-town creation in more ways than one—as she perceived her: "I think she's basically an introvert.... She

Percy Adlon filming *Salmonberries*. J. Huenergasdt, *Arctic Sounder*, Kotzebue, Alaska.

Shooting on location, however, posed problems for Adlon, as it had for Ewing Scott and Van Dyke before him. Not only did the production staff have trouble finding local extras, but locating hundreds of jars of salmonberries to decorate the set created a major challenge. Nineteen-ninety was a bad year for the arctic crop. Nevertheless residents came through, and the crew constructed the set from an even mix of glass "berry beads" and the real thing.

Equipment failure also posed problems, not to mention a blizzard during the last week of filming: "Despite a wind chill factor of minus 50 degrees, the Hollywood folks went ahead and set up a mock festival out on the ice, prompting some locals to wonder how authentic such a scene would be when most arctic residents stay inside during such weather" (Creed and Andrews 1990:15). In fact, Adlon was elated with the opportunity to film the "high drama" of the storm. "I love this kind of weather," the director said with a satisfied smile the morning after the winds subsided and local filming ended (Creed and Andrews 1990:15).

Although this focus on nature's power over human existence is familiar to audiences of Eskimo films, it is considered a risky departure from mainstream Hollywood movies. Adlon, who created dozens of documentaries before moving over to feature films, is well-known for his attention to setting. *Salmonberries* deploys the Alaska landscape in much the same way his best-known film, *Baghdad Cafe*, makes use of the harsh, barren environment of California's Mohave Desert: "I like minimal landscapes.… the warmth of the desert has many of the same elements as the cold of the Arctic," Adlon contends. "Nature is star number one here," said Zech, the German actress. "Here the first thing is you must survive, because nature is so strong" (Creed and Andrews 1990:15).

In fact, critics judged *Salmonberries'* visual evocation of Alaska, rather than Eskimos, its most salient feature, awarding it Le Grand Prix des Ameriques—the top prize of the 1991 Montreal World Film Festival. According to Richard Gay, a festival vice president, visually stunning shots of Alaska set the film apart: "I think that's one of the reasons [Adlon] made the film. It's surely one of the reasons we chose the film" (Freedman 1991). On the other hand, Gerald Peary, a Boston-based freelance reviewer, was unimpressed by the film's portrayal of Kotzebue locals. In his words they were "kind of macho, old-buzzard men and stereotyped spiritual Eskimos in this gloomy ice-cube spot that nobody should live in.… I thought it was a lousy movie" (Freedman 1991).

Adlon admitted to limited knowledge of Alaska native peoples, depending on an outsider's point of view to tell a credible story. In his opinion, "Cultures are not so different around the world.… This is just another variation on the theme of the human condition. I'm telling the story of a German woman and how she sees this world. It's through her eyes" (Creed and Andrews 1990:15). Adlon drew on a range of Alaska natives to create the eclectic mix of characters that is one of *Salmonberries'* distinguishing features. He also wove Iñupiaq and Yup'ik singing and drumming into the musical score to reinforce the authenticity of his production. As he sees no harm in placing Yup'ik and Aleut actors in an Iñupiaq setting, he auditioned a Yup'ik dance group as a possible accompaniment.

By the time he finished his film, Adlon spent between $500,000 and $750,000 in Alaska out of a total production budget of $3 million, much of the cost associated with shipping film equipment to Kotzebue. Times have changed since Ewing Scott scraped together $5,000 to produce *Igloo* sixty years ago. Adlon's California film crew was also substantial. Pelmele Pictures took fifty-four rooms in the local hotel, and the management had to import tofu and extra fruits for the fifteen vegetarians. Just as the chef of the Roosevelt Hotel accompanied Van Dyke to prepare meals for his crew while filming *Eskimo*, k.d. lang brought along her own recipes for the hotel cook (Freedman 1990a:2).

Adlon's film has enjoyed moderate success, although it is not as authentic as some Alaskans had hoped. To his credit Adlon, who strives for artistic recognition over financial success, has tried to overcome the tendency of mass arts, which tend to be allegorical, to emphasize types over individuals. Whatever its merits and flaws, *Salmonberries* is the first major commercial fiction film to show Alaska natives as Alaska natives. That an Aleut, a Tlingit, and a Yup'ik Eskimo play Iñupiat is a minor distraction. This is also the first time since Talu's performance in *Frozen Justice* that a film has focused on an Alaska Eskimo of mixed parentage. Ray Mala, ironically, part Iñupiat and part Jewish, played a pure-blood Canadian Inuit in *Igloo* and *Eskimo,* whereas in *Salmonberries* a nonnative Canadian singer plays a mixed-blood Alaska Eskimo. We can only wonder if the future will see a film in which an Alaska Eskimo will take the leading role as an Alaska Eskimo.

On Shifting Ground

At the same time Adlon was in Los Angeles planning his arctic expedition, no fewer than seven other feature film projects with Eskimo themes were in the works. Two of these, *Map of the Human Heart* (1993) and *Shadow of the Wolf* (1993), were filmed in the Canadian Arctic with more and less success. *Shadow of the Wolf,* a Canada-France co-production directed by French producer Jacques Dorfmann, employed a plethora of Inuit extras. But the principal stars—the rebellious hunter, his lovely wife, and his shaman father—are played by nonnatives Lou Diamond Phillips, Jennifer Tilly, and Toshiro Mifune, all speaking rudimentary English in the "me Tarzan, you Jane" tradition.[3] Despite a budget of $32 million, the film was a box-office disaster.

Map of the Human Heart, by New Zealand-born filmmaker Vincent Ward, makes much better use of its arctic theme. Robert Joamie and Jason Scott Lee

(Japanese, not Inuit) portray the half-white, half-Inuit Avik, first as a child in 1931 sent for treatment for tuberculosis to a Montreal children's home and later as an adult flying bombers over Europe during World War II. The film is crowded with stunning images, so many that the story line does not always manage to hold them together. It is remarkable, however, in its attempt to portray an Inuit caught between the traditional world into which he was born and the upheavals of the twentieth century. Like Adlon in *Salmonberries,* Ward uses film to explore the idea of mixed race, "people that are neither and both one race and/or another.... And never finding it easy to settle as a result" (Sheehan 1993).

Back in Alaska, in spring 1990, director August Cominto of the Scena Group in Rome moved his cameras and crew to Barrow to shoot the film *The Great Hunter.* The film stars Harvey Keitel, of *Mean Street* fame. The plot concerns a biologist who is murdered while studying arctic wildlife, and Keitel plays the friend who comes to the Arctic to find out what happened (Patkotak 1990:5). Cora Leavitt and Rossman Peetook of Wainwright portray the couple that Keitel winters with in their large, comfortable igloo. A local company, Ukpeagvik Iñupiat Corporation, built the igloo. With labor at $22 an hour, the finished snowhouse was worth about $4,000 (Patkotak 1990). Although filmed in Alaska and featuring Iñupiat in supporting roles, the film is once again a fictive presentation of the eastern Canadian Arctic. Although the film's off-camera direction was in Italian, the eclectic cast, featuring Americans and Europeans as well as Iñupiat, all spoke in English.

3. Linda Billington of the *Anchorage Daily News* (1993) quipped: "Sure the folks in the background—the ones who don't have much to say—seem to be actual Inuit; but the foreground looks as though some casting agent checked out the available B-list actors and said, 'Hey, these guys can pass for Eskimos. Just give Lou shaggy long hair, Jenny a good tan, and ol' Tosh a beard and weird headband, then drape 'em all in fur parkas. No sweat.'"

Not only did Cominto follow in Disney's tracks in featuring Rossman Peetook, he settled on the old Disney location, known locally as "Hollywood" for its propensity to attract moviemakers. Just off the pack ice with gentle slopes to break the wind, the site is ideal. Cominto had considered Nome for filming, but decided it did not have enough snow. Between ten and fifty people traveled daily by snowmachine out to the site, located ten miles from Barrow. Coordinating this exodus was no easy task, as whaling was under way, and snowmachines needed to transport the crew were in short supply (Patkotak 1990).

Because the film was shot outside Barrow, most people had no idea what was actually going on. One exception was Mabel Pederson, whom Scena hired as local coordinator. Pederson rounded up the authentic props the movie required, including a seal, caribou skins, and snowmachines. She also purchased fish shipped in from Anchorage to hang on the drying racks outside the Hollywood igloo. Longtime Barrow resident Elise Patkotak (1990) described one day of filming in which ten local whites were employed as the mean nonnative hunters out to hurt the hero. Most said they came for the experience, to see how movies were made, and to make a little money on a spring Sunday (from $130 to $250 for the day). They judged the project a whole lot of hurry-up-and-wait, but they liked the donuts and coffee and the chance to see how films happen. Few, however, will probably ever see the film, which was released in Europe but not in the United States.

A third international crew arrived in Bethel in July 1992 to shoot sequences for a family-made movie *Friends*. *Friends* tells the story of two boys searching the world for treasure. The "treasure," according to the film's executive director, turns out to be the "heart and soul" of the indigenous peoples the boys encounter. The film is being shot in six locations all over the world, including Madagascar, Southeast Asia, New York, and Alaska. German filmmaker Roderick Thomson and his ten-person crew traveled to Bethel and coastal villages Toksook Bay

and Tununak for location filming. According to the Bethel paper, *The Tundra Drums,* they wrote the story as they went along and hoped to sell their finished film to the Disney Channel (Faubion 1992:21).

Yet another film about Alaska, although not shot in the state, is *North* (1994), a Rob Reiner slapstick comedy about a nine-year-old boy who wants respect. The gimmicky film takes the form of a dream in which the boy advertises for a better family. An igloo-dwelling Eskimo couple applies, and the boy travels to Alaska to interview them. The filmmakers scouted Nome and Kotzebue for locations, but rejected both for logistical reasons. Similarly, they considered having actual Eskimos actually speaking Iñupiaq or Yup'ik, but decided otherwise. Instead Anthony Quinn makes his Eskimo comeback as the grandfather. Reviewers almost universally hated the film. *North* did not merely employ stereotypes, it was one.

Another candidate for the Disney Channel, the movie *Spirit Dog* was filmed in Boulder, Colorado, in April 1993. *Spirit Dog* is a children's story with environmental concerns and an Alaska setting. The ninety-minute film tells the story of a boy and his dog who try to stop pollution from poisoning local streams and killing animals and people. The boy discovers that evil Mr. Smith is stashing toxic waste in the sacred hills near the village of Nunaput. When his dog gets sick, the child goes to the Eskimo trapper Ray to cure it. With Ray's help, good conquers evil and Mr. Smith (Raven in disguise, according to the script) is overcome.

Like *North*, *Spirit Dog* was filmed outside Alaska. Unlike *North*, *Spirit Dog* used Alaska Eskimos to portray Alaska Eskimos, with good results. Casting director Judy Belshe was adamant about using only Eskimos to play Eskimos and traveled to Bethel for interviews with more than thirty locals (Kennedy 1992:20). After an extended search, the part of Ray was given to George Charles, a cosmopolitan Yup'ik Eskimo from Bethel attending graduate school in religious studies at the University of California Santa

George Charles, who plays Ray in *Spirit Dog*, in shaman coat with Jon Paul Nicoll. Corwin Bell, Centre Productions.

Barbara. Charles has been involved in media off and on for many years, including working for KYUK in Bethel during its early years. He auditioned for an antifreeze commercial in 1969, but they gave the part to a Japanese. *Spirit Dog* was his first experience working in front of a camera.

The most recent foray north is one of the most unusual. Warner Brothers arrived in Valdez in May 1993 to begin shooting the action adventure film *On Deadly Ground,* featuring martial arts star Steven Seagal, who wrote the screenplay and is making his directing debut. The Alaska Film Office estimates that *On Deadly Ground* will be the largest film production Alaska has seen, pumping more than $10 million into the state and hiring more than one hundred Alaskans. A casting handout summarized the story line: "Hard-bitten oil firefighter Forrest Taft joins forces with an Eskimo tribe when he is sent into a deathtrap by smarmy oil tycoon Sean Jennings [played by Michael Caine]. After learning

that Jennings plans to annihilate the ecology of Northern Alaska by deliberately creating an environmental catastrophe, Forrest and Sedna [since changed to Masu], an Eskimo tribeswoman, fight their way across icy terrain, pursued by an army of mercenaries, intent on stopping Jennings from creating a hell on earth."

Warner Brothers scouted all over the state before deciding to film their $30 million extravaganza in Valdez. Nome was their first choice, and they planned to begin shooting in March. But going to and from the site posed a logistical nightmare, and the film was first canceled and then reset for Valdez. They chose Valdez in part because they could do both the oil company shots as well as the Eskimo village scenes in one place, saving hundreds of thousands of dollars in setup costs. The company obtained permits from the State to use the park at the foot of Worthington Glacier as the site for the Eskimo village, and shooting began May 17, under blue skies and on white snow. Although the sky stayed blue, the snow rapidly began to disappear in the sunny weather. Warner Brothers had to hire a "snow crew" at Teamster wages to keep the Eskimo village looking "politically correct."

Seagal plays the part of Forrest in the film, which also includes three Eskimo principals: Forrest's lady-love, Masu, the shaman Silook,[4] and Silook's apprentice. Although the story is set in the present, none of the Eskimo principals have last names. Chinese actress Joan Chen, star of *Twin Peaks*, plays Masu, but Yup'ik Eskimos Irvin Brink and Charlie Kairaiuak play Silook and the apprentice.

Originally Seagal had planned that a "real Eskimo" play Masu as well. Warner Brothers advertised for "an Eskimo woman mid 20s to mid 30s with long black hair flowing from a beautiful round and moca colored face." Previous acting experience won out over authenticity, and they hired the glamorous Chen for the part. Her character was originally named Sedna, one of several names for the Canadian Inuit woman of the sea (*takanaluk arnaluk,* literally "the woman down there"), from whom all sea mammals are said to originate.[5] When Seagal realized the cosmological implications (and Canadian origin) of his choice of name, he changed it to Masu.

Charlie Kairaiuak, raised in Chefornak and presently living in Anchorage, was originally hired by Seagal as "authenticity consultant." Right away he advised Seagal not to include the old ceremonies, which might stir ambivalent feelings in native viewers. Instead, traditional native spirituality could be referenced by signs, including a medicine necklace and two shaman masks, both of which Kairaiuak

made and loaned to Warner Brothers for the occasion.

Seagal felt strongly that Silook at least should be authentic. Seagal's minions had been looking for a shaman for months, calling frantically all over the state. Scouts checked out a number of leads. In their inquiries they indicated a preference for an Iñupiaq shaman but said a Yup'ik one would do. Then Kairaiuak suggested contacting Irvin Brink, a respected leader in the village of Kasigluk and an active member of the Russian Orthodox Church. Brink was flown to Anchorage for a screen test. His weathered face perfectly matched the image Seagal had in mind, and he was offered the part.

After consulting with other village elders, Brink accepted. For him and his wife it was not a matter of trying out or competing. When Brink arrived in Valdez, Kairaiuak introduced the Yup'ik elder as chief of his community. Although the designation "chief" does not exist in Yup'ik political rhetoric, the name stuck. On the set Irvin Brink was referred to as either Chief Irvin or just plain "Chief." Neither this nickname nor his screen role as shaman seemed to trouble him. Christian missionaries rigorously suppressed shamanism in western Alaska at the turn of the century, and up until recently no respected Yup'ik elder, let alone someone active in the church, would have considered pretending to be an *angalkuq* (shaman). But with the recent nationwide reevaluation of native spirituality, more and more Yup'ik men and women, the Brinks and Kairaiuak included, are both owning and actively reinterpreting their past. In the process many reject the missionary equation between shamanism and devil-worship and instead see the shamans of the past as powerful spiritual leaders.

Kairaiuak's character in the film was not in the original script. He created his own part when he pointed out to Seagal that every shaman had an apprentice, an accessory Silook lacked. With the casting of Kairaiuak and "Chief Irvin" in these key roles, the Yup'ik language dominates a glacial landscape

---

4. Silook is also the name of the star of *Encyclopaedia Britannica's Eskimo Children*.

5. Sedna had once been human, but her father flung her into the sea during a storm to save his own life, severing her finger joints as she clung to the gunwale of his boat. The fingers became sea mammals, and Sedna sank to the bottom of the sea, where she resides as the respected and feared protectress of its creatures.

Joan Chen perfects her "Eskimo" look before filming *On Deadly Ground.*

Mrs. Irvin Brink in costume on the set of *On Deadly Ground.*

Yup'ik elder Irvin Brink and Charlie Kairaiuak on the set of *On Deadly Ground.*

and emerges from Iñupiaq clothing. The complications of location hunting produced this striking bricolage. In January, when the plan was to shoot the film in northwest Alaska, a casting director set up shop in Nome to interview Iñupiat for several roles, and wardrobe hired local women to fashion Iñupiaq-style mukluks and cotton dresses. Although the location changed, the costumes had already been made, and in the film an eclectic mix of Eskimo extras wears an equally eclectic mix of Iñupiaq, Yup'ik, and Inuit-style clothing based on pan-Eskimo themes gleaned from illustrations in Edward Nelson's *Eskimo About Bering Strait* (1899), John Murdoch's *Ethnological Results of the Point Barrow Expedition* (1892), and William Fitzhugh and Aron Crowell's *Crossroads of Continents* (1988).

The Eskimos appear in two varieties of clothing—heavy reindeer-skin parkas and pants for the outdoor village scenes, and leather shirts and cloth anoraks indoors. The member of the wardrobe team who supervised the Nome seamstresses later moved to Soldotna, where she worked with local women to produce the reindeer clothing. Not only did she need parkas and pants in various shapes and styles for Seagal, Chin, Silook, and all the extras, each piece of clothing Seagal used had to be made in identical sets of six for himself and his stand-ins. No two reindeer skins are alike, let alone the half-dozen needed for each parka. Wardrobe was firm, however, pointing out that every minor flaw and variation would appear magnified when the film was blown up for the big screen.

Work was not completed by the time the costumes arrived in Valdez. Wardrobe hired local women to stitch over the machine-done seams of the light leather shirts to "rough them up and make them look hand done." In fact Yup'ik and Iñupiaq women are expert seamstresses who pride themselves on their neat and invisible stitches. In the past Yup'ik mothers admonished their daughters to take care not to let their stitches show, lest the animals see their sloppy stitchery and find them "scary."

According to Clara Agartak of Nelson Island, "When making raingear care was taken to make each stitch perfect. It had to be perfectly sewn. And the stitches of his raingear if not made perfectly would be abhorrently conspicuous. And he would be so terrifying to the seal that it would never be caught by such a hunter. Even though a hunter is far away he would be that terrifying."

The thirty-odd extras hired to complete the Eskimo cast are as diverse as the clothes they wear. They include Yup'ik, Iñupiat, Aleut, Japanese, Chinese, Korean, and Filipino. Many of the Alaskans were not hired until a week before shooting started. Yupiit on the set include Olin Napoleon from Hooper Bay, now living in Anchorage attending the University of Alaska. The older couple Mary and Mark Hiratsuka had lived in Dillingham until four years ago when his health required them to move to Anchorage. Their son, working in Valdez, encouraged them to audition. A dozen members of the King Island dance group, some living in Nome and others in Anchorage, were also hired both to perform during the interior scenes as well as to stand around the Eskimo village and make it look populated.

Warner Brothers also hired two more experienced Iñupiaq actors, Rossman Peetook and Gabe Muktoyuk, Sr., of Nome. This is Peetook's fourth film, and he more than anyone else is familiar with the moviemaking routine—including long hours and long waits between scenes. He commented that he expected working on this film to be different from his earlier experiences working with Disney, but it was the same. Although Muktoyuk had never been in a film, he said that his experience doing the Luden's Cough Drop commercial several years before had helped him know what to expect. Both enjoyed the trip to Valdez and the change of pace. These men, like Irvin Brink of Kasigluk, are respected members of their communities for whom filmmaking is an interesting vacation, not an avocation. Rossman Peetook is a successful whaling cap-

Iñupiaq actor Rossman Peetook on the set of *On Deadly Ground.*

Japanese actresses decked in furs on the set of *On Deadly Ground.*

tain, and Irvin Brink preaches regularly in the local church. Their transient status as Hollywood stars is but a small part of very full lives.

Warner Brothers wanted visual variety in the Eskimo village scenes. Several slender Oriental actresses from New York contrast nicely with the rotund Alaska natives, old and young, and make the village more Hollywood-beautiful. Conversely, casting chose a gigantic young Japanese sumo wrestler to counter the taut features of the Iñupiaq men. Casting consciously sought after fat, and the net effect was a "heavy" look on the set in keeping with the classic Eskimo image. A minor problem is that the sumo wrestler looks just that—a sumo wrestler in fur clothing.

After the cast was assembled, Kairaiuak taught the Oriental extras a handful of Yup'ik phrases that they could utter at appropriate moments. The King Island dancers also worked with the Japanese and Chinese women to teach them the rudiments of Eskimo dancing. These efforts helped to meld the "Eskimo" extras into a working unit, although Alaska audiences find the results contrived.

As with the Hollywood beauties brought up to Teller for the making of *Eskimo* in the 1930s, the professional actresses appeared on the set with neatly coiffured hair and perfect makeup. Wardrobe personnel confided that they had tried for days to get the hairdresser to do something more realistic, but routine Hollywood style prevailed.

The dialogue that the Eskimos utter is as heterogeneous as the mix of actors and clothing styles. Kairaiuak and Brink speak to each other in Yup'ik and, like Ray Mala's Iñupiaq on the set of *Eskimo,* it rings real. Joan Chen speaks in both Yup'ik and English. This is not surprising as, according to the story line, she left her tribe to study law. What is surprising (if she is really supposed to be Eskimo) is the violent passion with which she utters her lines. For example, when her father is shot by one of the mercenaries, she kneels at his side, momentarily overcome with grief. Within seconds, however, she turns on the mercenary and yells, "I'll see you dead for this." Fair Eskimo maidens have never spoken less coyly in screen history.

Seagal's typically violent, shoot-'em-up shows run on cablevision and are well known to Yup'ik and Iñupiaq teenagers. With this film he hopes to move out of grade-B action films into stronger stuff. This is unlikely. Following its release in February 1994, the film was universally panned, eliciting reviews with titles like "On deadly movie" and "Seagal's directing career on shaky ground."

When asked what drew him to Alaska and Alaska Eskimos, Seagal contended that Native American spirituality was the initial attraction. Kevin Costner had already used an Indian theme, so Seagal placed his story further north. Before he arrived in Alaska, Seagal was unaware that a man named Van Dyke had made a movie called *Eskimo.* Seagal is not alone in his ignorance, as few contemporary filmmakers have seen these Alaska classics. After viewing *Eskimo,* Seagal commented that a comparable film had not been done for fifty years, but as soon as he decided to make a movie in Alaska, everybody else did, too. In fact, Seagal was following a trend, not leading one.

The evolution of the film's title gives a cameo portrait of the dynamics of the Seagal image. Seagal originally named his screenplay *Rainbow Warrior,* later changed to *Spirit Warrior,* referring to the hero's mythical, superhuman stature among the Eskimos who befriend him. He intended the title to reflect the combination of strength and spirituality which he saw his character, Forrest, embodying. Just as he was ignorant of *Eskimo,* he was unaware that the environmental organization Greenpeace has trademarked the name of their flagship which was blown up in 1985 by French intelligence agents. In fact, they are

in the process of making a movie about Greenpeace, titled *Warriors of the Rainbow.* Trans-Atlantic Enterprises, the group producing the film, complained to actor-writer-director-producer Seagal, and he reluctantly changed his original title to *On Deadly Ground,* a title more in keeping with the cadence of his previous blockbusters *Under Siege, Hard to Kill,* and *Above the Law.*

The Eskimo set Warner Brothers manufactured for the film is a *tour de force* in Hollywood re-creation. An elaborate, nineteenth-century Eskimo village—a dozen grey-brown sod and log structures of various shapes accoutered with drying racks, meat caches, kayaks, and dogsleds—was assembled at the foot of Worthington Glacier. It looks like the set from *Eskimo,* preserved intact for half a century. On closer inspection, however, it is *Eskimo's* set with a difference. Whereas the Eskimo village Freuchen helped reconstruct near Teller was fabricated from local materials after patterns familiar to Freuchen from his years of experience in the Arctic, Seagal's set is made entirely of Styrofoam and plastic. Nothing is real—not the sod or the logs or the weathered planks. Even the walrus skull hanging from a peg is manmade, and the painted rubber tusks bend to the touch. Members of the film crew maintained that the grey-brown structures were designed to match the color palette of the fur clothing. Echoing Flaherty seventy years before, one remarked that sometimes the colors have to be "off" to look real on screen.

The collection of dwellings is as incredible as the costumes. Each house is unique, and none remains faithful to the models on which they were based. Igloo-shaped sod houses with models of mastodon tusks embedded in their walls sit beside huts of weathered boards and Chukchi *iaranga*-style tents with sod walls and canvas roofs. Caribou and moose antlers adorn the walls, and reindeer skins cover the entryways. Incense burns in the chimneys to make them appear in use. Plastic salmon strips hang on fishracks in the snow, so realistic that birds regularly came to investigate.

This fantastic village covered more than an acre and cost $3 million to construct. Made in a Hollywood warehouse, it was first shipped to Nome, then to Anchorage, and finally to Valdez, where a dozen Teamsters spent a week assembling it. After the shoot it was sent back to Hollywood, where it joined a growing collection of Eskimo props available for future productions. True, Iñupiaq or Yup'ik villagers could have built a collection of semisubterranean sod structures for a fraction of the money Warner Brothers spent on their prefabricated set, and real salmon and walrus skulls might have served as well as plastic. Warner Brothers would have saved money, and the finished village would have looked much more authentic, if not so dramatic. In fact, Alaska Eskimos replaced their sod huts with contemporary houses, complete with electricity, running water, and, of course, TV reception, many years ago. Seagal's movie set is undeniably more picturesque and also undeniably implausible. The sod houses that provided the models for Warner Brothers' imaginative re-creation exist only in historic photos and the memories of Yup'ik and Iñupiaq elders who used them in their youth. A notable exception is the sod encampment Toksook Bay villagers built in 1985 for a movie that was never made. At the same time that Warner Brothers was working away in their Los Angeles warehouse constructing prefab igloos, the wind and weather on the Bering Sea coast continued to work away dissolving the model upon which their reconstruction was based.

On the set, neither Charlie Kairaiuak nor Irvin Brink nor any of the Yup'ik or Iñupiaq extras seemed concerned about the incongruous props, the mismatch of helicopters and sod houses, submachine guns and reindeer suits. After all, this was the movies. Rather than focusing on the implausible mixing of past and present, they saw value in making the village set as historically accurate as possible. They wanted a realistic reconstruction. Kairaiuak spent hours talking to set designers to insure that the dance house interior occupying a

Valdez warehouse was properly accoutred with skins and a central firepit.

Like the interviews with Ray Mala when he returned to Hollywood, interviews with native actors help sell the movie. In an advertising video made during the filming at the Eskimo village, Kairaiuak and Brink, wearing the fur garments in which they appear on screen, stand side by side facing the camera. The cameraman asks Irvin Brink questions in English, which he answers in Yup'ik, Kairaiuak following with a translation. "Chief Irvin" stated eloquently his thankfulness for being in the film. He said that he did not come on his own, but that the other elders of his village told him to come. They wanted people to know that the Yup'ik life-style is still alive. Both Brink and Kairaiuak see the film as more than entertainment. It is an opportunity to show the non-Yup'ik world something about Yup'ik language, history, and tradition. The finished film, however, did little to realize this potential, and Yup'ik contributions were largely left on the cutting room floor.

On Deadly Ground is both like and unlike its predecessors. It is the first action/adventure film to feature Alaska Eskimos, and in its storyline the dominant culture has never been more dominant. Like *Eskimo, On Deadly Ground* deals with assault from without that results in disaster. This is something contemporary Alaska native actors can identify with. But whereas the Iñupiaq Mala starred in *Eskimo,* here the Eskimos require a white hero, one foot taller than their tallest man, to save them from evil interlopers.

One final irony—while "Northern Exposure" ignores actual geography and ethnic identity to catch the real flavor of Alaska, *On Deadly Ground* employs authentic traditions and Yup'ik dialogue as props in the creation of an elaborate, hegemonic fantasy. One show sees itself as ignoring reality to reveal truth while the other unabashedly exploits reality in the name of entertainment.

Real People Playing Real People

There was a day when anyone could play anything, and no one would say anything about it. Hollywood is getting into the real people, and I think realism in television is what it's really all about. (Judy Belshe, casting director for *Spirit Dog*, Kennedy 1992:20)

Hollywood's use of native actors to dramatize Eskimo lives has taken two steps forward and one step back. In the beginning Hollywood preferred to employ nonnatives, especially beautiful Japanese women, to portray the Eskimos necessary to move the plot along. Ray Mala was the notable exception. Today, some directors still feel compelled to use professional Japanese and Chinese actors to portray Alaska Eskimos. Anthony Quinn and Joan Chen can occasionally get jobs pretending to be Eskimos. But more and more filmmakers want that aura of authenticity that only the Great Land and the Real People can provide. In only three of the eight most recent films did nonnatives pretend to be Eskimos. And only two of the eight films were made on sets outside Alaska. Some might say this is three and two too many. But compared to previous decades, Alaska and Alaska Eskimos are being called on to represent themselves as never before.

Fifty years ago Alaska natives seldom were sought after to fill Eskimo roles and often found it awkward to take them when offered. While attending school in San Francisco in the 1930s, Sadie Neakok had the opportunity to act in *Eskimo*. She recalls: "My dad was so against it. I was the only Eskimo in San Francisco. I was seventeen years old, my last year in high school. I was going to have a great, exciting time being in that movie until my dad said, 'Not on your life!'" Although Charlie Brower kept his daughter clear of the silver screen for the time, Sadie took bit parts in a number of movies after she returned to Barrow. Her favorite was the Norwegian production *The Life of Young George Seal*,

in which her husband Nate played the protagonist, magically transformed by makeup from youth to old age in the course of the picture. Sadie was the local magistrate and a well-respected Barrow resident, and her house became a stopping-off point for all the various film crews that passed through over the years—"so many I don't remember them. We'd be getting two and three dollars every time we showed up. They always had us searching around for old fur clothing to wear. It was fun. We didn't mind, we had nothing else to do" (personal communication; see also Blackman 1989:89-92).

Like Sadie Neakok, some of the Eskimos involved in the filming of *Salmonberries* still viewed their part in the movie-making process as a lark, as time off from real life. Happenstance led Oscar Kawagley of Bethel to try out for the part. He was attending graduate school at the University of British Columbia in Vancouver when he was called by a friend; he reluctantly auditioned and got the part the next day. Likewise Olin Napoleon saw a newspaper ad for auditions for Seagal's film in Valdez. He drove down one Saturday, tried out, and was later notified he had a part.

On the other hand, Jane Lind, a professional actress, was ecstatic when she landed her part and views *Salmonberries* as an opportunity to correct the false images of the past. Lind's Iñupiaq character in the film is an educated woman seeking more education, another atypical Hollywood Eskimo pursuit. Speaking about stereotyping, she remarked, "John Wayne killed us in more ways than one." She recalled how she and her siblings would cheer on the cowboys against the Indians in westerns shown in their village when she was a child: "My father would say, 'What are you doing?'" (Creed and Andrews 1990:14).

Adlon chose Lind after a long search. During auditions in Seattle, no one suited his vision until he received a FAX of Lind's photograph from New York, an image that so intrigued him, he had her flown out immediately and gave her the part. A native of the Alaska Peninsula, Lind began formal theatrical training in New York City in the late 1960s, and she views acting as part of her cultural heritage: "We're a people of dance and storytelling.… We came from that place of ceremony, from that place of ritual, which to me, performance is all about." She recalls the annual Alutiiq masking ritual, combining traditional Alutiiq and Russian orthodox practices into a unique cultural tradition, as influential in her career choice (Creed and Andrews 1990:14).

Although an experienced actress, Lind had never worked in front of the camera before her role in *Salmonberries.* Both Adlon and Conners gave her advice and support. Lind, in turn, encouraged fellow natives in *Salmonberries* who had no previous acting experience. For Oscar Kawagley, who plays Lind's father in the movie, "More than anyone else, Jane really put me at ease.… She'd crack jokes on the set and I'd relax. It really helped me get into my part." Adlon also hired George Barril, a Tlingit from Juneau, to play the sheriff of Kotzebue. Although the director told him to be himself, he still felt inadequate and went to Lind for help: "I had never met an Alaska Native who was in the business.… She worked with me for about four hours one night. I told her I was really grateful" (Creed and Andrews 1990:14).

Salmonberries potentially sets new direction for Hollywood feature films in Alaska as it explores the age-old universal theme of the human search for identity in arctic surrounds. In Lind's view, "Percy Adlon is not glorifying Natives by any means, but he's not deglorifying us either.… He might not succeed in this movie, but the attempt is genuine" (Creed and Andrews 1990:15). Lind views the film as an important opportunity for recognition of a native character and is especially intrigued by the film's potential of showing the uniqueness of Alaska natives. Insofar as Adlon has successfully elaborated this uniqueness, he has been among the first to do so.

Lind is not the only Alaska native whose interest in theater has translated into an interest in film.

Aleut actress Jane Lind while filming *Salmonberries.* Jim Magdanz, *Arctic Sounder,* Kotzebue, Alaska.

When the casting agent for *Spirit Dog* came to Bethel, Anastasia Cooke, who has always been interested in theater and appeared in high school plays, auditioned for a part. She agrees with Lind's estimation of acting: "Theater has been part of the Yup'ik life-style since Yup'iks have been around. They used to dance and do theatrical things with masks in the old steambaths and in the mud houses." She sees no conflict between traditional Yup'ik values and the assertiveness actors need to succeed in their profession: "Your traditional values you hold within you. Whether or not you're outspoken, you can still be traditional, I think." Chevak-born Earl Atchak, both an actor and a playwright, joined Cook at the *Spirit Dog* auditions. Atchak sees theater as a way for Yup'ik people to maintain their identity: "Acting does a lot of things. It gives you an identity. It lets you see who you are and where you come from.

If your grandfather taught you singing and dancing, you show it to other people around the world" (Kennedy 1992:4).

Evelyn Day has no formal theater experience. But the former Kotzebue resident expressed confidence that her life's experiences qualify her as an actor: "I'm a recovering alcoholic and an addict. I was good at hiding myself and not showing the pain. And I still have all of those wonderful qualities," she quipped (Kennedy 1992:4).

Although he has never appeared in a feature film, Chuna McIntyre of Eek is one of Alaska's best-known Yup'ik performers, and he and members of the *Nunamta* dance troupe have appeared in numerous publicity spots and public relations films. Most recently he acted in a BBC film on snow geese. They filmed Chuna in full regalia sitting by a fire in a California wetlands, with the sounds of geese in the background. He tells a story of snow geese transforming into humans and then back into geese. Chuna's rendition of the traditional Yup'ik tale or *quliraq* provides the film's "native perspective." In another film Chuna performed traditional Yup'ik dancing for the camera. He recalled how tiring it was to repeat the same sequence so the filmmaker could get the desired angle. But he took this in stride. Chuna sees himself as an artist, and he views filmmakers as artists as well. At the same time, he relishes the opportunity to represent Yup'ik culture before the camera to a wider audience: "We get to say things and we have to be forceful. We need to look at it, take it for what it's worth, and enjoy it. Film is OK because it has dance. We present that dance to the people, we make it present. It's an heirloom, and we put it in front of people."

Chuna finds these ventures especially enjoyable because they provide an opportunity to interact with people. Like Charlie Kairaiuak he finds satisfaction in giving viewers a look at his heritage: "It's great that there is interest for our traditions and dances. It makes us want to do it more. It's not a one-way deal, but a great exchange. They want to

Yup'ik actor George Charles and the cast of *Spirit Dog* on location in Boulder, Colorado. George Charles.

appreciate our history. That, to me, is a great, great thing—the appreciation of the people. That's always been true everywhere we go. That's why we reconstruct dance accoutrements, which are museum-quality pieces. We take great pains to create them correctly. When people see them, they realize how amazing they are." Like Charlie Kairaiuak, Chuna sees himself as using the tangible to make an intangible cultural heritage visible to the world at large.

George Charles, playing the part of Ray in *Spirit Dog*, provides an increasingly common scenario for Alaska Eskimo involvement in other peoples' depictions of Alaska Eskimos. George took the basic screenplay of *Spirit Dog* and "Yup'ikized" it, which is apparently just what the Disney Channel people had in mind. He named the fictional village Nunaput (from *nuna*, literally "our land") and added Yup'ik dialogue throughout. He referenced traditional Yup'ik values, as talked about today in western Alaska, telling the boy about *ellam yua* ("the person of the universe") and *yuyaraq* ("the way of the human being"). The boy learns from Ray that if you do good things for widows and orphans, those good deeds come back to you. He teaches the boy to be a *nukalpiaq* ("good provider") and in the end tells him, "We don't say goodbye but *piuraa* ("stay as you are"). Like both Chuna and Kairaiuak, Charles viewed his filmmaking activity as a good opportunity to "get the word out" about Yup'ik tradition. He knew the director was looking for more authenticity and enjoyed providing it.

In fall 1993, the *Anchorage Daily News* came out with yet another article announcing that "Hollywood is again casting about Alaska for native actors it hopes will add authenticity to a movie set in the Far North" (Curran 1993). This time the film was a sequel to the successful 1991 release *White Fang* called *The Myth of the White Wolf,* and the local talent agency Northern Stars was searching for native actors to fill six Tlingit roles. Although they wanted to use as many Tlingits as possible, the casting was not limited to Indians, and Eskimos were welcome to apply.[6]

Diane Benson has run Northern Stars since 1989 and in 1994 had more than two-hundred people in her talent bank, including eighty-five Alaska natives. She is Tlingit and, because of Disney's search when casting *White Fang,* has mostly Tlingit on the rosters. She frankly admits that she gets requests for all kinds of things, including the stereotyped Indian and Eskimo: "I deal with that reality but at the same time try to get across to the industry that we come in all shapes and sizes." Over the last half-decade, she has worked to gather a cadre of knowledgeable people and so diminish the possibility of producers taking advantage of the native acting community. Seagal contacted her during the casting of *On*

Deadly Ground, and she supplied some talent, but was unhappy with the results. On the other hand, both native principals in *Spirit Dog* were Northern Stars talent, and Benson remembers working with Centre Productions as a great experience.

As Iñupiaq and Yup'ik actors enter the international arena, some are not as concerned that they corner all available Eskimo parts as they are that, like Ray Mala in *The Tuttles of Tahiti,* they get a chance to play other roles. Jack Abraham, a Yup'ik maskmaker and playwright, auditioned for both *Spirit Dog* and *On Deadly Ground.* But he lacked the requisite appearance of authenticity and did not get a part. As he wants experience in the film business, he told his agent to look for parts as an Indian or Filipino, and he hopes that he can "do indigenous" in the future. Iñupiaq television personality Jeanie Greene, on the other hand, sees her greatest recent success as a low-budget local production about Alaska men in which she portrays, "just a human, just a woman, a woman who happens to be native."

As Alaska native involvement in film reaches an all-time high, Northern Stars' Tony Vita, sounded a sober note: "Any Alaska natives hoping to be the Athapaskan answer to Bette Davis or the Aleut Al Pacino shouldn't be fooled by Hollywood's recent interest in the state and its people. It's kind of a fluke to have two major motion pictures trying to cast up here one after the other. It's not going to get any easier trying to make a living as an actor up here" (Curran 1993).

In sum, no big-budget commercial films featuring Eskimos were made in Alaska in the 1980s. Between 1990 and 1993, however, a motley group of filmmakers made no less than four feature films and a handful of smaller projects. They range in budget from $2 to $32 million, and directors include a German, an Italian, and martial arts star Steven Seagal. All employ Yup'ik and Iñupiaq actors in both small and large roles. Most Eskimos portray Eskimos, but sometimes, like Jeanie Greene, they play men and women "who just happen to be native." These films

6. Holly Churchill, a Haida from Ketchikan, whom Disney Studios hired to make authentic cedar clothing for the film remarked, "I'm an American girl, and I'm happy to be in a Disney film. My weaving is an extension of me" (Koepping 1993).

Kuskokwim Community College students' game show at KYUK. James Barker.

continue to dramatize the traditional snow-house dwelling, skin-wearing native alongside such innovations as Ed the moviemaker and Avik the bomber pilot. Times are changing, and Alaska natives are beginning to take control over the way they are imaged in film. This take-over is not angry and violent, but quiet and ironic. Authenticity helps sell films, so filmmakers are seeking out Eskimos as never before. So far Yup'ik and Iñupiaq men and women work in small ways within the industry to authenticate, rather than transform, their screen image.

It appears the furry, friendly Eskimo image will die hard. One wonders when Yup'ik and Iñupiaq cinematographers will point their cameras south, making movies about the people who have persistently chosen to portray them in a primitive light?

Eskimos in the Audience

In the beginning films featuring Alaska Eskimos were viewed primarily by people with no knowledge of them. New Yorkers buying a ticket to see *Eskimo* in 1933 entered the Astor Theater with a handful of preconceptions and the expectation that they be both diverted and amused. They may have seen Flaherty's *Nanook* a decade before or read newspaper reports of Peary's conquest of the Pole, but the majority still associated Eskimos with igloos and primitive passions. They were unprepared to learn anything new about Alaska from *Eskimo,* let alone to view critically the film's dramatic representation.

In the half-century since, Alaska has become better known to U.S. citizens generally, although this knowledge has not usually extended to any in-depth understanding of its native people. Even residents in Anchorage and Fairbanks repeatedly demonstrate their ignorance of the way of life of the Yup'ik and Iñupiaq men and women living scattered along Alaska's north and west coasts. Ignorance is relative, however, and they do know enough to be alternately amused and irritated by Seagal's flagrant mixing of centuries.

Alaska natives are equally divided in their reaction to the films in which they star. Today some Hooper Bay residents find value in *Alaskan Eskimo,* and people in Teller and Wales still enjoy *Eskimo.* Yet several point to Anthony Quinn's portrayal of Inuk as offensive. Steve Kaleak remembered seeing both *Eskimo* and *Savage Innocents* at the Barrow showhall when he was younger. He loved the first film and felt the second discriminated against Eskimos. Commenting on Quinn's performance, Chuna McIntyre remarked, "They try to sensationalize everything. So bad!"

There is not, nor has there ever been, one Alaska Eskimo reaction to these films. Some take them in stride ("After all, it's only a movie"), while others view their portrayals more cynically. For example, while Kotzebue residents initially kept Adlon and his crew at arm's length, *Salmonberries* has been well received. On the other hand, although Yup'ik and Inupiaq actors involved in making *On Deadly Ground* enjoyed the project, many Alaska natives find the finished film disappointing. A dream sequence complete with topless dancing and throat-singing (a practice unknown in Alaska) is particularly offensive, even to Charlie Kairaiuak whose job it was to insure authenticity: "It's not tradition to throat-chant in a naked way. I couldn't change what Hollywood calls artistic license of the director." In another jarring scene, Joan Chen flees with Seagal on horseback. "Can you ride good," he asks her. "Of course, I'm a Native American," she responds. Diane Benson was appalled. "You have a Chinese actress playing a Yup'ik princess riding horseback. And

why? Because she's a Native American" (Enge 1994). *Anchorage Daily News* columnist Mike Doogan (1994) summed it up for all Alaskans, native and nonnative: "*On Deadly Ground* is a treasure. What else can you call a film that gets absolutely everything wrong?"

Documentary and Hollywood gambits will continue in Alaska, and Alaska native audiences will continue to argue their merits. Although Yup'ik and Iñupiaq objections are unlikely to prevent Seagal-like escapades in the future (especially if such fantasies make money at the box office), Alaska Eskimos today have the potential to create an alternative.

Thawing the Eskimo Image

On what basis are we to judge the successes and failures of films about Alaska Eskimos, both past and present, Hollywood and ethnographic? Certainly, much that we would like to know about Eskimos the films neglect to tell us. Yet we cannot criticize ethnographic films for not being analytical monographs translated into celluloid any more than we can fault Hollywood movies for not being true to life (Heider 1976:12). On "Hollywood scapegoating" Marsden and Nachbar (1988:608) contend: "There is as much danger of obscuring the truth about American Indians through these critical rantings about how Hollywood has warped the American imagination on the topic of Native Americans as there is in relying on movies for total knowledge about the world."

No film can be exhaustive any more than it can be absolutely realistic. Film is always more and less than reality. Hollywood never aimed for realism in the first place, and ethnographic filmmakers are increasingly aware that the film rendition of any indigenous people is just as much a constructed text as is a written book, with the same attendant problems of narrative and focus, editing, and reflexivity (Marcus and Fischer 1986:75).

Films omit things, this is inevitable, but they can

teach us things that books cannot. In an age when visual media vie with books for the public eye, abolishing the harmful stereotype of the noble Eskimo, admirable but doomed, may be one thing film can accomplish.

The film representation of American Indians peaked between 1909 and 1915, before Eskimos made their Hollywood debut. By the early 1920s, Indians already had become a staple of the Saturday afternoon serial and one of the central icons of the Hollywood rendition of the American West (Stedman 1982:110).

When Eskimos were popularized, beginning with *Nanook* in 1922, they instantly became what Indians were not—noble survivors, peaceful and happy as opposed to the violent and angry Indians of the Wild West. For all their admirable traits, the film Eskimo was from the first but a reflection of the American imagination. Whereas the Indian stood in the path of civilization, the Eskimo stood at its foundation—"essential man" enduring in the face of a harsh and unforgiving environment. Yet this total goodness was also less than human. The portrayal of the American Indian as the paradigmatic "bad guy" has been devastating. The reverse image of Eskimos as inescapably good is equally harmful.

Van Valin hinted at the falseness of the stereotypical igloo-dwelling Eskimo when he showed the sod houses Barrow residents called home. His footage of barges landing supplies, commercial reindeer herding, and the processing of whalebone for sale gave revealing snapshots of Alaska Eskimos early in the twentieth century. Hollywood did not follow Van Valin's lead. When moviemakers first came to Alaska in the late 1920s, their goal was to use contemporary Alaska Eskimos to depict a preconceived, primitive central Canadian past. No producer ever seriously considered Ray Mala's script, "Modern Eskimo," preferring Peter Freuchen's primitive, precontact *Eskimo*.

From the beginning Hollywood unconsciously imputed inferiority to Eskimos and then sentimen-

tally or melodramatically ennobled this inferiority out of existence (Pearce 1953:175). In both *Igloo* and *Eskimo* the details of Mala's life explain only how Eskimos differ from white men—they rub noses, they share wives, they abandon infants and the elderly. Thirty years later in *Savage Innocents,* Anthony Quinn's Inuk does the same. These summary traits do not tell us what Eskimos are but what civilized men supposedly are not.

In *Igloo* and *Eskimo* Mala portrayed nature's nobleman, a notch above his "civilized" counterparts. In *Eskimo* his savage nobility brings his downfall. The film was an unprecedented hit for some of the same reasons Longfellow's *Hiawatha* was a popular triumph (Pearce 1953:194-95). The Noble Eskimo could be idealized because he was not a real threat. Contemplating Eskimo nobility, especially in the Olympian body of Ray Mala, was like contemplating one's childhood. Whereas the savage Indian was part of history, the noble Eskimo was part of prehistory, admirable yet doomed.

Following *Igloo* and *Eskimo*, Hollywood continued to look north, although rarely at Eskimos. When they did, the results ranged from fine cinematography to the worst imaginable studio constructions. After Mala's success, Alaska Eskimos have until recently figured in remarkably few feature films. In the last seventy-five years during which Americans have been watching movies, studios have produced more than 200 feature-length films about Alaska and the Yukon, most between 1914 and 1955 (Norris 1992:53). Of these only forty featured Alaska Eskimos and most in only a peripheral way. Except for *Eskimo* and Disney's "People and Places" series, all have evaded critical acclaim.

Price (1973:168-69) argues that Eskimos largely escaped the stereotyped portrayal of Indians. As evidence, he points to the academy awards won by *Eskimo* (1934) and *Alaskan Eskimo* (1949). Films about Eskimos, he says, "are particularly noted for their creativity in the field of documentary ethnocinematography, a tradition that is very careful about the use of stereotypes." He cites two reasons. The first is that Eskimos have kept their "traditional" language and culture into the modern era where it is available for "realistic" portrayal on film and video. Yet as we have seen, when Alaska Eskimos first appeared in the movies, Hollywood cast them in the role of their Canadian brethren.

Price also notes that because of the extreme character of the arctic environment, people remain fascinated by the Eskimo solution to problems of cultural adaptation into the present day. And, in fact, this is the focus of the majority of films in which Eskimos appear, both Hollywood and documentary. Whereas more than a million Indians on reservations have been virtually ignored, Point Hope in northwest Alaska has been filmed a half-dozen times, beginning with *Igloo* in 1930. Filmmakers have also visited Emmonak in southwest Alaska and Barrow's "Hollywood" again and again.

Price (1973:169) cites Flaherty's work as setting precedent for the "relatively realistic" portrayal of Eskimos: "He let the story develop out of the lives of the people in their daily struggle for survival in a harsh environment." Flaherty actually chose this focus. It was not inevitable from the situation. In making this choice the "father of documentary" immortalized the ultimate Eskimo survivor that has dominated movies ever since.

No one can deny Flaherty's contribution: He was the first to make an Eskimo come alive as a human being on screen. Yet Flaherty's Nanook lived in a timeless zone, as have the majority of movie Eskimos in the years that followed. Only in the 1970s and 1980s—in films sponsored by Alaska native groups, in locally generated documentaries such as those produced by KYUK, and in the ethnographic films of Elder and Kamerling—is this ahistoricism addressed. Not only have these groups produced unique film images, but they suggest the possible transformation of the filmmaking process into a collaborative endeavor in which the passive objects of past representations become authors in acts of self-representation.

Ideas about Eskimos, just like ideas about anything else, derive from a particular cultural context and historical moment, and they change over time. Until the 1920s, the dominant idea about Eskimos was that like other Native Americans, they would not endure as distinct peoples (Clifton 1989:1). Since then, an unprecedented political and cultural renaissance has taken root and grown beyond all expectation. Just as Native American efforts in general focus on issues of cultural pluralism and resistance to assimilation (Clifton 1989:3), films and videos about Alaska Eskimos since the 1970s, especially those by the Alaska Federation of Natives, the Inuit Circumpolar Conference, and KYUK, take self-determination and cultural integrity as their themes. The past two decades have seen the birth of the idea of the Inuit with a commonality of interest and purpose, and film and video have been tools in this process.

How effectively these new tools can be used remains to be seen. The worldwide production of indigenous media is a complicated combination of local interests positioned in the global village (Ginsberg 1991). The impact of Iñupiaq and Yup'ik productions, like those of the Inuit Broadcasting Corporation, the Kayapo of Brazil, and Australian Aborigines, will depend on links to the larger society, both to fund their work and, as important, distribute it. *On Deadly Ground* has reached millions of viewers, while the audience for KYUK's documentary productions is a fraction that size and that of Andrew Chikoyak's *Once Our Way* virtually nonexistent.

Movies will continue to play an active role in the affirmation of Alaska Eskimo identity and power. What other avenues might film pursue? A plethora of films detail Eskimos surviving. This theme will die hard. Yet today's Iñupiat and Yupiit are not merely surviving—they are actively working to create new and innovative futures.

To date, no one has attempted a film series comparable to the Netsilik about a single Yup'ik or Iñupiaq community. A video production that followed modern Alaska Eskimos through their annual cycle could do more to educate nonnatives on the meaning and significance of subsistence in contemporary rural Alaska than any written rhetoric. Such a series could be produced on video at a lower cost than on film. Along with adequate funding, it would require a dedicated, knowledgeable production crew and the willingness of Yup'ik and Iñupiaq people to share their lives.

Both ethnographic and commercial films have the potential to teach new ways of seeing and to evoke empathy, albeit in different ways. This potential has yet to be realized for the much-filmed Alaska Eskimos. Limited funding and distribution, and the tenacity of the formula Eskimo, have constrained even experienced, sensitive producers like Elder and Kamerling and KYUK's Alexie Isaac. Documentaries like Lipton's *Village of No River* and Hollywood extravaganzas like Seagal's *On Deadly Ground* continue to display Eskimo exoticism and to deny their individuality. Films can broadcast the essential humanity of Eskimo peoples at the same time that they portray the actual details of their lives. Flaherty stressed Eskimo humanity over an accurate portrayal of their way of life. Documentary gives us snapshots of "real Eskimos" at a distance that denies their humanity. Humanity and reality are equally essential, and both ethnographic films and Hollywood movies can profit by aiming in the direction of the "Real People."

FILMOGRAPHY

Commercial Films

La Conquête du Pôle
   (The Conquest of the Pole)   George Méliès 1912

Carnegie Museum Alaska-
   Siberian Expedition   F. E. Kleinschmidt 1912

Nanook of the North   Revlon Frères 1922   Robert Flaherty (W&D)

The Frozen North   Buster Keaton Prod. 1922   Buster Keaton (W&D)

Adventures in the Far North   F. E. Kleinschmidt 1923

The Eskimo   Fox Films 1923   S. Summerville (P)

The Alaskan   Paramount 1924   Adolf Zukor and Jesse Lasky (P)/Herbert Brenon (D)

Kivalina of the Ice Lands   B.C.R. Productions 1925   Earl Rossman (P&D)

Justice of the Far North   Columbia 1926   Norman Dawn (W&D)

Alaskan Adventures   Pathé Exchange 1926   C.C. Griffin (P)/Capt. Jack Robertson (D)

Primitive Love   1926   F. E. Kleinschmidt

Frozen Justice   Fox Films 1929   Allan Dwan (D)

Igloo   Universal 1932   Ewing Scott (D)

Eskimo   MGM 1934   W. S. Van Dyke (D)

S.O.S. Iceberg   Universal 1933   Arnold Frank/Taj Garnett (D)

The Wedding of Palo   Rasmussen 1937   Knud Rasmussen (D)

Call of the Yukon   Republic Pictures 1938   Armand Schoefer (P)/B. Reaves Eason (D)

Girl from God's Country   Republic Pictures 1940   Armand Schoefer (P)/Sidney Salkov (D)

Petticoat Fever   MGM 1936   Frank Davis (P)/George Fitzmaurice (D)

Arctic Manhunt   Universal 1949   Leonard Goldstein (P)/Ewing Scott (D)

Arctic Fury   Columbia 1949   Boris Petroff (P)/Norman Dawn (D)

Arctic Flight   Monogram 1952   Lindsley Parsons (P)/Lew Landers (D)

Red Snow   Columbia 1952   Boris Petroff (P&D)

Abbott and Costello:
   Lost in Alaska   Universal 1952   Howard Christie (P)/Jean Yarbrough (D)

Back to God's Country   Universal 1953   Howard Christie (P)/Joseph Pevney (D)

Ice Palace   Warner Brothers 1959   Henry Blake (P)/Vincent Sherman (D)

The Savage Innocents   Paramount 1960   Meleno Malenotti (P)/Nicholas Ray (D)

North of the Sun   Eastman International 1960   Gordon Eastman (D)

North of the Yukon   Yukon Pictures 1967   Jon Doudman (P&D)

Snow Bear	Walt Disney 1970 James Algar (P)/ Michael Williamson (D)
Two Against the Arctic	Walt Disney 1974 James Algar (P)/ Robert Clouse (D)
White Dawn	Paramount 1974 Martin Ransohoff (P)/Phillip Kaufman (D)
Never Cry Wolf	Walt Disney 1983 Lewis Allen, Jack Couffer, Joseph Strick (P)/ Carroll Ballard (D)
Salmonberries	Pelmele Pictures 1991 Percey Adlon (P&D)
The Great Hunter	Scena 1991 Martin Lanfergin (P)/ Jeff Daugherty (D)
Shadow of the Wolf	Triumph Pictures 1993 Claude Leger (P)/ Jacques Dorfmann (D)
Map of the Human Heart	Ward 1993 Tim Bevan (P)/ Vincent Ward (P&D)
Spirit Dog	Centre Productions 1994 John Hillard (P&D)
On Deadly Ground	Warner Brothers 1994 Steven Seagal (P&D)

Documentary and Ethnographic Films and Videos

Tip Top of the Earth	Van Valin 1919
Eskimo Trails	Twentieth Century Fox 1940 Truman Talley (P)/Father Hubbard/ Lowell Thomas (D)
Eskimo Children	Encyclopedia Britanica Films 1941 Henry Collins Jr. (P)
Return of the Musk Oxen	Alaska Department of Fish and Game, Information and Education Section 1943
Little Diomede	Northern Films 1947
Alaskan Eskimo	Walt Disney 1949 Alfred Milotte (photography)/Ben Sharpsteen (P)/ James Algar (D)
Eskimo Hunters of Northwest Alaska	United World Films 1949 Louis de Rochemont (P)
Tigera: Ageless City of the Arctic	BFA Educational Media 1955
Alaskan Sled Dog	Walt Disney 1956 Fred and Sara Machetanz (photography)/ Ben Sharpsteen (P)
Life in Cold Lands	Coronet Films 1956
Alaska: America's Brightest Star	Alaska Chamber of Commerce 1959 Lowell Thomas, Jr. (P)/Lillian Jones (D)
Eskimo Family	Encyclopedia Britanica Films 1960 Edmund Carpenter (P)
Customs of the Eskimo	A.V. Educational Films 1960
Native Alaska	Indiana University 1961
Elisha Rock: Seal Hunter	Vagabond Films 1962 Don Hobard (P&D)
Alaska Movie Trails	Kodak 1960s James Steeb/Charles Kingsley

Eskimo River Village	Northern Films 1962 Louis R. Huber (P&D)
Netsilik Eskimo Series	Education Development Center, National Film Board of Canada 1968
	Quentin Bell (P)/Asen Balikci
The Children of Eek and	
Their Art	British Petroleum, Commercial Films Division 1969
Alaska: End of the Last	
Frontier	Xerox Films 1970 Pierre Streit (P&D)
Eskimos:	
A Changing Culture	BFA Educational Media 1971 Wayne Mitchell (P&D)
River Is Boss	Sky River 1971 John Tenney (P)/Art Marks (D)
Maggie Lind: History of the	
Kuskokwim and Life in	
the Bethel Area	Sky River
Education in Eskimo:	
An Approach to	
Bilingual Education	Bureau of Indian Affairs 1971
The Emerging Eskimo	Larry Brayton 1972 Larry Brayton (P&D)
People of the Yukon Delta	Aaron Productions 1972 Matthew Aaron (P&D)
Suguat: A Bristol Bay	
Yup'ik Eskimo Doll Story	Yup'ik Language Workshop 1972 R. A Emmert (D)/University of Alaska
	Division of Media Services (P)
Peter and the Wolf in	
Yup'ik Eskimo	KUAC 1973
The Alaskan Eskimo: A Way	
of Life	Films North, Alaska Federation of Natives 1973 Rod Thompson (P&D)
Early Days Ago	Alaska Federation of Natives 1975 Alva I. Cox, Jr. (P)/Albert Maysles (D)
Our Land, Our Life	Davidson 1976 Art Davidson (P&D)
Festival of the Whale	KUAC 1976 Moses Wassilie (P&D)
Tununermiut:	
The People of Tununak	ANHFP 1973 Leonard Kamerling/Andrew Chikoyak
At the Time of Whaling	ANHFP 1974 Sarah Elder/Leonard Kamerling
On the Spring Ice	ANHFP 1976 Sarah Elder/Leonard Kamerling
From the First People	ANHFP 1976 Sarah Elder/Leonard Kamerling
Overture on Ice	ANHFP 1983 Sarah Elder/Leonard Kamerling
Every Day Choices	ANHFP 1985 Sarah Elder/Leonard Kamerling
From the Elders	ANHFP 1987 Katrina Waters/Sarah Elder/Leonard Kamerling

Uksuum Cauyai:		
Drums of Winter	ANHFP 1989	Sarah Elder/Leonard Kamerling
Inuit	Bo Boudart 1977	Bo Boudart (P&D)
Hunger Knows No Law	Bo Boudart 1978	Bo Boudart (P&D)
The Sea Is Our Life	Bo Boudart 1979	Bo Boudart (P&D)
Umealit, the Whale Hunters	Time-Life Films 1980	Bo Boudart (P)/Russell Gilman (D)
Rope to Our Roots	Inuit Life Foundation 1981	Bo Boudart (P&D)
Stebbins Kotlik Potlatch	Kawerak 1979	Kawerak Adult Basic Education Services
Village of No River	Newark Museum 1981	Stuart Hersh (P&D)/Barbara Lipton (W)
Agnes of Tununak	Alaska Film Studies 1981	
No Word for Rape	1981	M. R. Katzke (P&D)
You Can't Grow Potatoes Up There!	Kinetic Film Enterprise 1981	
Iñupiatun: In the Manner of the Eskimo	1981	Peter Haynes/Harold Tichenor (P&D)
21st Annual World Eskimo-Indian Olympics	PBS 1983	Skip Blumberg (P&D)
Alaska: The Yup'ik Eskimos	Chevron USA 1985	Larry Landsburgh (P&D)/Gail Evanari (P)
Shungnak: A Village Profile	Northwest Arctic TV Center 1985	Daniel Housberg (D)
Iñupiat Eskimo Healing Series	Northwest Arctic TV Center 1985	Nellie Moore (P)/Daniel Housberg (D)
Iñupiat Legends of the Northwest Arctic Series	Northwest Arctic TV Center (ongoing)	
Iñupiat Eskimo Technology Series	Northwest Arctic TV Center	
The People of Ukpiagvik	University of Alaska Anchorage 1985	Bob Jenkins/Carrol Hodge (P&D)
Inua: Return of the Spirit	Alaska Department of Education 1985	
Issues of Native Self Governance	University of Alaska Division of Media Services 1987	
The Last Hunters	BBC Enterprises 1988	Graham Johnston (P)
The Reindeer Queen	Alaska Public TV 1991	Marie Brooks (P&D)
Alaska Native Spirit Profiles	Syntax Productions 1991	

KYUK Video Productions

The Way We Live
  (4-part series)   KYUK 1981 Steve Gaber/John McDonald/Alexie Isaac

   Blackfish Trapping
   The Way Dance Sticks
     Were Used
   The Way They Have Seal
     Party Years Ago
   The Way They Used Dog
     Mushing for Living

St. Marys Potlatch	KYUK 1981	Alexie Isaac
Russian Mission, Yukon	KYUK 1982	Alexie Isaac
They Never Asked Our Fathers	KYUK 1982	John McDonald/Corey Flintoff/Alexie Isaac
Archaeology Series	KYUK 1983	Steve Gaber/John McDonald/Alexie Isaac
Somebody's Taking Pictures	KYUK 1983	Corey Flintoff/John McDonald
Racing the Wind	KYUK 1983	Corey Flintoff/John McDonald
The People of Kashunak	KYUK 1983	William Sharpsteen
A Matter of Trust	KYUK 1983	William Sharpsteen/Byran Murray
Yup'ik Schoolroom	KYUK 1983	William Sharpsteen
Traditional Migration	KYUK 1983	William Sharpsteen
Long Distance Medicine	KYUK 1983	William Sharpsteen
A Dancing People	KYUK 1983	Alexie Isaac/Corey Flintoff
Eyes of the Spirit	KYUK 1983	Alexie Isaac/Corey Flintoff
Old Dances, New Dances	KYUK 1984	Mike Martz
Just a Small Fishery	KYUK 1984	Mike Martz/Richard Goldstein
Yup'ik Antigone	KYUK 1985	John McDonald/Alexie Isaac
Parlez-vous Yup'ik?	KYUK 1985	John McDonald/Richard Goldstein
From Hand to Hand: Bethel Native Artist Profiles	KYUK 1985	Gretchen McManus
We of the River	KYUK 1985	John McDonald/Richard Goldstein
The Issue Is Children: Child Sexual Abuse	KYUK 1985	Richard Goldstein/Mike Martz
Hard Time and Treatment: Child Molesters	KYUK 1985	Richard Goldstein/Mike Martz

Revved Up, Roughed Up:		
Three Wheelin' in Alaska	KYUK 1986	John McDonald/Richard Goldstein
Let's Eat (3-part series):	KYUK 1986	Richard Goldstein/Mike Martz
Harvest of the Seasons		
Making Choices		
The Price You Pay		
Siberian Odyssey	KYUK 1987	
Legends of the Tundra	KYUK 1987	
Living and Working in		
Bethel, Alaska:		
The PHS Hospital	KYUK 1987	Chuck Bradley/Richard Goldstein
Crossing Paths:		
Artists in the Schools	KYUK 1987	Gretchen McManus/Richard Goldstein
Just Dancing	KYUK 1987	Alexie Isaac
1987 Yup'ik Dance Festival	KYUK 1987	Alexie Isaac
Following the Star	KYUK 1987	Alexie Isaac
One Vision, Many Voices	KYUK 1988	Mike Martz/Richard Goldstein
The Kanakanak Hospital	KYUK 1989	Richard Trotto
Cross on the Yukon	KYUK 1990	Mike Martz/Richard Goldstein
The Toughest Trail	KYUK 1991	Richard Trotto/ Mike Lane
Drowning:		
Can We Turn the Tide?	KYUK 1991	Rhonda McBride
The Fastest Trail	KYUK 1992	Richard Trotto/Mike Lane
Camai Dance Festival		
Highlights	KYUK 1992	Dean Swope
Having Your Baby in Bethel	KYUK 1992	Richard Totto
Tales of the Tundra	KYUK 1993	Richard Trotto, Jerry Brigham
A Video for all Seasons	KYUK 1984, 1985, 1986, 1988, 1990, 1991, 1992,	
	1993 Various Producers	

Viewing Facilities:

Motion Picture, Broadcasting and Recorded Sound Division, Library of Congress

Film and Television Archive, University of California Los Angeles

Media Services, Rasmuson Library, University of Alaska Fairbanks

Museum of Modern Art Film Archives

George Eastman House, Rochester, New York

REFERENCES

Aberle, David
1982   *Peyote Religion among the Navaho.* Chicago: University of Chicago Press.

Agos, Alicia
1993   "Pulling Together the Rural Alaska News." *Anchorage Daily News,* "We Alaskans," January 31, p. F-5.

Alaska Journal (Anchorage)
1984   "The Alaska-Yukon-Pacific Exposition of 1909: Photographs by Frank Nowell." Summer, pp. 8-14.

Alaska State Film Library
1989   Letter from Gordon Hills. May 17. Anchorage.

Alexander, Rosemarie
1992   Cultural Impact of Television on Indigenous Alaskans. Project Description, School of Journalism, Michigan State University.

Allen, Everett S.
1962   *Arctic Odyssey: The Life of Rear Admiral Donald B. MacMillan.* New York: Dodd, Mead and Company.

American Museum
1909   "The Mural Decorations of the Eskimo Hall." *American Museum Journal* 9(7):211-26.

Anchorage Daily News
1988   "A People in Peril." Newspaper series. January-February.

Arnold, Gary
1974   "The White Dawn." Film review. *The Post* (Broadcasting and Recorded Sound Division, Library of Congress, Washington, D.C.).

Balikci, Asen
1984   "Illustres Sauvages." *Le Monde Aujourd'hui.* July 15-16.
1986   "Anthropologists and Ethnographic Filmmaking." Manuscript. University of Montreal, Quebec.
1989   "Anthropology, Film and the Arctic Peoples: The First Forman Lecture." *Anthropology Today* 5(2): 4-10.
1989   *Arctic Dreams.* Film script. Commission on Visual Anthropology, University of Montreal, Quebec, Canada.

Balikci, Asen, and Quentin Brown
1966   "Ethnographic Filming and the Netsilik Eskimos." In *Educational Services Incorporated Quarterly Report* (Spring-Summer), pp. 19-23. Newton, Mass.: Educational Services, Inc.

Barnouw, Erik
1983   *Documentary: A History of the Non-Fiction Film.* Oxford: Oxford University Press.

Bataille, Gretchen M., and Charles L. P. Silet
1980   *The Pretend Indians: Images of Native Americans in the Movies.* Ames: Iowa State University Press.

Beach, Rex
1906   *The Spoilers.* New York: Harper and Brothers.
1909   *The Silver Horde.* New York: Harper and Brothers.

Beaglehole, J. C., ed.
1967   *The Voyage of the Resolution and Discovery, 1776-1780.* Cambridge: The University Press.

Beechey, Frederick W.
1832   *Narrative of a Voyage to the Pacific and Beering's Strait to Co-operate with the Polar Expeditions; Performed in His Majesty's Ship "Blossom," under the Command of Captain F. W. Beechey, in the Years 1825, 26, 27, 28.* 2 vols. London: Colburn and Bentley.

Benedict, Burton
1983   *The Anthropology of World's Fairs: San Francisco's Panama Pacific International Exposition of 1915.* Lowie Museum of Anthropology. Berkeley, Calif.: Scholar Press.

Berkhofer, Robert F., Jr.
1978   *The White Man's Indian: Images of the American Indian from Columbus to the Present.* New York: Alfred Knopf.

Berthon, Ted Le
1932   "An Eskimo Beholds Hollywood." *The New Movie Magazine,* May, p. 12.

Billington, Linda
1993   "Hollywoodisms Cast a Shadow on 'Eskimo' Movie." *Anchorage Daily News,* April 9, p. H-9.

Blackman, Harold
1945   "The Mukluk Shuffle." *Alaska Sportsman,* July, p. 18.

Blackman, Margaret B.
1989   *Sadie Brower Neakok: An Iñupiaq Woman.* Seattle: University of Washington Press; Vancouver, B.C.: Douglas and McIntyre.

Bliss, Laura
1992   "KYUK: Broadcasting from Bethel." Television program for Channel 2 News (Anchorage), April 6.

Bloom, Daniel
1990 "Letter to the Editor." *Tundra Times* (Anchorage), June 18, pp. 2-3.

Bodenhorn, Barbara
1990 "'I'm Not the Great Hunter, My Wife Is': Iñupiat and Anthropological Models of Gender." *Études/Inuit/Studies* 14(1-2):55-74.

Bongard, David
1952 "Lost in Alaska." Film review. *Los Angeles Daily News,* August 14.

Boyum, Joy Gould
1974 "From an Epic of Adventure to Tragedy." Film review. *Wall Street Journal,* July 29.

Breen, Joseph
1951 Letter to Petroff. January 26. Production Code Administration censorship files on *Red Snow.* Special Collections, Academy of Motion Picture Arts and Sciences.
1952 Letter to William Gordon. December 30. Production Code Administration censorship files on *Back to God's Country.* Special Collections, Academy of Motion Picture Arts and Sciences.

Briggs, Jean
1983 "Review of *Village of No River." American Anthropologist* 85(1):234.

Brigham, Jerry
1991 "Tundra Terror Theater: From Rats to RATNET. *KYUK Anniversary Edition,* September 26, p. 8. Bethel Broadcasting, Inc., Bethel, Alaska.

Brower, Charles
n.d. "The Northernmost America: An Autobiography." Typescript, 895 pp. Stefansson Collection, Dartmouth College Library.

Brownlow, Kevin
1979 *The War, the West, and the Wilderness.* New York: Alfred Knopf.

Buliard, Roger
1951 *Inuk.* New York: Farrar, Straus, and Young, Inc.

Burch, Ernest S., Jr.
1974 "Eskimo Warfare in Northwest Alaska." *Anthropological Papers of the University of Alaska* 16(2):1-14.
1975 *Eskimo Kinsmen: Changing Family Relations in Northwest Alaska.* American Ethnological Society Monograph 59. San Francisco: West.
1980 "Traditional Eskimo Societies in Northwest Alaska." *Senri Ethnological Studies* 4:253-304.
1988 *The Eskimo.* Norman: University of Oklahoma Press.

Burroughs, John
1904 "In Green Alaska." In John Burroughs, *Far and Near.* Boston: Houghton, Mifflin and Company.

Burton, Mary June
1937 "The Clock Never Stops for Priests." *Los Angeles Times Sunday Magazine,* May 2, p. 4.

Calder-Marshall, Arthur
1963 *The Innocent Eye: The Life of Robert J. Flaherty.* London: W. H. Allen and Company.

Cameron, Kate
1936 "A Spirited Farce on the Capitol Screen." *News,* March 21.

Campbell
1894 *Campbell's Illustrated History of the World's Columbian Exposition.* Vol. 1. Boston: E. Gately and Company.

Cannom, Robert
1948 *Van Dyke and the Mythical City of Hollywood.* Culver City, Calif.: Murray and Gee, Inc.

Carey, Richard Adams
1987 "On the Corner of Hollywood and Quinhagak." *Harvard Magazine,* September-October, pp. 10-15.

Carpenter, Edmund
1972 *Oh! What a Blow That Phantom Gave Me.* New York: Holt, Rinehart and Winston.

Carrighar, Sally
1953 *Icebound Summer.* New York: Alfred Knopf.

Chalfen, Richard
1992 "Discovery and Resistance Conference." *American Anthropological Association Newsletter* 33(9):15.

Champlin, Charles
1974 "White Dawn of the Eskimo's Despoliation." *Los Angeles Times,* July 21.

Chance, Norman
1984 "Alaska Eskimo Modernization." In *The Handbook of North American Indians,* vol 5: *Arctic,* ed. David Damas, pp. 646-56. Washington, D.C.: Smithsonian Institution.

Christopher, Robert
1988 "Narrators of the Arctic." *American Review of Canadian Studies* 18(3):259-69.

Clifford, James
1988 *The Predicament of Culture: Twentieth-Century Ethnography, Literature, and Art.* Cambridge: Harvard University Press.

Clifton, James, ed.

1989 *Being and Becoming Indian: Biographical Studies of North American Frontiers.* Chicago: Dorsey Press.

Coles, Robert

1977 "Distances." In Robert Coles, *The Last and First Eskimos.* Boston: New York Graphic Society.

Colin, Susi

1987 "The Wild Man and the Indian in Early Sixteenth Century Book Illustration." In *Indians and Europe: An Interdisciplinary Collection of Essays,* ed. Christian F. Feest. Aachen, Germany: Rader-Verlag.

Collier, John Jr.

1973 *Alaskan Eskimo Education: A Film Analysis of Cultural Confrontation in the Schools.* Case Studies in Education and Culture. George and Louise Spindler, general editors. New York: Holt, Rinehart and Winston, Inc.

Collins, Henry B., Jr.

1984 "History of Research Before 1945." In *Handbook of North American Indians,* vol. 5: *Arctic,* ed. David Damas, pp. 8-16. Washington, D.C.: Smithsonian Institution.

Condon, Richard G.

1989 "The History and Development of Arctic Photography." *Arctic Anthropology* 26(1):46-87.

Cook, James, and James King

1784 *A Voyage to the Pacific Ocean.* 3 vols. and atlas. London: G. Nicol and T. Cadell.

Coons, Robbin

1932 "Hot Weather Release Due for *Igloo.*" Mala Collection, University of Alaska Archives, Anchorage.

Crantz, David.

1767 *The History of Greenland.* 2 vols. London: Brethren's Society.

Creed, John, and Susan Andrews

1990 "Aleut Thespian Lands First Big Break in Home State. *Tundra Drums,* November 29, pp. 14-15. Bethel, Alaska.

1990 "Hollywood Movie Shot in Kotzebue Profiles Two Cultures." *Tundra Drums,* November 29, p. 15. Bethel, Alaska.

Crewe, Regina

1933 "Review of *Eskimo.*" *New York Times,* November 16.

Cross, Charles R.

1992 "Where the Hell Is Cicely, Alaska?" *Anchorage Daily News,* "We Alaskans," June 7, p. C-10.

Curran, Hugh

1993 "Hollywood's Looking for the Real Thing." *Anchorage Daily News,* May 9, p. B-1.

Curwood, James

1919 *Swift Lightning: A Story of Wild-Life Adventure in the Frozen North.* New York: Grosset and Dunlap.

Daily News Staff

1991 "Didn't Robert Redford Start Out This Way?" *Anchorage Daily News,* August 6, p. B-6.

Damas, David

1984 "Introduction." In *Handbook of North American Indians,* vol. 5: *Arctic,* ed. David Damas, pp. 1-7. Washington, D.C.: Smithsonian Institution.

de Brigard, Emilie

1975 "The History of Ethnographic Film." In *Principles of Visual Anthropology,* ed. Paul Hockings, pp. 13-43. Paris: Mouton Publishers.

Delehanty, Thornton

1936 "Drab Comedy at the Capital." *Post,* March 21.

Deloria, Vine, Jr.

1989 "Fantasy and Technique: The Indian Realities of Michael Harner and Lynn Andrews." Paper presented at the Eighty-eighth Annual Meeting of the American Anthropological Association, Washington, D.C.

Devlin, Theresa Demientieff

1989 "Life at the Mission Was Exciting, but Nothing Could Top Seeing Mom and Dad." *Tundra Times* (Anchorage), August 21, pp. 8-9.

Doogan, Mike

1990 "There's More Cartoon in the Eskimo than Eskimo in the Cartoon." *Anchorage Daily News,* December 28, p. E-1.

1994 "On Deadly Movie: Steven Seagal Makes an Accidental Classic." *Anchorage Daily News,* February 25.

Dorr, John H.

1974 "White Dawn." Film review. *Hollywood Reporter* (Los Angeles, Calif.), July 17.

Ducker, James H.

1989 "Out of Harm's Way." Manuscript. Anchorage, Alaska.

1991 "Curriculum for a New Culture: Federal Schooling at Bethel and Along the Kuskokwim." Paper prepared for the Bureau of Land Management, Anchorage, Alaska.

Education Development Center

1968 The Netsilik Eskimos Series. Cambridge,

Mass.: Education Development Center, Inc.

Enge, Marilee.
1994   "Seagal's *On Deadly Ground* Beats up Believ-
        ability." *Anchorage Daily News,* February 23.

Faubion, Michael
1992   "New York Film Crew Documents Story of
        Yup'ik Bible." *Tundra Drums* (Bethel, Alaska),
        June 18, p. 9.
1992   "Family Company Brings Family Film-
        making to Delta." *Tundra Drums* (Bethel,
        Alaska), July 30, p. 21.

Fienup-Riordan, Ann
1983   *The Nelson Island Eskimo.* Anchorage: Alaska
        Pacific University Press.
1984   "Regional Groups on the Yukon-Kuskokwim
        Delta." In *The Central Yup'ik Eskimos,* ed.
        Ernest S. Burch, Jr. Supplementary issue of
        Études/Inuit/Studies 8:63-93.
1986a   *When Our Bad Season Comes: A Cultural
        Account of Subsistence Harvesting and Harvest
        Disruption on the Yukon Delta.* Prepared for
        the Alaska Council on Science and Technol-
        ogy. Aurora vol. 1. Alaska Anthropological
        Association.
1986b   "The Real People: The Concept of
        Personhood among the Yup'ik Eskimos of
        Western Alaska." *Études/Inuit/Studies* 10(1-
        2):261-70.
1988   *The Yup'ik Eskimos as Described in the Travel
        Journals and Ethnographic Accounts of John
        and Edith Kilbuck, 1885-1900.* Kingston,
        Ontario: Limestone Press.
1990   *Eskimo Essays: Yup'ik Lives and How We See
        Them.* New Brunswick, N.J.: Rutgers Univer-
        sity Press.
1991   *The Real People and the Children of Thunder:
        The Yup'ik Eskimo Encounter with Moravian
        Missionaries John and Edith Kilbuck.* Norman:
        University of Oklahoma Press.

Films North
1973   *The Alaskan Eskimo: A Way of Life.* Filmscript.
        Anchorage, Alaska.

Fitzhugh, William W., and Aron Crowell
1988   *Crossroads of Continents: Cultures of Siberia
        and Alaska.* Washington, D.C.: Smithsonian
        Institution Press.

Flaherty, Frances
1960   *The Odyssey of a Filmmaker: Robert Flaherty's
        Story:* Urbana, Ill.: Beta Phi Mu.

Flaherty, Robert
1949   BBC Talk, London, July 24.
1950   *Robert Flaherty Talking in Cinema 1950.*

Edited by Roger Manvell. London: Pelican

Fortuine, Robert
1989   *Chills and Fever: Health and Disease in the
        Early History of Alaska.* Fairbanks: University
        of Alaska Press.

Freedman, Donna
1990a   "Hollywood in Kotzebue." *Anchorage Daily
        News,* October 30, p. H-2.
1990b   "Readers to L.A. Producers of *Northern
        Exposure:* 'Get Real.'" *Anchorage Daily News,*
        July 23, p. D-2.
1991   "*Salmonberries* Wins Top Prize at Film Fest."
        Anchorage Daily News, September 5, p. G-3.

Freuchen, Peter
1929   *Die Flucht ins Weisse Land.* Berlin: Safari-
        Verlag.
1931   *Eskimo.* New York: Grossett and Dunlap.
1953   *Vagrant Viking: My Life and Adventures.*
        Trans. Johan Hambro. New York: Julian
        Messner, Inc.

Gilbert, Susan
1989   "Film Notes." In *Changing Views: Filming the
        Peoples of the North Pacific Rim.* National
        Museum of Natural History and Human
        Studies Film Archives, Smithsonian Institu-
        tion.

Gilbreth, Frank Jr., and Ernestine Gilbreth Carey
1948   *Cheaper by the Dozen.* New York: Harper and
        Row.

Ginsburg, Faye
1991   "Indigenous Media: Faustian Contract or
        Global Village?" *Cultural Anthropology* 6(1):
        92-112.

Gordon, George Byron
1906-7 "Notes on the Western Eskimo." *Transac-
        tions of the Free Museum of Science and Art
        (University of Pennsylvania)* 2:69-101.

Graburn, Nelson
1969   *Eskimos without Igloos: Social and Economic
        Development in Sugluk.* Boston: Little Brown.
1982   "Television and the Canadian Inuit." *Études/
        Inuit/Studies* 6(1):7-17.

Grierson, John
1932   "First Principles of Documentary." *Cinema
        Quarterly* (Winter).

Griffith, Richard
1953   *The World of Robert Flaherty.* New York:
        Duell, Sloan and Pearce.

Griffiths, George H., and Carolyn Ramsey
1942   *The Eskimos: Teacher's Handbook for Use with
        the Instructional Sound Film "Eskimo Chil-
        dren".* New York: ERPI Classroom Films, Inc.

Hakluyt, Richard
1589 *The Principal Navigations, Voyages, Traffiques and Discoveries of the English Nation in Twelve Volumes.* Vol. 7. Reprint. New York: Augustus M. Kelley, 1969.

Hall, Mordaunt
1933 "Drama of the Frozen North." *New York Times Film Review,* November 15, p. 1000.
1933 "Review of *S.O.S. Iceberg.*" *The New York Times,* September 25.

Hall, Stuart
1992 "Cultural Studies and Its Theoretical Legacies." In *Cultural Studies,* ed. L. Grossberg, C. Nelson, and P. Treichler. pp. 277-94. New York: Routledge.

Haraway, Donna
1989 *Primate Visions: Gender, Race, and Nature in the World of Modern Science.* New York: Routledge.
1992 "Primate Re-visions." Paper presented at the Ninety-first Annual Meeting of the American Anthropological Association, San Francisco.

Harper, Kenn
1986 *Give Me My Father's Body: The Life of Minik, the New York Eskimo.* Frobisher Bay, NWT.:Blacklead Books.

Harris, Christopher
1993 "A World-class Movie Mess." *Globe Mail* (Toronto), March 10, p. A-9.

Healy, Michael A.
1887 "Report of the Cruise of the Steamer 'Corwin.'" In *Report of the Cruise of the Revenue Marine Steamer 'Corwin' in the Arctic Ocean, 1885,* pp. 5-20. Washington, D.C.: U.S. Government Printing Office.
1889 *Report of the Cruise of the Revenue Marine Steamer 'Corwin' in the Arctic Ocean in the Year 1884.* Washington, D.C.: U.S. Government Printing Office.

Hegeman, Susan
1989 "History, Ethnography, Myth: Some Notes on the 'Indian Centered' Narrative." *Social Text* 18(2):144-60.

Heider, Karl G.
1976 *Ethnographic Film.* Austin: University of Texas Press.

Herald (Los Angeles)
1949 "*Arctic Fury.*" Film review. October 1.

Hill, Robin Mackey
1994 "Producer Takes 'Heartbeat' to Viewers Nationwide," *The Tundra Drums* (Bethel, Alaska), May 5, p. 27.

Hockings, Paul
1975 *Principles of Visual Anthropology.* The Hague: Mouton Publishers.

Hollywood Citizen News (Los Angeles)
1961 "Anthony Quinn Fine in Film on Eskimos." February 16.

Hollywood Reporter (Los Angeles)
1933 "'*Eskimo*' Is Great." October 16.
1949 "Arctic Film: '*Flying Doctor*' Lost in Icy Wilderness." May 6.
1953 "The Alaskan Eskimo." March 4.

Hollywood Spectator (Los Angeles)
1933 "Van Dyke Shoots a Saga." December 9.

Hooper, Calvin L.
1881 *Report of the Cruise of the U.S. Revenue Steamer Corwin in the Arctic Ocean, November 1, 1880.* Washington, D.C.: U.S. Government Printing Office.

Houston, James
1971 *White Dawn.* New York: Harcourt Brace Jovanovich.

Hubbard Collection
1991 Biographical Sketch of Bernard Hubbard, S.J. Box I, f. 42. Santa Clara University Archives, Santa Clara, Calif.

Hughes, Charles C., ed.
1972 *Make Men of Them: Introductory Readings for Cultural Anthropology.* Chicago: Rand McNally and Company.

Hunter, Don
1992 "Swedish Chain-Saw Company Films Igloo Commercial." *Anchorage Daily News,* November 1, p. B-7.

Idiens, Dale
1987 "Eskimos in Scotland." In *Indians and Europe,* ed. Christian F. Feest. Aachen, Germany: Rader Verlag.

Jacobson, Steven
1984 *Yup'ik Eskimo Dictionary.* Fairbanks: Alaska Native Language Center, University of Alaska.

Jody, Marilyn
1969 "Alaska in the American Literary Imagination: A Literary History of Frontier Alaska with a Bibliographical Guide to the Study of Alaska Literature." Ph.D. diss., Department of English, Indiana University.

Johnson, Erskine
1933 "*Eskimo* Vivid Story of Primitive Passions." *Los Angeles Times,* November 25.

Johnson, Susan Hackley
1979 "When Moviemakers Look North." *Alaska Journal* (Winter), pp. 12-23.

Joseph, Robert

1949 "Revised Arctic Saga Becomes Hot Property." *New York Times,* July 17.

Kan, Sergei

1988 "The Russian Orthodox Church in Alaska." In *Handbook of North American Indians,* vol. 4: *History of Indian-White Relations,* ed. Wilcomb Washburn, pp. 506-21. Washington, D.C.: Smithsonian Institution.

Kane, Elisha Kent

1856 *Arctic Explorations.* 2 vols. Philadelphia: Childs and Peterson.

Kennedy, Geoff

1992 "Some Roles Still Up in Cable Movie 'Spirit Dog.'" *Tundra Drums* (Bethel, Alaska), January 21, p. 20.

1992 "Actors Take a Shot at Eskimo Roles." *Tundra Drums* (Bethel, Alaska), December 24, p. 4.

Kennedy, Timothy

1971 "SKYRIVER: An Experiment in Change." *The Village Voice* (New York) 1(4):1-2.

1982 "Beyond Advocacy: A Facilitative Approach to Public Participation." *Journal of the University Film and Video Association* 34(3):33-46.

Kilbuck, Edith

1890 Journal to her father, January 17. Kilbuck Collection, Moravian Archives, Bethlehem, Pennsylvania.

King, Jonathan

1990 "Eskimos at Expos: The Development of an Enduring Stereotype at Expositions in the United States, 1893-1909." Paper presented at the Seventh Inuit Studies Conference, Fairbanks, Alaska.

Kipling, Rudyard

1895 *The Second Jungle Book.* New York: Century Company.

Knight, Arthur

1961 "Review of *The Savage Innocents.*" *The Saturday Review,* January 28.

Koepping, Gerrit

1993 "Ketchikan Artist Weaves Cedar Clothes for Disney." *Ketchikan Daily News* (reprinted in *Anchorage Daily News,* July 20, p. E-4).

Kotzebue, Otto von

1821 *A Voyage of Discovery into the South Sea and Beering's Straits for the Purpose of Exploring a North-East Passage, Undertaken in the Years 1815-1818.* 3 vols. London: Longman, Hurst, Rees, Orme, and Brown.

Krauss, Michael E.

1980 *Alaskan Native Languages: Past, Present and Future.* Fairbanks: Alaska Native Language Center, University of Alaska.

Kretch, Shepard III

1989 *A Victorian Earl in the Arctic: The Travels and Collections of the Fifth Earl of Lonsdale, 1888-89.* Seattle: University of Washington Press.

KYUK-TV, Bethel (Alaska) Broadcasting Inc.

1991 "Yup'ik Interviews Gather Wisdom of Elders." *KYUK Anniversary Edition,* September 26, p. 17.

Lantis, Margaret

1984 "Aleut." In *Handbook of North American Indians,* vol. 5: *Arctic,* ed. David Damas, pp. 161-84. Washington, D.C.: Smithsonian Institution.

Lee, Stacy L.

1990a "Locals Livid Over Lang's Subsistence Views." *Arctic Sounder* (Kotzebue, Alaska) 15 (16), November 21.

1990b "Extras, extras, read all about it! You can be in a local movie." *Arctic Sounder* (Kotzebue, Alaska) 15 (13), October 10.

London, Jack

1902 *Children of the Frost.* New York: Macmillan Company.

1903 *The Call of the Wild.* New York: Macmillan Company.

1905 *White Fang.* New York: Macmillan Company.

Los Angeles Times

1934 "They Willingly Share Their Wives." Part 4, p. 16. Annual Midwinter Number.

1948 "Earth's Ends Unearth Talent for Hollywood." December 12.

1949 "Eskimo Girl Flies Here for Movie Role." December 1, p. I-10.

Low, Rachel

1949 *History of the British Film,* vol. 2: 1906-14. London: Allen and Unwin.

Loy, Wesley

1992 "Lights, Camera, Alaska! Filmmakers Say It's Worth the Effort." *Anchorage Daily News,* September 6, pp. E-1, 9, 11.

1993 "Hollywood Discovers New Star in Alaska." *Alaska: The Magazine of Life on the Last Frontier* (Anchorage), March, pp. 28-35.

Lyon, George F.

1824 *The Private Journal of Captain G. F. Lyon.* London: John Murray.

Mala, Ray

1929 "Modern Eskimos." Manuscript. Mala Collection, University of Alaska Anchorage, Archives.

Malaurie, Jean
1982 *The Last Kings of Thule.* Trans. Adrienne Foulke. Chicago: University of Chicago Press.
Marcus, George E., and Michael M. J. Fischer
1985 *Anthropology as Cultural Critique: An Experimental Moment in the Human Sciences.* Chicago: University of Chicago Press.
Marsden, Michael T., and Jack G. Nachbar
1988 "The Indian in the Movies." In *Handbook of North American Indians,* vol. 4: *History of Indian-White Relations,* ed. Wilcomb E. Washburn, pp. 607-16. Washington, D.C.: Smithsonian Institution.
McBride, Rhonda
1991 "Broadcasting on the Last Frontier." *KYUK Anniversary Edition,* September 26, p. 2. Bethel Broadcasting, Inc., Bethel, Alaska.
1991 "Reporter Finds Bush News Full of Daily Surprises." *KYUK Anniversary Edition,* September 26, pp. 6, 21. Bethel Broadcasting, Inc., Bethel, Alaska.
McCall's Magazine
1960 "The Savage Innocents." Film review. December.
Michael, Henry N., ed.
1967 *Lieutenant Zagoskin's Travels in Russian America, 1842-1844.* Toronto: University of Toronto Press.
Michaels, Eric
1985a "How Video Has Helped a Group of Aborigines in Australia." *Media Development* 1:16018.
1985b "Constraints on Knowledge in an Economy of Oral Information." *Current Anthropology* 26(4):505-10.
Mikkelson, Ejnar
1922 *Frozen Justice.* New York: Alfred Knopf.
Milotte, Alfred
1946 Journal. Milotte Collection, Alaska and Polar Regions Department, Rasmuson Library, University of Alaska Fairbanks.
1949 Letter to Don Foster, Alaska Native Service, July 17. Box 3, Milotte Collection, Alaska and Polar Regions Department, Rasmuson Library, University of Alaska Fairbanks.
Mishkin, Leo
1936 "Screen Presents: *Petticoat Fever* Returns to B'way, A Slight Farce Made Cute by Movies. *Morning Telegraph,* March 21.
Morin, Edgar
1956 *Le Cinéma ou l'homme imaginaire.* Paris: Les Editions de Minuit.

Morrow, Phyllis, and Chase Hensel
1992 "Hidden Dissension: Minority-Majority Relationships and the Use of Contested Terminology." *Arctic Anthropology* 29(1):39-53
Mowat, Farley
1963 *Never Cry Wolf.* New York: Atlantic Monthly Press.
Muir, John
1917 *The Cruise of the Corwin,* ed. William F. Bade. New York: Houghton Mifflin.
Murdoch, John
1887 "On Some Popular Errors in Regard to Eskimos." *American Naturalist* 21:9-16.
1892 "Ethnological Results of the Point Barrow Expedition." *Ninth Annual Report of the Bureau of Ethnology for the Years 1887-1888.* Reprinted 1983. Washington, D.C.: Smithsonian Institution Press.
Napoleon, Harold
1990 "Yuuyaraq: The Way of the Human Being." *Northern Notes* 3(May):1-35.
Nelson, Edward W.
1882 "A Sledge Journey in the Delta of the Yukon, Northern Alaska." *Proceedings of the Royal Geographical Society* (n.s.) 4:669-70.
1899 *The Eskimo about Bering Strait.* Bureau of American Ethnology Annual Report for 1896-1897, vol. 18, no. 1. Reprinted 1983. Washington, D.C.: Smithsonian Institution.
New York American
1934 "Review of Eskimo."
New York Herald Tribune
1961 "Icy Hunt for Food and Love." January 15.
New York Times
1932 "Igloo." Film review, July 2, p. 845.
1940 "Girl From God's Country." Film review. December 9, p. 1731.
Norris, Frank
1992 "Popular Images in the North in Literature and Film." *Northern Review* (Yukon College, Whitehorse, NWT) 8-9:53-82.
Office of Telecommunications, Juneau
1975a *Alaska Education Experiment: Final Report Executive Summary.* Alaska ATS-6 Health/ Education Telecommunications Experiment. Office of the Governor of the State of Alaska.
1975b *Alaska Education Experiment: Final Report, vol. 1.* Alaska ATS-6 Health/Education Telecommunications Experiment. Office of the Governor of the State of Alaska.

Oliver, W. E.

1932 "'Igloo' True, Powerful Story of Eskimo Tribe." *Los Angeles Evening Herald and Express,* June 1.

Oswalt, Wendell H.

1979 *Eskimos and Explorers.* Novato, Calif.: Chandler and Sharp.

1990 *Bashful No Longer: An Alaskan Eskimo Ethnohistory, 1778-1988.* Norman: University of Oklahoma Press.

Owletuck, George N.

1991 Letter to the Editor. *Tundra Times* (Anchorage, Alaska), November 11, p. 3.

Paramount Pictures

1974 Press Book for *White Dawn.* Los Angeles.

Parry, William E.

1828 *Journals of the First, Second and Third Voyages for the Discovery of a North-West Passage.* 5 vols. London: John Murray.

Patkotak, Elise Sereni

1990 "Barrow Goes Hollywood: Tinseltown on the Ice." *Northland News* (Fairbanks, Alaska) 6(6):4-7.

Pearce, Roy Harvey

1953 *Savagism and Civilization: A Study of the Indian and the American Mind.* Baltimore: Johns Hopkins University Press.

Peary, Robert E.

1898 *Northward over the Great Ice.* New York: Frederick A. Stokes.

1910 *The North Pole.* New York: Frederick A. Stokes.

Pelswick, Rose

1936 "*Petticoat Fever:* Charming People Perform in Diverting Picture Shown at Capitol." *Evening Journal,* March 21.

Phillips, Natalie

1992 "Doctors Find Cicely Is All in Their Heads." *Anchorage Daily News,* July 21, p. A-1.

Pratt, Kenneth L.

1984 "Classification of Eskimo Groupings in the Yukon-Kuskokwim Region: A Critical Analysis." In *The Central Yup'ik Eskimos,* ed. Ernest S. Burch, Jr. Supplementary issue of *Études/Inuit/Studies* 8:45-61.

Preloran, Jorge

1975 "Documenting the Human Condition." In *Principles of Visual Anthropology,* ed. Paul Hockings, pp. 103-7. Paris: Mouton Publishers.

Price, John A.

1973 "The Stereotyping of North American Indians in Motion Pictures." *Ethnohistory* 20(2):153-71.

Prucha, Francis P.

1988 "Two Roads to Conversion: Protestant and Catholic Missionaries in the Pacific Northwest." *Pacific Northwest Quarterly* 79(4):130-37.

Pytte, Alyson

1991 "Eskimo Pie Gets a Genuine Eskimo: The Ice Cream Bar Was Born in Iowa; the TV Actor Was Born in Shishmaref." *Anchorage Daily News,* November 12, p. A-1.

Rechetnik, Sidney

1960 "The Savage Innocents." Film review. *Motion Picture World,* October 1. Los Angeles.

Rock, Howard

1962 "Arctic Survival: Inaccurate Textbooks Create Igloo Myths in Alaska." *Tundra Times* (Anchorage, Alaska), November 19. (reprinted January 23, 1974).

Rogers, George W.

1969 "The Cross-cultural Economic Situation in the North: The Alaska Case." Paper presented at the Conference on Cross-cultural Education in the North, Montreal, Canada.

Rotha, Paul

1983 *Robert J. Flaherty: A Biography.* Philadelphia: University of Pennsylvania Press.

Rouch, Jean

1975 "The Camera and Man." In *Principles of Visual Anthropology,* ed. Paul Hockings, pp. 83-102. The Hague: Mouton Publishers.

Ruby, Jay

1979 "'The Aggie Will Come First': The Dymystification of Robert Flaherty." In *Robert Flaherty: Photographer/Filmmaker. The Inuit 1910-1922.* Vancouver, B.C.: Vancouver Art Gallery.

1980 "*Nanook of the North* Press Kit." *Studies in Visual Communication* 6(2):61-76.

1990 "Eye-Witnessing Humanism: Ethnography and Film." *Commission on Visual Anthropology Review,* Fall, pp. 12-16. Montreal, Canada.

1993 "The Viewer Viewed: The Reception of Ethnographic Films." Manuscript, Temple University, Mifflintown, Penn.

Ruesch, Hans

1950 *Top of the World.* New York: Pocketbook Edition, Simon and Schuster.

Ruskin, Evey

1984 "Memories of a Movie Star: Ray Mala's Life in Pictures." *Alaska Journal,* Spring, pp. 34-39.

Sadoul, Georges
1966 *Histore du cinéma mondial des origines a nos jours.* 8th ed. Paris: Flammarion.

Sahlins, Marshall
1985 *Islands of History.* Chicago: University of Chicago Press.

Said, Edward
1978 *Orientalism.* London: Pantheon.

Sharpsteen, Ben
1946 Letter to Alfred Milotte, August 13. Milotte Collection, Alaska and Polar Regions Department, Rasmuson Library, University of Alaska Fairbanks.

Sheehan, Henry
1993 "Filmmaker's Culture Shock Echoed in Tale of Eskimo." *Los Angeles Times Syndicate* (reprinted *Anchorage Daily News,* April 13, p. F-3).

Shinkwin, Anne D., and Mary Pete.
1984 "Yup'ik Eskimo Societies: A Case Study." In *The Central Yup'ik Eskimos,* ed. Ernest S. Burch, Jr. Supplementary issue of *Études/Inuit/Studies* 8:95-112.

Shurlock, Geoffrey
1959 Letter to Luigi Luraschi, Paramount Pictures. June 8. Production Code Administration censorship files on *Savage Innocents.* Special Collections, Academy of Motion Picture Arts and Sciences.

Simpson, John
1875 "The Western Eskimo." In *A Selection of Papers on Arctic Geography and Ethnology,* pp. 233-75. London: John Murray.

Smith, Cecil
1970 "Polar Bear Actors Discover the Arctic in Disney 2-parter." *Los Angeles Times TV News,* November 1.

Spokesman Review (Spokane, Wash.)
1939 "Glacier Priest to Speak Here." April 23.

Stage Magazine
1940 "The Wedding of Palo." Film review.

Stedman, Raymond William
1982 *Shadows of the Indian: Stereotypes in American Culture.* Norman: University of Oklahoma Press.

Stefansson, Vilhjalmur
1922 "Nanook of the North: An Educational Movie." Stefansson Papers, Mss. 98:36-10. Dartmouth College Library, Hanover, N.H.
1928 *The Standardization of Error.* London: Kegan Paul.

1932 "Igloo." Stefansson Papers, Mss. 98:36-6. Dartmouth College Library, Hanover, N.H.

Steward, Julian
1938 *Basin Plateau Aboriginal Sociopolitical Groups.* Bulletin 120, Bureau of American Ethnology, Smithsonian Institution. Washington, D.C.: U.S. Government Printing Office.

Stinson, Charles
1961 "*The Savage Innocents* Accurate but Awkward." *Los Angeles Times,* February 17.

Stoney, George M.
1900 *Naval Explorations in Alaska: An Account of Two Naval Expeditions to Northern Alaska, with Official Maps of the Country Explored.* Annapolis, Md.: U.S. Naval Institute.

Stromberg, Hunt
1932 Telegram to Ray Wise, July 22. Mala Collection, University of Alaska Anchorage Archives.

Sturtevant, William C., and David B. Quinn
1987 "This New Prey: Eskimos in Europe in 1567, 1576, 1577." In *Indians and Europe,* ed. Christian F. Feest ed. Aachen, Germany: Rader Verlag.

Teacher, Lawrence, and Richard E. Nicholls, eds.
1981 *The Unabridged Jack London.* Philadelphia: Running Press.

Tetpon, John
1991 "Film Depicts Natives as 'Good Guys.'" *Tundra Times* (Anchorage), July 15, p. 3.

Tilden, George
1933 "Into a White Hell for a Movie." Mala Collection, University of Alaska Anchorage, Archives.

Thomson, Lori
1991 "A Bit of Tinsel Town Livens the Day." *Anchorage Daily News,* July 30, p. B-6.

Tundra Drums (Bethel, Alaska)
1991 "KYUK Reporter Sends 'Berry Good' Message Over National Airwaves." September 5, p. 5.

Tundra Times (Anchorage)
1990 "Greatland Dancers Audition for 'Salmonberries' Movie." October 8, p. 7.
1991 "KYUK Wins Community Service Award." July 1, p. 6.
1991 "KYUK Radio Presents Yup'ik News Service." October 14, p. 8.
1993 "Grande Dame of Tourism: Helen Seveck Passes On." January 6, p. 1.

Turner, Terrance
1990 "Visual Media, Cultural Politics, and Anthropological Practice: Some Implications of

Recent Uses of Film and Video Among the Kayapo of Brazil." In *Commission on Visual Anthropology Review,* pp. 10-12, *Bulletin d'Information* (Spring), University of Montreal, Quebec.

Twitchell, Peter
1992 "Letter to the Editor: Powerful Voice." *Tundra Drums* (Bethel, Alaska), April 9, p. 3.

U.S. Department of Interior
1967 *Alaska Natural Resources and the Ramparts Project.* Washington, D.C.: U.S. Government Printing Office.

U.S. Federal Field Committee for Development Planning in Alaska.
1968 *Alaska Natives and the Land.* Washington, D.C.: U.S. Government Printing Office.

Van Valin, William
1941 *Eskimoland Speaks.* Caldwell, Idaho: Caxton Printers.

Vancouver Art Gallery
1979 *Robert Flaherty: Photographer/Filmmaker. The Inuit 1910-1922.* Vancouver, B.C.: Vancouver Art Gallery.

VanStone, James
1964 "Some Aspects of Religious Change Among Native Inhabitants in West Alaska and the Northwest Territories." *Arctic Anthropology* 2(2):21-24.
1973 "V. S. Khromchenko's Coastal Explorations in Southwestern Alaska, 1882." Trans. David H. Kraus. *Fieldiana: Anthropology* 64. Chicago: Field Museum of Natural History.
1977 "A. F. Kashevarov's Coastal Explorations in Northwest Alaska, 1838." Trans. David H. Kraus. *Fieldiana: Anthropology* 69. Chicago: Field Museum of Natural History.
1978 "E. W. Nelson's Notes on the Indians of the Yukon and Innoko Rivers." *Fieldiana: Anthropology* 70. Chicago: Field Museum of Natural History.
1983 "Protective Hide Body Armor of the Historic Chukchi and Siberian Eskimos." *Études/Inuit/Studies* 7:3-24.
1984 "Exploration and Contact History of Western Alaska." In *Handbook of North American Indians,* vol. 5: *Arctic,* ed. David Damas, pp. 149-60. Washington, D.C.: Smithsonian Institution.
1988 *Russian Exploration in Southwest Alaska: The Travel Journals of Petr Korsakovskiy (1818) and Ivan Ya. Vasilev (1829).* Trans. David H. Kraus. Rasmuson Library Historical Transla-

tion Series, vol. 4. Fairbanks: University of Alaska Press.

Variety (Los Angeles)
1923 "Adventures in Far North." Film review, September 13.
1926 "Justice of the Far North." Film review, November 3.
1932 "Igloo." Film review. July 26.
1933 "Eskimo." Film review. November 21.
1949 "Arctic Manhunt." Film review, September 15.
1960 "The Savage Innocents." Film review. June 29.

Walt Disney Pictures
1983 Publicity from *Never Cry Wolf.* Broadcasting and Recorded Sound Division, Library of Congress, Washington, D.C.

Warren, Elaine
1983 "A Nerd Survives the North: Charles Martin Smith's Life Changed after 'Wolf.'" *Los Angeles Herald Examiner,* October 25, p. C-1.

Weakland, John H.
1975 "Feature Films as Cultural Documents." In *Principles of Visual Anthropology,* ed. Paul Hockings, pp. 231-51. The Hague: Mouton Publishers.

Weatherford, Elizabeth
1990 "Native Visions: The Growth of Indigenous Media." *Aperture,* pp. 58-61.

Whitaker, Alma
1932 "Movies in the North." *Los Angeles Times Sunday Magazine,* July 17, p. 3.

Whitehead, Peter J. P.
1987 "Earliest Extant Painting of Greenlanders." In *Indians and Europe,* ed. Christian F. Feest. Aachen, Germany: Rader Verlag.

Wolf, Eric R.
1982 *Europe and the People without History.* Berkeley: University of California Press.

Wolfe, Robert
1982 "Alaska's Great Sickness, 1900: An Epidemic of Measles and Influenza in a Virgin Soil Population." *Proceedings of the American Philosophical Society* 126:90-121.

Wooley, Chris B.
1990 Iñupiat Images: The North Slope Photographs of William Van Valin and Leo Hansen. Paper presented at the Seventeenth Annual Meeting of the Alaska Anthropological Association, Anchorage.

Worth, Sol, and John Adair
1972 *Through Navajo Eyes.* Bloomington: Indiana University Press.

Wright, Robin K.

1987   "The Traveling Exhibition of Captain Samuel Hadlock, Jr.: Eskimos in Europe, 1822-1826." In *Indians and Europe,* ed. Christian F. Feest. Aachen, Germany: Rader Verlag.

Yacowar, Maurice

1974   "Aspects of the Familiar: A Defense of Minority Group Stereotyping in the Popular Film." *Literature Film Quarterly* 2:129-39.

Young, Scott

1989   *Murder in a Cold Climate.* New York: Viking Press.

INDEX

Charles, George, 193, 203-4

Cheaper by the Dozen, 13

Chechahcos (1923), 57

Chen, Joan, 195, 196, 197, 198, 201, 206

Chevak, Alaska, 149, 180

Chigliak, Ed, 188

Chikoyak, Andrew, 154, 163, 186, 208

Children of Eek and Their Art (1969), 145

Chukchi Peninsula, 18

Cicely, Alaska, 187, 188, 189

Cinematographers: collaboration with anthropologists, 150-51, 154; European, 3; *See also* Film

Cinema vérité, 155

Civilization: ladder of, 31, 40, 46; march of, 135, 167, 207; Western, 32

Climate, 18. *See also* Environment

Collecting. *See* Museum collections

Collins, Henry B., Jr., 137, 148

Columbia Pictures, 60, 92

Columbus, Christopher, 8, 10

The Conquest of the Pole (1912), 40

Conversion. *See* Missionaries

Cook, Captain James, 24

Corporation for Public Broadcasting, 182, 183

Costello, Lou. *See Lost in Alaska* (1952)

Crime, 29

Culture: change, 35; identity, 36, 162-67, 208-9; revitalization, 35

Cup'ik language, 180n

Curwood, James Oliver, 90, 105

Dances with Wolves (1990), 132, 187

Darwinism, 8; Social, 27

DeMille, Cecil B., 56

De Roussellet, Guy Marie, 152

Disease, 29. *See* Epidemics

Disney Channel, xv, 203. *See also* Walt Disney

Documentary: appearance of, 121, 128, 129, 130-31, 142; film, xiv, xv, 40-41, 47-55, 87, 109-10, 133, 135-50, 206, 207, 208, 209

Donald Duck, 141

Drowning: Can We Turn the Tide? (1991), 183

Drums of Winter. See Uksuum Cauyai: Drums of Winter

Early Days Ago (1975), 163

Eastman, Gordon, 109

Economic development, 34

Edison, Thomas, 40, 50

Education, 30-32, 147, 149; bilingual, 183

Eek, 145, 149

Elder, Sarah, 150, 154-61, 170, 208, 209

The Emerging Eskimos (1972), 147-48

Emmonak, Alaska, 155, 156, 160, 164, 174, 208

Encyclopedia Britannica, 135, 137-38, 145

The End of the Road, 166

Environment, 15, 16, 74, 143

Epidemics, 29, 30, 64, 66, 95, 105, 143

Eskimo (1934), xvi, 70, 167, 169, 201, 205, 207; compared to other films, 98, 99, 109, 110, 116, 121, 126, 128, 130, 131, 132, 135, 199, 200; making of, 71-81, 93, 97, 187; reception of, 81-83, 85-86, 206; storyline, 82-83

Eskimo Children (1941), 137-38, 144

Eskimo Hunters of Northwest Alaska (1949), 144, 145

Eskimo Pie, 177

Eskimos: adaptability of, 137, 147, 153; as Alaskan resource, 146; assimilation of, 30-34, 162; childlike, ix, x, 8, 23, 40, 43, 46, 62, 69, 76, 85, 116, 118, 163; contradictory images of, 4-5, 13; "corrupted by civilization," 87, 116, 120, 123, 126, 130; designation of, xvi-xvii; etiquette, 116-17, 148; exhibitions of, x, 7, 12, 39-40, 43, 46; happy, 74, 138, 144, 177, 185; history of representation of, 4, 130-33, 204-9; humorous images of, 11, 115, 132; in literature, 7, 10-11; interaction with nonnatives, 28-36; mixed blood, 60, 192; names, 49, 122; peaceful, ix, 135, 177, 185, 207; played by nonnatives, 78, 81, 100, 116-17, 119, 128, 132, 192, 193, 195, 197-98, 201; Polar, 27; presumed inferiority of, 60-62; primitive, 4-5, 9, 15, 54, 56, 62, 67, 93, 119, 137, 138, 140, 142, 144-47; pure, ix, 52, 62, 93, 128, 132; realistic portrayal of, 133, 208; smiling, 74, 123, 124, 135, 139; social organization, 18, 32; speaking English, 90, 118; *vs.* Indians, 5-6, 8, 12-15, 28, 53-55, 56, 133; villainous, 93, 99. *See also* Inuit; Inupiat; Primitive; Yup'ik Eskimos

Eskimos: A Changing Culture (1971), 147

Eskimo Springtime, 135

Eskimo Summer, 145, 151

Eskimo Territorial Guard, 92, 93

Eskimo Trails (1940), 135-36, 144

Eskimo Winter, 136, 145

"Essential men," ix, 52, 67, 116, 120, 207. *See also* Eskimos: history of representation of; "Natural men"

Ethnographic film, xiv, 40, 135, 150-61, 206, 208, 209; definition of, 151

Evanari, Gail, 149

Every Day Choices (1985), 156, 159-60

Exhibitions. *See* Eskimos: exhibitions of

Exploration: films, x, 39-47, 56; literature, 7-8, 10-11, 39; voyages, 22-24, 28, 29

Extras. *See* Inuit: as "extras"; Iñupiat: as "extras"
Eyes of the Spirit (1983), 182, 186

Ferber, Edna, 105
"Fiction of realism," 128, 129, 133, 142, 153. *See also*
    Documentary: appearance of
Film: awards, 161; costumes, 197; editing, 158; ex-
    otic locations for, 57, 98; expeditions, 87, 130,
    144, 186; history of, xvi, 57; lectures, 40, 135, 145;
    narrated, 109-10, 122, 137, 144, 148, 149, 150;
    production costs, 70, 92, 105, 123, 129, 186, 191,
    192, 194; production standards, 131; reenact-
    ment, 48-52, 128-29, 151, 153; script, 65; tool of
    empowerment, 39, 162. *See also* Documentary:
    film; Ethnographic film; Exploration: films; Film-
    making
Filmmaking: collaboration with Alaska natives, 58,
    162, 208; community determined, 155-56, 171;
    on location, 191, 197, 199. *See also* Studio pro-
    duction
Fishing, 16; commercial, 25, 27, 32
Flaherty, Robert, xii, 3, 41, 47-55, 56, 87, 99, 130,
    133, 135, 141, 144, 152, 153, 199n, 209; influence
    of, 65, 118, 205, 208, 209. *See also Nanook of the
    North*
Fox, John, S.J., 140, 142, 143
Fox Studio, 60, 65, 66
Frank, Arnold, 97
Franklin, Sir John, 24
Freuchen, Peter, 90, 97, 199, 207; participation in
    making *Eskimo,* 71-87
Friends, 193
Frobisher, Martin, 10-11
Frobisher Bay, 128-29, 169. *See also* Iqaluit
    (Frobisher Bay)
From Hand to Hand (1985), 182
From the Elders (1987), 156, 159
From the First People (1976), 156
Frozen Justice (1929), 60-63, 66, 130, 192
The Frozen North (1922), 57-59, 115

Gambell, Alaska 156, 157
Ginsburg, Faye, 162n
The Girl Alaska (1919), 57
Girl from God's Country (1940), 90, 92
Gold Rush, 57; Klondike, 27; Nome, 25, 33, 130
Gordon, George Byron, 14, 25, 44
Granville, Fred LeRoy, 43
"Great Death." *See* Epidemics
The Great Hunter (1991), 192
Greene, Jeanie, 176, 177
Greenland, 15, 20, 43, 71, 97, 98, 166, 204; song

duel, 98. *See also* Inuit: Greenlandic
Griffith, D. W., 56

Haraway, Donna, ix, x, xiii, 120
"Heartbeat Alaska," 176
Herding. *See* Reindeer herding
High Arctic. *See* Arctic
Hollywood: Camp, 77-78, 208; Eskimo, xiii, 191,
    198; scapegoating, 206
Hooper Bay, Alaska, 139-44, 206
Houses: frame, 15, 95; snow, 50, 77, 135, 143, 153,
    205; sod, 15, 199. *See also* Igloos
Houston, James, 125, 126, 129
Hubbard, Bernard, S.J., 135-36
Hudson's Bay Company, 90
Hunger Knows No Law (1978), 165, 166
The Hunters (1958), 154, 155
Hunting: film depiction of, 54, 68, 79, 83, 92-93,
    110, 158. *See also* Sea mammals

Ice Palace (1959), 105-8, 131, 132, 188
Igloo, Alaska, 115
Igloo (1932), 62, 64-71, 72, 79, 82, 83, 85, 89, 97;
    compared to other films, 99, 109, 110, 131, 135,
    191, 192, 207, 208; footage used in other films,
    92, 105; reception of, 69-71
Igloos, 15, 46, 58, 59, 67, 69, 70, 71, 79, 81, 87, 93,
    105, 110, 113-15, 121, 128, 129, 137, 177, 189,
    192, 193, 199, 200, 205, 207; papier mâché, 27,
    39. *See also* Houses: snow
Ince, Thomas, 56
Indians, 44, 201; as contradictory idea, xvi; Holly-
    wood, 159, 167, 199, 206; in literature, 26; origi-
    nal romantic image of, 6; pretending to be
    Eskimos, 179, 188; real, 134; history of represen-
    tation, 4-11, 56-57, 119, 124, 132-33, 207; savage,
    x, 5, 13, 15; similar to Eskimos, 126, 167, 176; *vs.*
    Eskimos, 5-9, 12-15, 53-55, 56, 115, 133, 207,
    208. *See also* Athapascan; Tlingit
Indigenous media, 162n, 186, 208
Infanticide, 68-69, 86, 116, 207
Inuit: as "extras," 128; Baffin Island, 10, 125, 128;
    Canadian, 11, 21, 39, 113, 123, 129, 153, 208;
    dialogue, 129; Greenlandic, 10-11, 21, 22, 24, 39,
    80, 118; Hudson Bay, 48, 49; identity, 162-67,
    208-9; Labrador, 39; represented by Alaska Eski-
    mos, xvii; view of themselves, 54-55, 126
Inuit (1977), 166
Inuit Broadcasting Corporation, 180, 186, 208
Inuit Circumpolar Conference, 162, 166, 208
Inuktitut, 49n, 180
Iñupiaq language, 20, 58, 74-75; on screen, 85, 90,

Rousseau, Jean Jacques, 8
Royal Canadian Mounted Police, 83, 130
Ruby, Jay, 48, 148n
Ruesch, Hans, 116, 118
Russian American Company, 23
Russian Mission, Yukon (1981), 183

Said, Edward, x
Sailor Song (1991), 3
St. Lawrence Island, 18, 156
Salmonberries (1991), 3, 189-92, 201-2
Salomonie, Joanasis, 127, 129
Savage Innocents (1960), 116-20; compared to other
    films, 121, 126, 128, 130, 131, 132, 206, 207
Savagism, 6. *See also* Indians: savage; Noble Savage;
    Wildmen
Savoonga, Alaska, 156
Scott, Ewing, 66, 67, 88, 92, 100, 103, 109, 129, 191
The Sea Is Our Life (1979), 165-66
Sea lions, 111
Sea mammals, 15-16, 74, 111. *See also* Hunting
Seagal, Steven, 194-200, 204, 206
Seattle, 27
Senilicide, 68, 69, 86, 207
Sesame Street, xv, 177
Seveck, Chester, 105, 108
Seveck, Helen, 105, 108
Sex and violence, 131-32
Shadow of the Wolf (1993), 192
Show Hall, 167
Shungnak, Alaska, 156
Silet, Charles, 132
Silook, Susie, 122
Sky River Project, 164
Slapins, Andres, xvi
Sleetmute, Alaska, 144, 188
Smith, Marty, 122
Snow Bear (1970), 121-22, 131, 169
S.O.S. Iceberg (1933), 97-98
Sovereignty movement, 35
Spirit Dog (1994), 193-94, 202, 203-4
Stefansson, Vilhjalmur, 42, 43; critique of *Igloo*, 69-
    71; critique of *Nanook*, 48-51, 152
Stereotypes, 207, 208; breaking, 176; sexual, 62. *See*
    also Eskimos: history of representation of
Studio production, 60, 66, 113
Subsistence, 35, 182, 183; activities, 15, 44, 209; con-
    flict with commercial interests, 148, 184, 189; film
    definition of, 149
Subtitles, 85
Suicide, 29, 183, 190
Survival of the fittest, 27

Synchronous sound, 150-51, 157

Teachers. *See* Education
Television, xv, 95, 121, 130n, 153, 167, 169-86, 189;
    Alaska native broadcasters, 176-77; commercials,
    177-78; effects of, 169-70; introduction of, 144,
    147; viewer defined programming, 171-72. *See*
    also KIMO-TV, Anchorage; KUAC-TV, Fairbanks;
    KYUK-TV, Bethel
Teller, 72, 74, 95, 109, 206
Tetpon, John, 176
They Never Asked Our Fathers (1982), 186
Thomas, Lowell, 42, 137, 146
Thoreau, Henry David, 25
Thurston, Carol, 100, 103
Tip Top of the Earth (1919), 43-47. *See also* Van Valin,
    William
Tlingit, 13, 170, 171, 172, 188, 202
Trade, 33; fur, 28-29, 74. *See also* Russian American
    Company
Trader Horn (1930), 74, 75, 79, 87
Traditional Migrations (1983), 182
Trapping, 27, 32
Travel films, 41-47, 52, 135-36. *See also* Exploration:
    films
"Tundra Terror Theater," 185
Tununak, Alaska, 154, 163
Tununermiut: The People of Tunuuak (1973), 154-58,
    164
Turner, Terrance, 186
Twentieth Century Fox, 135
Twitchell, Peter, 169, 176
Two Against the Arctic (1974), 122-23, 131

Uksuum Cauyai: Drums of Winter (1989), 156, 158,
    160, 164
Unalakleet, Alaska, 18, 144, 145
Ungava Peninsula, 48, 49, 50, 54
Universal Pictures, 62, 97, 105

Valdez, Alaska, 3, 194
Van Dyke, W. S., 109, 132, 165, 191, 199; directing
    Eskimo, 71-87
Van Valin, William, xii, 43-47, 48, 52, 56, 118, 144,
    207, 208, 209
Video, 132, 149, 150, 153, 160, 167, 171; documen-
    tary, 173, 179. *See also* KYUK-TV, Bethel
Village of No River (1981), xvi, 148-49, 164, 185, 209
Violence. *See* Sex and violence

Wales, 71, 72, 206
Walt Disney, 109, 121-25, 130, 132; filming Alaska

natives, 135, 139-44, 145, 153, 165, 169, 187, 193, 204, 207

Wanamaker Expedition, 43, 44

Ward, Vincent, 192

Warfare, bow and arrow, 22, 29, 143

Warner Brothers, 3, 187, 194, 197, 200

War on Poverty, 34

Wassilie, Moses, 170-71

Waters, Katrina, 159

Wedding of Palo (1937), xvi, 98-99

We of the River (1985), 182

Whaling: commercial, 24, 27, 30, 95, 125-26; filming of, 44, 45, 66, 67, 77, 109, 156, 165, 179; subsistence, 15-16, 177. *See also* Sea mammals

White Dawn (1974), 3, 125-30, 131, 132, 169

Wife-sharing, 83, 85-87, 116, 118, 129, 207

Wild men, 11. *See also* Savagism

Wise, Ray. *See* Mala, Ray

"The Wonderful World of Disney," 121-23, 131. *See also* Walt Disney

World War II, 33, 95, 109, 130, 150

Worth, Sol, 186

Yukon Eskimos, 13

Yukon River, 16, 18; Delta, 26-27

Yup'ik Eskimos, 18; dances of, 140-42, 143, 160; Kuskokwim, 14, 25, 30; relationship to land, 185; Siberian, 27, 44; Yukon, 13. *See also* Eskimos

Yup'ik language: distribution, 18; in film dialogue, 197, 203; programming in, 172, 180, 182; vitality of, 169-70

Yup'ik Schoolroom (1983), 183

Zagoskin, Lavrentii, 23